JAMES VI AND I

PROFILES IN POWER
General Editor: Keith Robbins

. . . . .

JAMES VI AND I

Roger Lockyer

LONGMAN
London and New York

Addison Wesley Longman Limited
Edinburgh Gate,
Harlow, Essex CM20 2JE, United Kingdom
and Associated Companies throughout the world.

*Published in the United States of America
by Addison Wesley Longman, New York.*

First published 1998

Visit Addison Wesley Longman on the world wide web at
http://www.awl-he.com

ISBN 0-582-27962-3 CSD
ISBN 0-582-27961-5 PPR

British Library Cataloguing in Publication Data

A catalogue entry for this title is available from the British Library

Library of Congress Cataloging-in-Publication Data

Lockyer, Roger.
James VI and I / Roger Lockyer.
p.   cm. — (Profiles in power)
Includes bibliographical references and index.
ISBN 0–582–27962–3. — ISBN 0–582–27961–5 (pbk.)
1. James I, King of England, 1566–1625.   2. Great Britain—
History—James I, 1603–1625.   3. Great Britain—Kings and rulers—
Biography.   4. Scotland—History—James VI, 1567–1625.
5. Scotland—Kings and rulers—Biography.   I. Title.   II. Series:
Profiles in power (London, England)
DA391.L63   1998
941.06′1′092—dc21
[B]   98–5726
                                                            CIP

Set by 35 in 10.5/12pt Baskerville
Produced by Addison Wesley Longman Singapore (Pte) Ltd
Printed in Singapore

CONTENTS

LIST OF MAPS

NOTE ON PUNCTUATION

For clarification, the author has used double quotation marks for primary source material, and single quotation marks for material quoted from secondary sources.

Chapter 1

KING OF SCOTLAND

'James I slobbered at the mouth and had favourites: he was thus a Bad King.'[1] This pithy judgment on the first Stuart, passed by Sellar and Yeatman in their classic history of England, *1066 and All That*, first published in 1930, is based on a view of James VI & I as a windbag, a man of unsavoury morals and a political failure, that has a long pedigree. It was first given general currency by Sir Walter Scott in *The Fortunes of Nigel*, published in 1822. 'He was deeply learned, without possessing useful knowledge; sagacious in many individual cases, without having real wisdom; fond of his power, and desirous to maintain and augment it, yet willing to resign the direction of that, and of himself, to the most unworthy favourites; a big and bold asserter of his rights in words, yet one who tamely saw them trampled on in deeds; a lover of negotiations, in which he was always outwitted; and one who feared war, where conquest might have been easy. He was fond of his dignity, while he was perpetually degrading it by undue familiarity; capable of much public labour, yet often neglecting it for the meanest amusement; a wit, though a pedant; and a scholar, though fond of the conversation of the ignorant and uneducated.'[2]

Scott's critical view of James, along with his antithetical manner, was echoed by Lord Macaulay, writing a quarter of a century later. 'The indignation excited by his claims', declared Macaulay, 'and the scorn excited by his concessions went on growing together. By his fondness for worthless minions, and by the sanction which he gave to their tyranny and rapacity, he kept discontent constantly alive. His cowardice, his childishness, his pedantry, his ungainly person and manners, his provincial accent made him an object of derision. Even in his virtues and

1

accomplishments there was something eminently unkingly . . . It was no light thing that, on the very eve of the decisive struggle between our kings and their parliaments, royalty should be exhibited to the world stammering, slobbering, shedding unmanly tears, trembling at a drawn sword, and talking in the style alternately of a buffoon and of a pedagogue.'[3]

Although Scott and Macaulay gave wide currency and canonical sanction to the conventional view of James VI & I, they were not the first proponents of it. They based their interpretation upon three principal sources: Sir Anthony Weldon's *Court and Character of King James*, Arthur Wilson's *The Life and Reign of King James I*, and Francis Osborne's *Traditional Memoirs of the Reign of King James the First*. Sir Anthony Weldon was born into the royal circle, for his father and uncle both held posts in the King's household as, respectively, Clerk of the Green Cloth and Clerk of the Kitchen. Weldon succeeded his father in office and was subsequently knighted by James I. In 1617, when the King decided to revisit his native land, Weldon went with him, but Scotland made a poor impression on a man who, in the words of Sir Walter Scott, had been 'educated, as it were, among the flesh-pots of the English Court'.[4] He vented his spleen and boredom in writing what he called *A Perfect Description of the People and Country of Scotland*, but it was not exactly an impartial account. 'For the country,' said Weldon, 'I must confess it is too good for those that possess it, and too bad for others to be at the charge to conquer it. The ground might be fruitful had they wit to manure it. The beasts be generally small, women only excepted, of which sort there are none greater in the whole world. There is great deal of fowl too – as foul houses, foul sheets, foul linen, foul dishes and pots, foul trenchers and napkins', and so on.[5] Weldon was no doubt pleased with this masterpiece of invective, but in a careless moment he wrapped it up in one of the Board of Green Cloth's records. By this means it came to the attention of James I, who promptly dismissed him from the royal service.

It might be thought that Weldon had got what he deserved, but this was not his view. Weldon took with him into private life a sense of grievance over what he regarded as unjust treatment, and nurtured his revenge by writing an *exposé* of James's Court which, had it been done today, would be snapped up by the tabloid press. Weldon apparently considered publishing his witty lampoon, but was dissuaded from taking this risky step.

However, the outbreak of civil war – in which Weldon embraced the parliamentary cause – and the subsequent collapse of the royal government, removed the need for discretion, and in 1650 the *Court and Character of King James I* appeared in print. By this time Weldon was dead, but his book was eagerly snapped up and became a best-seller. Bishop Goodman, who wrote what he intended as a counterblast to Weldon's salvo, declared that he had never read 'a more malicious-minded author, nor any who had such poor and mean observations'.[6] But unfortunately for Goodman and other of James's defenders, Weldon was a gifted polemicist whose malice sharpened the edge of his style. His description of James's Court entered the popular imagination and provided one of the foundations upon which the traditional interpretation of James's reign was constructed.

Arthur Wilson, born in 1595, grew to maturity after James had ascended the English throne, and served in the household of the third Earl of Essex, whose private life was exposed to public view when his wife demanded an annulment of their marriage. She did so because of her obsession with Robert Carr, the King's favourite, whom she wanted as her new husband, but in the widely reported legal proceedings she based her case on Essex's alleged impotence. Subsequently Wilson entered the service of the Earl of Warwick, who, like Essex, was out of sympathy with many aspects of early Stuart rule. Given these links it is hardly surprising that Wilson's *Life and Reign of King James I* is distinctly biassed against its subject. Anthony à Wood, the Oxford antiquary whose autobiography begins in the middle years of the seventeenth century, had good grounds for observing that 'a partial, presbyterian vein . . . constantly goes through the whole work, it being the genius of those people to pry more than they should into the courts and comportments of princes, to take occasion thereupon to traduce and bespatter them'.[7]

Francis Osborne, two years older than Wilson, began his career as Master of the Horse to William Herbert, third Earl of Pembroke, who, although he served James loyally as Lord Chamberlain, was by no means uncritical of his sovereign. When the civil war broke out, Osborne's sympathies were with the King's opponents, and he married the sister of a colonel in the parliamentary army. Osborne's *Traditional Memoirs* are not so scurrilous as Weldon's *Court and Character*, but they propagated the belief that many of the problems which confronted Charles I were inherited from his father. In Osborne's words, 'I found not only the imprudent commissions, but voluntary omissions of King James so much instrumental in the promotion of our present evils, as it may justly be said, he, like Adam, by bringing the crown into so great a necessity through a profuse prodigality, became the original of his son's fall.'[8] Osborne blamed James above all for his largesse towards 'the beggarly rabble' that attended him 'not only at his first coming out of Scotland, but through his whole reign . . . His too palpable partiality towards his countrymen rendered him no higher place than of a king-in-law, not a prince of any natural affections to the people of this nation.'[9]

Weldon, Wilson and Osborne, between them, created the traditional disparaging view of James as a ruler – at least of England. Yet in normal circumstances their writings would never have seen the light of day. If the Personal Rule of Charles I had been successful, if royal authority had been strengthened instead of weakened, these highly critical accounts would have remained private. Had they been preserved at all they might have been published many years later, but they would probably have been destroyed as too dangerous and incriminating. In short, the interpretation of James's reign which they established as authentic derives from a unique combination of circumstances, one which made possible the dissemination of works which consisted, in the words of one of Wilson's critics, of 'truth and falsehood finely put together'.[10] A similar situation might have arisen with respect to Elizabeth I if civil war had broken out in the 1590s and her many critics had been given free rein. How different our view of the Elizabethan age would be if we depended upon such (unwritten, or at least unknown) masterpieces of vituperation as Sir Walter Ralegh's *Secret History of the Court of Queen Elizabeth* or Sir Francis Bacon's *The Viper's Eye: Passages upon the Life and Times of her Late Majesty*.

The traditional version of the reign of James I is now more than 150 years old, yet only in recent decades has it come under scrutiny. The standard biography of the first Stuart sovereign of Britain is still that produced in 1956 by David Harris Willson, which remains firmly within the established parameters: indeed, Willson makes no attempt to conceal his distaste for the king whose character and reign he chose, somewhat surprisingly, to describe and dissect.[11] Marc Schwarz, who in 1974 published an article reconsidering James's reputation, commented on the remarkable staying power of the conventional version, but added that the picture emerging from current research was 'a much different one'.[12] This was indeed the case, for by the time Schwarz's article appeared, significant revisionist interpretations were beginning to modify the older view. In the area of foreign policy, Charles Carter claimed that the King's approach was both subtle and well thought out, and that far from being the puppet of Gondomar, the Spanish ambassador to England, James was as much the deceiver as the deceived.[13] Meanwhile, Mark Curtis, D.E. Kennedy and Stuart Babbage had set in train a revaluation of James's religious policy that still continues,[14] as witness the article by Kenneth Fincham and Peter Lake, published in 1985, which acclaims James's success in containing 'inherently antithetical tendencies within his ecclesiastical regime'.[15] In the field of government and policy-making, 1981 saw the publication of a biography of the Duke of Buckingham, which broke with precedent by treating Macaulay's 'worthless minion' as a serious politician.[16] In the following year came Linda Peck's study of the Earl of Northampton, usually regarded as an unscrupulous and self-seeking manipulator, which showed him to have been both an efficient administrator and a committed proponent of reform.[17] It was Linda Peck who organised a conference on 'The Mental World of the Jacobean Court' at the Folger Shakespeare Library in Washington in 1988 which marked a watershed in the reinterpretation of James's reign. She also edited the invaluable collection of papers given at the conference, which was published, under the same title, in 1991.[18]

One of the most important papers, on James's political writings, was written by Jenny Wormald, a leading figure in Jacobean studies. She had the initial advantage of looking at James from the Scottish viewpoint, and in an article provocatively entitled 'James VI & I: Two Kings or One?' she dealt with the contrast between James's perceived success in Scotland and his apparent failure in England.[19] By the time her article appeared, in 1983, Maurice Lee had already published a study of Scotland under James, which showed just how much he achieved there.[20] James did so with the co-operation of the Scottish Parliament, which was effectively under royal control, but in England, as Jenny Wormald showed, he had to deal with a larger body, more formal, more concerned with the preservation of its rights and privileges, and frequently intransigent. It seemed unlikely that revisionism could do much to dispel the assumption that James was constantly at loggerheads with his English parliaments, yet when Conrad Russell published a book on this theme in 1979 he made the heretical assertion that James was by no means a failure; on the contrary, he was 'as successful as Queen Elizabeth, or even more so'.[21] Not all historians have been converted to this view, but they increasingly acknowledge James's many positive qualities, not least his detestation of extremism and his search for a middle way in both religion and politics.

.   .   .

James Stuart was born on 19 June 1566 in Edinburgh Castle, at a time when Scotland was in the throes of a religious revolution. The old catholic order had been identified not only with the monarchy but also with France, for James's grandfather, James V, had married Mary of Guise, who came from one of the most distinguished French noble houses. Their daughter and James's mother, Mary Stuart, was born only a few days before James V's death in 1542 (at which point she immediately became Queen of Scotland), and in the struggle for power that followed, Mary of Guise stood for the French and catholic interest. It was through the assistance given to her by French troops that she eventually established herself as regent, and in 1548 she sent her daughter to France as prospective bride for the dauphin, the future Francis II.

The most difficult problem with which Mary of Guise had to deal, as *de facto* ruler of Scotland, was that created by the return in 1559 of John Knox, the outspoken champion of Scottish protestantism, who had been ministering to the congregation of English protestant exiles in Geneva, where John Calvin had set up a model of 'reformed' religious practice. Knox's return coincided with the accession of the protestant Elizabeth I to the English throne, following the death of the catholic Mary Tudor in November 1558. The leading protestant nobles in Scotland, who had formed themselves into the 'Band of the Lords of the Congregation', took heart from this dramatic change of fortune, for they could now look for support from south of the border. Their new-found optimism was soon put to the test, for in October 1559 they seized control of Edinburgh and declared Mary of Guise to be no longer regent. Mary, however, had the support of French troops, and soon drove them out. But at this point, as the Lords of the Congregation had hoped, Elizabeth intervened, and in January 1560 an English fleet anchored in the Firth of Forth. The French risked being cut off from their homeland and therefore agreed to negotiate – a process made easier by the death of Mary of Guise in June 1560. Under the terms of the Treaty of Edinburgh, signed in July, French and English forces were to be withdrawn from Scotland, and the nature of the religious settlement there was to be decided by a Scottish Parliament.

This Parliament met in August 1560, and the members accepted a Confession of Faith, which abolished the mass and put an end to papal authority in Scotland. As in England, however, there was little or no attempt to dismantle the existing structure of the Church. Although the episcopate had been brought into low repute by the venality of many bishops and their obvious lack of spiritual qualities, it was allowed to survive, in large part because it had become a preserve of the nobles. If the Scottish throne had been occupied by a committed protestant of mature age, then a radical reconstruction of the Church might have been practical politics. Alternatively, a forceful catholic ruler might have been able to push through changes which would have revivified the existing Church and enabled it to meet the protestant challenge. But in 1560 the nominal ruler of Scotland was Mary Stuart, who returned to her native land a year later, following the death of her husband, Francis II. Mary never wavered in her catholic faith, but she was not temperamentally suited to leading a crusade on its behalf. The Scottish bishops, rather than waiting for such a lead, could have taken the initiative themselves by setting on foot a reform programme. Had they done so they might have preserved catholicism, or at least put up a more effective defence against the protestant assault, but unfortunately for the old faith they remained mired in all the old abuses.

In 1565 the widowed Queen of Scots married her cousin, Lord Darnley. His protestantism was not to her taste, but the big advantage of the match was that it would strengthen her claim to the English throne, since they were both direct descendants of the first Tudor, Henry VII. Mary could do little to enforce her claim while Elizabeth was alive, but in catholic eyes she, rather than the protestant Elizabeth, was the rightful ruler of England, and since Elizabeth's hold on power was, at this early stage in her reign, uncertain, Mary might not have to wait too long before coming into her inheritance. Meanwhile she remained Queen of Scotland and could look forward to many years of rule, provided she showed the appropriate qualities, which included restraint and decorum. Unfortunately for Mary, these were qualities in which, at this stage of her life, she was conspicuously lacking. She may have been genuinely in love with Darnley, but she quickly came to hate him, and whether or not she was party to his murder in February 1567 she showed no regret. She was now under the spell of James Hepburn, fourth Earl of Bothwell, and despite the widespread belief that he was Darnley's murderer, she married him. This prompted a revolt by a section of the Scottish nobility, which led to the collapse of her rule. In July 1567 she formally abdicated, and James, at the age of thirteen months, became king. In a coronation ceremony held at Stirling, "the royal robe was put on him, the crown put upon his head, the sword to his side, the sceptre in his hand. At the doing of every one of these particulars, there were prayers made in the mother tongue. Last of all was the blessing, pronounced by the bishop. And so the ceremony ended with triumph, fireworks and shooting of cannon and feasting."[22]

James, who had hardly known his mother, let alone his father, never saw her again, for she fled to England in May 1568. He was now undoubted king, but a king under tutelage, and his principal tutor was George Buchanan. On the face of it there could have been no better choice, for Buchanan was renowned throughout Europe as a poet, playwright and scholar. He taught Latin in Paris for several years and subsequently moved to Bordeaux, where he composed a number of tragedies. They were acted by his pupils, among them Michel de Montaigne, whose fame as an author was subsequently to eclipse his own. Buchanan was undoubtedly an effective teacher, but, as was the case with most of his contemporaries, he put the acquisition of learning above all other considerations and had no time for human frailties. Under Buchanan's direction, James was subjected to a regime that would have crushed a less spirited boy. Peter Young, the assistant tutor, described how "after morning prayers, his attention was devoted to the Greek authors, and he read a portion of the New Testament, Isocrates, or the *Apophthegmata* of Plutarch, and was exercised in the grammar rules. After breakfast he read Cicero, Livy, Justin,* or modern history. In the afternoon he applied himself to composition, and when his leisure would permit, to arithmetic or cosmography, which included geography and the doctrine of the sphere, or to logic or rhetoric."[23]

James was an intelligent boy and an eager scholar. Through the study of theology and the classics he entered a world which was more congenial than the one in which he actually lived. However, Buchanan's pedagogic skills could not bridge the gap of sixty years between the master and his pupil, particularly since ill health as well as the passage of time had hardened his spirit and shortened his temper. He took it for granted that to spare the rod was to spoil the child, and since he believed that kings should be servants of their people rather than masters he made it his duty to pounce on any signs of arrogance or wilfulness in his young charge. On one occasion the kindly Countess of Mar rescued the sobbing James from a severe beating and upbraided Buchanan for presuming to lay his hands on 'the Lord's anointed'. "Madam," replied the irate tutor, "I have whipped his arse; you may kiss it if you please."[24] Little wonder that James lived in fear of Buchanan. If Francis Osborne is to be believed, this fear lasted as long as James's life, for many years later the King 'used to say of a person in high place about him, that he ever trembled at his approach, it minded him so of his pedagogue'.[25]

James shared his schoolroom in Stirling Castle with a number of well-born contemporaries – among them John Erskine, subsequently second Earl of Mar – who became close friends. He was also on affectionate terms with Peter Young, who had none of Buchanan's acerbity; on the contrary he was "loath to offend the King at any time, carrying himself warily, as a man who had a mind of his own weal by keeping of His Majesty's favour".[26] These friendships brought warmth into James's life but they could not shield him from overbearing and authoritarian father substitutes. These included not only George Buchanan but also

---

* Justin Martyr, put to death in Rome c.165 for propagating the Christian faith, was the author of an *Apology* in which he attempted to reconcile Greek philosophy with Christian revelation. An edition of his works had recently been published by Robert Estienne, who was official printer to the King of France until 1551, when he went into exile in Geneva and embraced Calvinism.

James Douglas, fourth Earl of Morton, who became regent in 1572. Morton was a forceful personality with a fierce temper, and insisted upon absolute obedience to his will. One French observer referred to "the terrorism under which he [i.e. James] had been brought up" and added that for this reason the boy king was "timid with the great lords, seldom venturing to contradict them".[27] James's timidity, which was linked to his fear of violence and horror of weapons, became notorious, but it may have had its source in an event which took place before his birth. As Mary, Queen of Scots, found her husband, Darnley, increasingly repellent she turned for comfort to her Italian secretary, David Rizzio. This enraged Darnley, who contrived to be at a supper party in the Queen's apartments when a band of his supporters – Morton prominent among them – burst in, dragged away Rizzio, who was one of the guests, and stabbed him to death on the spot. Mary was six months pregnant at the time, and although the shock did not result in a miscarriage, as the conspirators may have hoped, it could have affected the unborn child.

By the time James came to the throne in 1567 a protestant Church or Kirk was already well established. Admittedly bishops, and indeed abbots, remained in existence, but they lacked any real authority. Since the Scottish Reformation had surged up from below, rather than being imposed by the ruler, the Kirk was left to make its own arrangements for self government, and adopted the presbyterian organisation set up by Calvin in Geneva. Presbyteries consisted of the local minister or ministers and elected laymen of good repute, known as elders, and they functioned either as a supplement or an alternative to the traditional parishes. Knox was a powerful advocate of the new system, having experienced it at first hand, but not until Andrew Melville returned from Geneva in 1574 did the Kirk fully embrace presbyterianism. Melville – like James's tutor, Buchanan, who was his friend and supporter – was a scholar with an international reputation. In his early twenties he had been appointed to the chair of humanity in the Genevan academy, the leading institute of learning in the protestant world, and had formed a close friendship with Calvin's successor, Theodore Beza. He returned to Scotland determined to eradicate the remaining vestiges of popery from the Kirk and to create in his native land a Church as pure in its doctrine and discipline as that of Geneva. In 1560 the first Book of Discipline, drawn up by the protestant leaders, had retained a form of episcopacy in the shape of 'superintendents', but in 1578 the second Book, of which Melville was the principal begetter, discarded episcopacy altogether and set up in its place a hierarchy of autonomous Church courts to impose discipline not only on ministers but on civil magistrates as well. If Melville had had his way, Scotland would have become a theocracy, and final authority would have resided in the general assembly of the Kirk.

In fact, the situation in Scotland in the 1580s was so confused that it was impossible to define where exactly authority was located. Morton's appointment as regent in 1572 gave the protestants much comfort, since despite his dissolute private life he was a close friend of John Knox, and delivered the eulogy at the reformer's funeral in November 1572. Morton, however, although a Calvinist in theology, was Erastian by temperament, and, as James Melville – the nephew of Andrew and an ardent reformer in his own right – recorded, his aim was to "bring in a conformity with England in governing of the Kirk by bishops and injunctions, without the which, he thought, neither the kingdom could be guided to his fantasy, nor stand in good agreement and liking with the neighbour land".[28] Morton was particularly distrustful of the general assembly of the Kirk, which acted as if it was the sovereign authority for state and Church alike, and he "would have had the name thereof changed, that he might abolish the privilege and force thereof".[29] The general assembly, of which Andrew Melville was elected moderator in 1578, riposted by drawing up the second Book of Discipline, already mentioned, and calling for an end to the appointment of bishops. Two years later, in 1580, it came out against episcopacy altogether, on the grounds that it lacked biblical sanction.

Morton had no time for such egalitarianism and scoffed at Melville's "oversea dreams [and] imitation of Geneva discipline and laws", warning him that "there will never be quietness in this country till half a dozen of you be hanged or banished".[30] Morton was not without supporters, including a section of the nobility, but the Calvinists prayed for his downfall and rallied behind those nobles whose opposition to the regent was based upon jealousy and self-interest rather than principle. The attitude of the young King was all-important, for without his support Morton could hardly retain power. But James was no longer as dependent upon Morton as he had been, for in 1579 his father's first cousin, Esmé Stuart, Seigneur d'Aubigny, arrived from the French Court. Aubigny, then in his thirties, was handsome, charming, and possessed of exquisite manners. To the young king he must have seemed like a visitor from another planet, a world far removed from the harsh masculinity of the Scottish Court. Responding to the warmth of Aubigny's attentions, James showed an infatuation worthy of his mother. Aubigny was created Earl and subsequently Duke of Lennox, and James gave him whatever lands and positions were in his gift. Sir Robert Bowes, Elizabeth I's agent in Scotland, informed her in March 1579 that the new earl had been "called to be one of the secret counsell, and carryeth the sway in court". Thereafter Lennox's influence steadily increased, and in September 1580 Bowes reported that he stood "so high in the King's favour and strong in counsell as few or none will openly withstand any thing that he would have forward".[31] This was the first indication of what was to become a marked feature of James's reign in both Scotland and England. Although he married and sired a number of children, James found his principal emotional – and conceivably sexual – fulfilment in handsome young men with fine French manners, on whom he lavished not only affection but money, places and titles. The political role of James's favourites will be considered later, but their closeness to the monarch gave them an importance which, even if it transcended their abilities, had to be taken into account by all those who sought office and power in James's kingdoms.

Aubigny's arrival in Scotland transformed the political situation, for one of the motives behind his mission was to wean James away from the dependence upon England which was central to Morton's policy. Aubigny moved with great skill to rally the opposition behind him. Not only did he win over James. By a well-timed conversion to protestantism he also made himself acceptable to the Calvinists. Factionalism, which was endemic among the Scottish nobles, now spread into all sections of society, and Bowes, in a despatch of April 1580, described how, at his arrival in Edinburgh, he had found "right strange humours, and matters standing in very doubtful condition. The nobility is no less in division than the people in fury." A few months later he reported that "this fire beginneth to rage mightily".[32] Among the first to be caught up in the flames was Morton. Aubigny, now Earl of Lennox, masterminded the *coup* which led to Morton's arrest and trial, on the charge of involvement in Darnley's murder. The verdict was a foregone conclusion, and in June 1581 Morton was publicly beheaded.

It took a great deal of craft on James's part, as well as stubbornness, to ward off English intervention on behalf of Morton and against Lennox. Robert Bowes urged James to demonstrate his regard for Elizabeth by breaking with Lennox, but while James gave assurances that he was "always willing . . . to write privately with his own hand to satisfy her Majesty therein, or do any other thing in his power to her highness' good contentment",[33] he not only retained the earl as his principal adviser but made him a duke, in August 1581. Bowes put James's attitude down to his tender years and his susceptibility to the advice of those around him, but Elizabeth, wounded in her pride and stung to anger, warned her young cousin that the error of his ways would "appear more foul when riper years and the inconvenience and prejudice he shall receive by the lack of her Majesty's favour – how light soever now it is weighed – shall lead him to know what it is to prefer an Earl of Lennox before a Queen of England".[34]

So blunt a warning was not lost on James, who already had the English succession in his sights, and he wrote to the Queen to tell her how "infinitely distressed" he would be "if anyone should think that I was unwilling to bear you the honour and the duty that I owe you". He begged her "to give me your good counsel and advice" and assured her that "in every matter wherein it pleases you to command me, you will always find me your very obedient son".[35] Yet in practice James had called Elizabeth's bluff, for she was preoccupied with negotiations for a possible French marriage and did not dare risk open intervention in Scotland. However, the Queen had made no secret of her support for Morton and she took the news of his overthrow badly. According to one account she was overheard saying to herself, "That false Scotch urchin, for whom I have done so much! To say to Morton the night before he arrested him, 'Father, no one else but you has reared me, and I will therefore defend you from your enemies', and then after this, the next day, to order him to be arrested, and his head smitten off! What can be expected from the double dealing of such an urchin as this?"[36] James was indeed a double dealer, but given the conflicting pressures on him he had little choice. In a poem written at about this time, and described as "the first verses that

ever the King made", he set out the philosophical justification
for his attitude:

> Since thought is free, think what thou will
>   O troubled heart to ease thy pain.
> Thought unrevealed can do no ill;
> But words passed out comes [sic] not again.
>   Be careful aye for to invent
>   The way to get thy own intent.[37]

James had got his own intent by advancing Lennox and elim-
inating Morton, but he could not keep his favourite in power
indefinitely. The Calvinists quickly repented of their alliance
with a man they now regarded as a crypto-papist and blamed
him for James's increasing assertiveness in matters concerning
the government of the Church. At a meeting of the general
assembly held at Perth in 1582 a list of articles was drawn up
which began with a blunt warning that James, "by device of some
counsellors", was being encouraged to assume "that spiritual
power and authority which properly appertains to Christ, as only
King and head of his Kirk; the ministry and execution whereof
is given to such only as bears [sic] office in the ecclesiastical
government of the same". When the leaders of the assembly
appeared at Court to present their complaints, one of James's
councillors demanded to know who would dare to support
such treasonable articles. "We dare", answered Andrew Melville,
"and will subscribe them, and give our lives in the cause."[38]

Melville's uncompromising stance, backed up by his fellow
delegates who immediately put their signatures to the list of
articles, prompted Lennox and the other Councillors present
with the King to take a softer line, "for they gathered thereon
that the Kirk had a back [i.e. backing]".[39] This was indeed the
case, for a number of lords, out of a mixture of motives ranging
from religious conviction to personal spite, were determined to
topple Lennox just as he had earlier toppled Morton. James was
little more than a pawn in this dangerous game. His situation
had been perceptively summarised by Bowes, who informed
Elizabeth that "the strife in the nobility and others about the
King at this present, is raised and nourished by the inordinate
desire occupying each several party and faction, to attain and
hold the ear and nearness of the King; which they would turn to
their own advantage, and for their private respects, according

to their several and secret intentions agreeable to their plots devised".[40] The conspiracy to get rid of Lennox reached its climax in August 1582, when James, who was hunting in the neighbourhood, was persuaded to enter Ruthven Castle, where its owner, the Earl of Gowrie, was present with the Master of Glamis and other protestant lords. Although James was treated with outward respect, it was made plain that he would not be allowed to leave the castle until he had ordered Lennox to quit the kingdom. James "grew into a passion, and after some threatening speeches burst forth into tears. The Master, seeing him weep, said: 'It is no matter of his tears. Better that bairns should weep than bearded men.' "[41] James never saw his favourite again. By early 1583 Lennox was back in Paris, and it was there, in May, that he died.

The Ruthven Raid was a watershed in James's life, for he was now isolated and had to work out his own salvation. He could not turn for advice even to his formidable tutor, for George Buchanan had died in late 1582. James came to terms with the situation by yielding to the demands of the Gowrie conspirators and apparently accepting their guidance. By doing so he lulled them into a sense of security, but he was secretly establishing contact with the anti-Gowrie group among the nobles and plotting a counter *coup*. This involved James in deception, in which he was already well versed. It also made demands upon his courage, for the stakes were so high that James's life was under threat. In June 1583 he secured the consent of his self-appointed guardians to go off on a hunting trip which brought him within range of St Andrews, where his supporters were gathered in strength. James sought refuge in the castle there, and by so doing emancipated himself from his captors. It was in St Andrews Castle, "newly fortified [and] well guarded", that Bowes found him in early July. Bowes reminded James of Elizabeth's advice that he should give equal access to all the Scots nobles, in order to dampen down the fires of faction. James, in reply, declared his intention "to draw the nobility unto unity and concord, and to be known to be (as he termed it) an universal King, indifferent to them all".[42] There is no reason to doubt that this was indeed James's aim, but he was not as yet well placed to achieve it. Bitter divisions among the leading nobles were a fact of life, and his escape from one group left him, inevitably, dependent upon another. His new counsellors were led by the charismatic but unscrupulous James Stewart,

Earl of Arran, whose principal concern was the pursuit of a vendetta against the men who had held the King prisoner. This culminated in the seizure of Gowrie, and his execution as a traitor in May 1584.

The subjugation of the nobility and the elevation of the crown above faction were clearly, at this stage, little more than long-term objectives, but James was committed to achieving them. He told Fontenay – an agent sent to him on behalf of his mother, Mary, held prisoner in England – that the irresponsibility of the Scottish aristocracy sprang from "the fact that for forty years or more they had only had for governors in this kingdom women, little children, and traitorous and avaricious regents, so that during the divisions and troubles happening in that time the nobility by an unbridled liberty had become so audacious in leaning on those who commanded them, that now it is not possible to subdue and reduce them all at once to their duty". Nevertheless, added James, he was determined that "little by little he would have them in good order".[43]

While James had to give up any immediate hope of bringing the nobles under closer royal control, he had a much better chance of achieving his parallel aim of subordinating the Kirk. The Ruthven Raid had given the green light to its leaders to renew the attack upon the bishops, which they had eagerly embarked on. Now, however, the tables were turned, and Andrew Melville, as the symbol of the Kirk's pretensions, was summoned before the King and Council to answer for his actions. Despite what his nephew described as "roarings of lions and messages of death", Melville refused to recant. Instead, he challenged the right of the secular authorities to take any action against the Kirk, which was a constituent estate of the kingdom of Christ, and reminded his accusers that he and his fellow presbyterians were "the ambassadors and messengers of a King and Council greater nor [i.e. than] they, and far above them!"[44] James's Councillors were unimpressed by this claim, and ordered Melville to be imprisoned; he only escaped this fate by fleeing south over the border into Berwick.

James and Arran were now free to bring the Kirk under royal control, and they used Parliament as their agent. The Scottish Parliament was much smaller than its English counterpart and its sessions were far shorter: in 1584 it sat for only two days, but nevertheless passed forty-nine acts. The main reason why legislation passed so quickly was that the parliamentary programme was prepared in advance by a body called the committee of the articles, to which James appointed his principal Councillors and officers of state. The King himself was a frequent attender at both the committee and Parliament, and it was virtually impossible for any matter to be discussed without either his overt approval or tacit consent. In 1584 James made it plain that he wished Parliament to muzzle the presbyterians, and it responded by passing what the Calvinists dubbed the 'Black Acts'. The most important of these confirmed "the royal power and authority over all [e]states, as well spiritual as temporal, within this realm", sanctioned the right of the King and his Councillors to summon before them all offenders, "of whatsoever degree or condition they be, spiritual or temporal", and made it a treasonable offence for anyone so summoned to "presume or take upon hand to decline the judgment" of King or Council. Another act forbade the holding of "councils, conventions or assemblies to . . . consult and determinate in any matter of estate, civil or ecclesiastical", without the King's prior approval. The power of the presbyterian clergy was further restrained by acts giving the bishops sole right to present to benefices and requiring all "ministers, readers and masters of colleges and schools" to make a written promise to show their "humble and dutiful submission and fidelity to our sovereign lord the King's Majesty", and likewise to give obedience to bishops or any other official appointed by the King "to have the exercise of the spiritual jurisdiction in our diocese". It was also made an offence "privately or publicly, in sermons, declamations or familiar conferences, to utter any false, untrue or slanderous speeches to the disdain, reproach and contempt of his Majesty, his Council and proceedings".[45]

The Black Acts did not end the struggle between James and the Kirk. Much depended upon the balance of power at Court, for religion and politics were so closely enmeshed that the overthrow of a principal minister would inevitably have implications for Church–state relations. In 1585 Arran was toppled by his enemies among the Scottish nobles, acting with English support, and James, seeing the need to keep a potentially explosive situation under control, issued a statement in which he denied any intention of constraining the Kirk. He still insisted on the need to retain episcopacy, but not "according to the traditions of men, or inventions of the Pope, but only according to God's word".[46] In practice, this meant that bishops could carry out their administrative duties only in conjunction with committees of ministers, and they were subject to censure by the general assembly of the Kirk. Although they were graced with the episcopal title and what little dignity went with it, the Scottish bishops remained ordinary ministers, with the usual parochial cares. Their status was further diminished in 1587 when James, faced with one of his recurring financial crises, secured from Parliament an Act of Annexation transferring to the crown the temporalities – i.e. the secular, as distinct from spiritual, revenues – of all benefices.

Episcopacy in Scotland, then, was a pale reflection of James's ideal, but he was content to bide his time while he dealt with more pressing matters. Principal among these was his marriage. In 1587 James became twenty-one, and it was both assumed and expected that he would shortly marry and provide an heir to the throne. The King of Denmark had two marriageable daughters, and James therefore despatched his old tutor, Peter Young, to Copenhagen, to see whether the elder one was available. Young returned with the news that she was already engaged, but that her younger sister, Anne, was well worth James's consideration, not least on account of her beauty. James was cautious in his response. By marrying into the Danish royal family he would increase his own prestige and that of his country, but such a prospect was not pleasing to Queen Elizabeth, who wanted to maintain James as a client and suppliant rather than deal with him on terms of equality. She also feared that such an alliance would give Scotland too favoured a position in the Baltic trade, on which England was dependent for naval supplies. Elizabeth would have preferred James to marry the sister of Henri de Navarre, the future Henri IV of France, at that time the champion of the French protestants. But the lady in question was eight years older than James, whereas Anne was eight years younger and much better looking. James, therefore, with the enthusiastic support of the merchants and burgesses of Edinburgh, decided to risk Elizabeth's wrath by asking for Anne's hand. The marriage took place, by proxy, at Copenhagen in August 1589, and a few weeks later Anne sailed for Scotland. However, her ship was driven off course by tempestuous weather and she was forced to seek shelter in Norway. When James heard the news he acted with all the impatience of an ardent lover and set out in person to seek his bride. Braving the storms, he sailed to Norway and met Anne at Oslo, where, in November, they went through another marriage ceremony. They stayed in Oslo until the new year and then journeyed overland – and over frozen seas – to Copenhagen, where James met his brother-in-law, the new King of Denmark, and was formally married for the third time. He and his bride were obviously enjoying themselves and did not return to Scotland until the summer of 1590.

James showed himself to be a considerate husband, at least until the birth of his eldest son, Prince Henry, in February 1594. Thereafter his insistence that the young prince should be placed under the guardianship of his old friend, the Earl of Mar, soured relations, and James increasingly went his own way and left Anne to do the same. When they came together, however, a degree of intimacy still prevailed, as was demonstrated by the fact that Anne, as well as experiencing a number of miscarriages, had seven children, of whom the last was born in 1606. Only three, however, survived infancy. Prince Henry grew into a healthy and athletic young man, but was struck down by typhoid in 1612 when he was eighteen. His younger brother, Charles (born in November 1600), lived to be King of Great Britain in succession to his father, but lost his life on the scaffold at the age of forty-eight; only Princess Elizabeth (born in August 1596), who married the Elector Palatine and spent one brief winter as Queen of Bohemia, came near achieving the psalmist's threescore years and ten, for she was sixty-five at the time of her death in London in 1662.

When James set sail for Norway he was accompanied by John Maitland of Thirlestane, who had taken the place of Arran as the King's principal adviser. James had shown his trust in Maitland, who was already Secretary of State, by appointing him Chancellor in 1587, but Maitland's dominance of the Scottish political scene was resented by the older nobility, particularly as he promoted the interests of the 'household' or bureaucratic elements among James's advisers – lawyers, lairds, and younger sons of noble families. James did not dare risk leaving so controversial a figure behind, for fear of an aristocratic *coup*. He also wanted to identify Maitland with the Danish match, since he knew that the Chancellor had been opposed to it and would have preferred a link with France. On the return of the royal party to Scotland, Maitland was elevated to the peerage, but this did not make him any more acceptable to the old nobility. The major challenge to him came from the Roman Catholic peers who held estates in the highlands, principal among them George Gordon, sixth Earl of Huntly. Maitland regarded such men as far more of a danger to the King than the presbyterians, and he persuaded James to move away from the policy of repression signalled by the Black Acts towards one of compromise and co-operation with the Kirk. He would also have liked the King to take a firm stand against the catholic peers, but James was reluctant to do so. He already had the English succession in mind, and did not want to alienate the English catholics, whose support he might need, by harsh treatment of their Scottish counterparts. For the same reason he wished to avoid doing anything which might lead to a papal excommunication. There was the further consideration that anti-catholic measures might provoke committed defenders of the old faith to take violent action against him, and the assassinations of William the Silent in 1584 and Henri III in 1589 showed that this was a very real risk.

Political considerations, as was so often the case with James, were intermingled with personal feelings. The Earl of Huntly, who was a few years older than James, had the combination of good looks and fine French manners to which the King was highly susceptible. Moreover, he was married to the daughter of Esmé Stuart, James's first favourite. In 1588, when the despatch of a Spanish armada against England sent catholic hopes in Scotland soaring, James appointed Huntly to command the royal guard and chose to ignore evidence that he was in treasonable communication with the King of Spain. Only in 1589, when Huntly and other catholic lords came out in open rebellion, was James driven into action. With the help of the protestant lords he raised an army and marched rapidly north. As he drew near Aberdeen, where Huntly was expected to make a stand, he spent a night in the field. "His Majesty would not so much as lie down on his bed", wrote one of his officers, "but went about like a good captain encouraging us."[47] Huntly's men were not prepared for this forceful riposte and deserted rather than fight, leaving the earl with no choice but surrender. However, he spent only a few months in prison before James ordered his release and allowed him to return to his estates.

The complexity of Scottish aristocratic factionalism is indicated by Huntly's alliance at this juncture with Francis Stewart, fifth Earl of Bothwell, who was one of his principal enemies. Bothwell, whose uncle had been the lover and then the husband of Mary, Queen of Scots, was handsome, intelligent and well read in several languages, but he had a highly unstable personality and pursued a wayward course regardless of the law or royal authority. He found the prospect of rebellion irresistible; hence his appearance alongside Huntly in 1589. When Bothwell first appeared at Court in the early 1580s he had been well received by the King, but James gradually came to distrust him. Distrust turned to fear and loathing when Bothwell was accused of consulting witches in order to raise a storm while the King was *en route* from Denmark to Scotland with his bride in 1590, and thereby imperil his life. James, like most of his contemporaries, believed in witchcraft. He later wrote a tract on it entitled *Daemonologie*, and in the *Basilicon Doron* he advised his son to include witchcraft – along with "wilful murder, incest . . . sodomy, poisoning, and false coin" – among those "horrible crimes that ye are bound in conscience never to forgive".[48] Just as God had his angels, so the Devil had his agents at work in the world, seeking to destroy those rulers whom God had appointed. James took an active part in the prosecution of the so-called witches, cross-examining them under torture. "Whatsoever hath been gotten from them", he boasted, "hath been done by me myself, not because I was more wise than others, but because I believed that such a vice did reign and ought to be suppressed."[49] In later years, once he was secure on the English throne, James came to doubt whether witchcraft existed, but in 1590 it appeared to pose a threat to his life that he could not ignore. Bothwell was arrested but escaped from captivity and took refuge in the lawless north of Scotland. He continued to enjoy the support of the militant Calvinists, with whom his cause was identified, and of many of the old nobility who resented the supremacy of the upstart Maitland. In December 1591 he made a raid upon the Palace of Holyrood House, where the King and Maitland were in residence, and James was only saved by the citizens of Edinburgh who came to his assistance. Six months later Bothwell tried to seize the King at Falkirk, and once again James was dependent upon the local people who flocked to his support.

While James was distracted first by his marriage and then by Bothwell, Huntly was engaged in the congenial pursuit of clan warfare. In February 1592 he outraged public opinion by launching a raid which culminated in the killing of his enemy, the popular Earl of Moray. Even then, James took no decisive action against him, and Huntly continued to solicit Spanish support. In December 1592 the arrest of a catholic courier led to the discovery of the 'Spanish blanks' – sheets of paper, signed at the bottom by Huntly and other catholic peers, on which Philip II was invited to write his terms for an invasion of Scotland. James summoned Huntly to St Andrews, so that the matter could be fully investigated, and when Huntly failed to appear he again raised troops and moved north. Huntly retreated rather than fight, but James did not pursue the campaign. As always where Huntly was concerned, he hoped to win over the earl by persuasion rather than force. This lack of decisiveness was attacked by the Kirk, which regarded it as a dereliction of duty, and led Queen Elizabeth to turn to Bothwell as a means of bringing pressure to bear upon the King. James was indignant when he heard this news. "Touching that vile man himself," he wrote to the English ambassador, "as his foul offences towards me are unpardonable and most to be abhorred for example's sake by all sovereign princes, so we most earnestly pray her to deliver him in case he have refuge any more within any part of her dominions, praying you to inform her plainly that if he be received or comforted hereafter in any part of her country I can no longer keep amity with her, but, by the contrary, will be enforced to join in friendship with her greatest enemies for my own safety."[50]

Elizabeth wrote a conciliatory reply, but did not abandon Bothwell. Her attempts to bring him and James closer together culminated in an extraordinary scene at the Palace of Holyrood House in July 1593. Not long after awakening, and while he was still dressing, James heard a noise in the adjoining chamber. When he went to investigate he found Bothwell kneeling in the room with a drawn sword before him. The offer of the sword was meant as a token of obedience, and Bothwell pleaded for pardon, but James feared yet another attempt upon his life and responded with cries of "Treason!" Only after the initial shock, and when the Duke of Lennox and other attendants made their appearance, did James agree to accept Bothwell's submission, on condition that he stood trial for his supposed contract with the witches, and until then kept away from Court. This seemed to be yet one more in the chain of episodes that demonstrated the King's inability to break out of the vicious circle of aristocratic factionalism, yet it was at times like these that James showed to best advantage. No sooner was he free to act than he recalled Maitland – who had retired from Court because he was so unpopular with all sections of society – and supported his efforts to build up a coalition of moderates prepared to rally behind the King.

It had become clear to James that he was not only putting at risk the English succession but also losing the support of his Scottish subjects by failing to take effective action against the northern earls. He had already begun mending his fences with the leaders of the Kirk, and in 1592 he gave his consent to the 'Golden Act' which annulled the Black Acts of 1584 and confirmed "all liberties, privileges, immunities and freedoms whatsoever given and granted . . . to the true and holy Kirk established within this realm". These included the right, "every year at the least, and oftener . . . as occasion and necessity shall require, to hold and keep general assemblies", though the timing of such meetings was to be left to the King or his deputy. Synodal and provincial assemblies were also given statutory confirmation, as were presbyteries, which now resumed the right to present ministers to livings "and to put order to all matters and causes ecclesiastical within their bounds, according to the discipline of the Kirk".[51] In many respects the legislation of 1592 merely acknowledged changes that had already taken place, for despite the passing of the Black Acts the number of presbyteries set up within the framework of the Scottish Church had multiplied, and they had a degree of vitality and public support which the bishops could not match. By the time the Golden Act was passed, Scottish episcopacy was at its nadir. To all intents and purposes it had ceased to exist.

The rapprochement between James and the presbyterians was signalled by the fact that when, in 1594, he once more led an army against the northern earls, he was accompanied by Andrew Melville. The advance guard of James's army was routed by Huntly at Glenlivet, but the earl had no stomach for a fight against the King and fled into the remote areas of the highlands. James continued his advance, burning down the houses of the rebels, and in March 1595 they surrendered and agreed to go into exile. A year later Huntly secretly returned, but was allowed to stay when he agreed to embrace the protestant faith. In June 1597 he was formally received into the Kirk, and shortly afterwards he was freed from the judgments pronounced against him for rebellion and given back his estates. A clear sign that he had been restored to royal favour came in April 1599 when the King created him a marquis. James had been much criticised for his failure to take resolute action against the dissident nobles, but his methods had paid off, for he had no further problem with the catholic lords.

Bothwell might have been more difficult to deal with, had he not demonstrated his utter lack of principles and convictions by joining Huntly in 1594. As a direct consequence of his betrayal of the Kirk he was excommunicated by the Edinburgh presbytery, acting at the King's command. He continued to roam about the highlands, but he was now an isolated and increasingly pathetic figure. By the end of 1595 he too had gone into exile, but unlike Huntly he never returned. He lingered on for nearly thirty years before dying in extreme poverty in Naples, a year before James I.

Bothwell's departure really marked the end of aristocratic factionalism in Scotland, except for the coda of the Gowrie Conspiracy on 5 August 1600. This extraordinary episode is so clouded with obscurity that it still defies explanation. All that can be said for certain is that the King spent the day hunting near Perth and then made his way to Gowrie House – the seat of John Ruthven, third Earl of Gowrie – where he was to take dinner. When the meal was over the King left the room, accompanied by Gowrie's brother, the Master of Ruthven, while Gowrie led the attendant lords into the garden. Sometime later it was reported that the King had left the house by a back way, and Gowrie went up to see whether this was the case. When he came down again he confirmed that the King had indeed left, but at this moment James's voice was heard shouting "Treason!" and his face briefly appeared at a turret window. The attendant lords rushed up to the room, where they found James apparently being assaulted by the Master of Ruthven, whom they killed on the spot. They then turned on Gowrie and killed him as well. The only eye-witness left alive was James, who put out an account of what had happened which was inconsistent and barely credible. When James summoned the five ministers of Edinburgh to hear his story and then relay it to their congregations, they expressed their scepticism and were promptly banished from the city.

Many people believed that James had arranged the whole incident in order to be rid of the Gowrie brothers. He had no reason to feel affection towards them. Their grandfather had played a prominent role in the assassination of Rizzio, while their father had held James prisoner in the Ruthven Raid, and had subsequently been executed. James might well have wanted to take his revenge on such a disloyal family, particularly since he was in debt to them to the tune of £80,000, but he could have done so without resorting to assassination. He accused one of the Edinburgh ministers who refused to believe his story of implying that he was a murderer, which James stoutly denied: "It is known very well that I was never bloodthirsty. If I would have taken their lives, I had causes enough. I needed not to hazard myself so."[52] It may be that the Gowrie brothers were planning to kidnap James, or that he assumed this to be the case and took fright. Whatever the truth behind the Gowrie Plot, it had such a traumatic impact upon the King that he kept its anniversary as a feast day for the rest of his life. In November 1605, writing to inform his brother-in-law, the King of Denmark, of the Gunpowder Plot, he compared it with the earlier occasion on which he had "escaped the impious and wicked hands of traitors bent on our destruction", and eighteen years later, when he penned a letter to Charles and Buckingham in Spain, he noted that he did so "upon the good fifth day of August".[53]

If the Gowrie Plot was an attempt to win power by seizing the King's person, it was a throwback to modes of behaviour which were now obsolete. By the close of the sixteenth century, and on the eve of his accession to the English throne, James had succeeded in his long-term aim of reducing the Scottish nobility to order, thereby allowing the rule of law to take precedence over the rivalry of factions. He had done this not so much by asserting his own authority as by waiting for his enemies to destroy themselves. The nobles, or at any rate a section of them, had clung, longer than other elements in Scottish society, to ideals of clan loyalty and personal bonds which were becoming increasingly outmoded. When, in 1598, James composed the *Basilicon Doron*, a manual on kingship drawn up by the King for the guidance of his eldest son and heir, he defined the "natural sickness" of the nobles as consisting in "a feckless arrogant conceit of their greatness and power". This had led them to overawe the "meaner sort", to "maintain their servants and dependers in any wrong", regardless of the law, and to engage in constant feuds, one against another. James advised his son not simply to "teach your nobility to keep your laws as precisely as the meanest" but also to acquaint himself with "all the honest men of your barons and gentlemen".[54] James had already shown Prince Henry the way. In the state, as in the Church, he had fostered the moderates, drawn primarily from the middle ranks of society, who wanted peace and good order above all other things, and looked to the crown to provide them. James had luck as well as judgment on his side, but by a combination of duplicity and pertinacity he had achieved a remarkable success.

The reduction of aristocratic power had been achieved only at the cost of conciliating the Melvillians in the Scottish Church and leaving episcopacy in limbo. James had not, however, given up all his influence in ecclesiastical matters. He retained the right to determine the time and place for meetings of the general assembly, and after the militants provoked a riot in Edinburgh in 1592 he outflanked them by summoning the next assembly to Perth. He was now deliberately cultivating the moderates among the Kirk's ministers, offering to pay their expenses in order to encourage them to attend meetings. By these means he gradually isolated the extremists and reduced their influence.

James derived strength from the fact that, as a protestant ruler, he offered the best chance of preserving and strengthening the reformed Church in Scotland. Although catholicism had been overthrown as the official religion of the state, it still had powerful adherents among sections of the nobility, as Huntly and his associates had demonstrated. And in Europe as a whole, catholicism was recovering from the initial impact of the Reformation and regaining lost ground. The French protestants, the Huguenots, who at one time had seemed an irresistible force, predestined for victory, were now fighting for their very existence. The Counter-Reformation movement had found secular champions, of whom the greatest – and, from the protestant viewpoint, the most threatening – was Philip II of Spain. The survival of protestantism depended in large part upon the survival of its staunchest defenders, the Dutch and the English, but their ability to resist was undermined by the expansion of Spanish power and their leaders were under constant threat – as was shown by the assassination of William the Silent in 1584 and the Babington Plot against Elizabeth in 1586.

Presbyterian leaders in Scotland would probably have preferred a theocracy along the lines of Geneva, and James had grounds for believing that they were crypto-republicans. But they had nothing to gain from overthrowing their protestant sovereign, even if this had been a practical possibility. It made far more sense to enlist him in their cause, but while their strategy may have been correct their tactics were at fault. Because they held such strong convictions and were so persuaded of the rightness of their position they tended to treat James as a child long after he had reached maturity. Men like Andrew Melville had a European reputation and were accustomed to being listened to with respect. Moreover, as God's messengers they claimed not merely a right but a positive duty to instruct the young King and tell him what to do. They treated him as they would have treated any member of their congregation, but they stood their ground all the more firmly because James could make decisions that affected the entire role of the Kirk in Scottish life. It never occurred to the hard-line presbyterians that what they regarded as no more than a statement of obvious truths might seem to James, and other people, a sign of intolerable intellectual arrogance. Nor did they ever seriously consider the possibility that James's own views on the role of a divinely appointed monarch might have something to be said for them, despite the fact that they were at variance with their own. James was amenable to learned argument, but they eschewed this in favour of browbeating and thereby stimulated the opposite reaction from the King to that which they were trying to produce.

This was shown most clearly and dramatically at a conference at Falkland Palace between the King and a commission from the general assembly in October 1596, following James's decision to allow the Earl of Huntly to take up residence again in Scotland. The commissioners had chosen James Melville, Andrew's nephew, to be their spokesman and to present their case "in a mild and smooth manner, which the King liked best of". But the conference had hardly begun when Andrew Melville, stung beyond endurance by what he regarded as the King's intransigence, intervened "in so zealous, powerful and irresistible a manner, that . . . [he] . . . bore him down, and uttered the commission as from the mighty God, calling the King but 'God's silly [i.e. simple] vassal;' and, taking him by the sleeve, says this in effect . . . 'Sir, we will humbly reverence Your Majesty always, namely in public, but since we have this occasion to be with Your Majesty in private, and the truth is, ye are brought in extreme danger both of your life and crown, and with you the country and Kirk of Christ is like to wreck, for not telling you the truth and giving of you a faithful counsel, we must discharge our duty therein or else be traitors both to Christ and you.

And, therefore, Sir, as divers times before, so now again, I must tell you, there is two kings and two kingdoms in Scotland. There is Christ Jesus the King, and his kingdom the Kirk, whose subject King James the Sixth is, and of whose kingdom not a king, nor a lord, nor a head, but a member.' "[55]

James kept his temper and the meeting ended amicably, but it can only have strengthened his belief that the Melvillians were a threat to his rule. In the *Basilicon Doron*, on which he was shortly to begin work, James inveighed against "some fiery spirited men in the ministry" who had "fed themselves with the hope to become *Tribuni plebis* [i.e. tribunes of the people]: and so, in a popular government by leading the people by the nose, to bear the sway of all the rule". He told his son to be on the alert against "these fanatic spirits" and to make sure that the principal men among them were excluded from his kingdom.[56] James would no doubt have liked to set his son an example in this respect, but exiling the Kirk's leaders at this stage would merely have confirmed their status as heroes and martyrs and made it more difficult for him to win over the moderate majority. He therefore preserved an uneasy *modus vivendi* with Andrew Melville and his fellow militants until his accession to the English throne.

While James had only limited success in curbing the militants in the Kirk, he managed to keep in being the shadow of episcopacy, even though he could not give it much substance. He took advantage of the fact that the Kirk needed to have representatives in Parliament to make sure its voice was heard. The general assembly, which appointed such representatives, referred to them only as 'commissioners' and insisted that their powers should be limited and carefully defined. James assured the Dundee assembly in 1598 that he had no intention of introducing "angelical nor papistical bishoprics, but only the best and wisest of their ministers, appointed by the general assembly".[57] In 1600, however, he persuaded a convention of commissioners to elect three bishops. Thereby, even if through the back door, he reinstated episcopacy in the Scottish Church. This represented the fulfilment of a long-held ambition, for James, from an early age, had regarded bishops as upholders of the royal authority, and he never wavered in his support for them, even when he had to make tactical concessions to their opponents. In the *Basilicon Doron* he advised his son to "entertain and advance the godly, learned and modest men of the ministry, whomof (God be praised) there lacketh not a sufficient number" and advance them to bishoprics and benefices. By so doing he would undermine the Kirk's insistence on the parity of ministers, "which can neither stand with the order of the Church, nor the peace of a commonweal and well ruled monarchy". He would also open the way to "re-establish the old institution of three estates in Parliament, which can no otherwise be done".[58]

By the time James began work on the *Basilicon Doron* the moment was fast approaching when he would leave Scotland to become King of England and, *ipso facto*, of Great Britain. The English succession was a matter of paramount importance for James, since it would free him from the constraints which impeded his rule in Scotland and elevate him in an instant to the upper ranks of the European princes. As early as April 1585, when he was only eighteen, he had by-passed his chief minister, the Earl of Arran, by opening up direct negotiations with Queen Elizabeth. He was duly rewarded when, in July 1586, Elizabeth agreed to pay him an annual pension of £4,000. A few months later, however, James's uncertain relationship with the ruler he addressed as "madame and dearest sister" entered its most difficult phase, for the ratification of the agreement coincided with the discovery of the Babington Plot against Elizabeth's life, in which James's mother, Mary Stuart, was involved. In October 1586 Mary was put on trial and found guilty. Only Elizabeth now stood between her and the block, and James used all the means at his disposal to persuade the Queen not to implement the death sentence. He sent messengers to the English Court to plead his case. He wrote to the Queen's favourite, the Earl of Leicester, protesting that while "my religion ever moved me to hate her [i.e. Mary's] course . . . my honour constrains me to insist for her life".[59] He also wrote directly to Elizabeth, to remind her of the danger of allowing human justice to strike down monarchs whom God himself had anointed and called gods."What thing, madame, can greatlier touch me in honour that [am] a king and a son than that my nearest neighbour, being in straitest [friend]ship with me, shall rigorously put to death a free sovereign prince and my natural mother . . . What monstrous thing is it that sovereign princes themselves should be the example-givers of their own sacred diadems' profaning."[60]

James had chosen his ground well. A straightforward plea on humanitarian grounds to save his mother would have had little impact on Elizabeth. But the Queen was susceptible to the argument that by permitting the execution of a monarch – albeit no longer a reigning one – she would endanger the entire institution of monarchy. Elizabeth, as is well known, delayed signing the death warrant, and even after she had done so she temporised about putting it into effect. The decisive action which led to Mary's execution in February 1587 was taken by Elizabeth's secretary, William Davison, whom the Queen promptly repudiated. By making Davison her scapegoat she freed herself from responsibility and was able to assure James that she had never intended the death of his mother. This enabled James to assure her that "considering your rank, sex, consanguinity, and long professed goodwill to the defunct, together with your many and solemn attestations of your innocency", he was willing "to judge honourably of your unspotted part therein". But he reminded her that in return he expected her to give him "such a full satisfaction in all respects as shall be a mean to strengthen and unite this isle, establish and maintain the true religion, and oblige me to be, as of before I was, your most loving and dearest brother".[61]

James's attitude towards his mother's execution, particularly the way in which he used his acquiescence in it as a bargaining counter to secure recognition of his right to succeed to the English throne, has contributed to the generally unfavourable picture of him. What became the standard view was summed up by the distinguished Victorian historian, Samuel Rawson Gardiner, when he declared that James's 'pressing the matter at such a time showed how little chivalry or even respect for decency there was in his nature'.[62] It is possible that if James had threatened to ally himself with England's principal enemy, the King of Spain, he might have made Elizabeth's ministers draw back from Mary's execution. But there was no certainty of this, and alliance with Philip II hardly made sense, since the Spanish champion of Counter-Reformation catholicism would have been happy to topple the heretic King of Scotland as well as the Queen of England. In practice there was little that James could do other than plead with Elizabeth to uphold the cause of monarchy to which she, no less than James and Mary, was committed.

After his pleas were rejected, James could have shown his anger by breaking with the Queen, but this once again would have been a pointless gesture, of no long-term benefit to James, to Scotland or to the protestant cause. James can be condemned for not showing greater overt affection for his mother, but Mary had abandoned him when he was a baby, and he had not seen her for nearly twenty years. It would have been gross hypocrisy on his part to have displayed a love that had never in fact existed. Moreover, as a direct consequence of Mary's selfish behaviour, James had been king virtually for his entire life, and had made the defence of kingship in general, and of his own in particular, the rudder by which he steered his course through the turbulent waters of Scottish politics and religion. Why should he suddenly have changed direction in order to make a gesture that would have been meaningless and, in its possible consequences, highly dangerous? James had learnt by long experience to accept and take advantage of conditions forced upon him by persons and circumstances over which he had no control. His reaction to the trial and execution of Mary, Queen of Scots, was in accord with the principles which had enabled him to survive and even to flourish. The triumph of those principles came in March 1603 when James peacefully ascended the English throne.

. . .

REFERENCES

1. Walter Carruthers Sellar and Robert Julian Yeatman, *1066 and All That*, 34th edn (Methuen, 1950), p. 61.
2. Sir Walter Scott, *The Fortunes of Nigel*, Waverley Novels, the Border Edition (1907), p. 83.
3. Thomas Babington Macaulay, *The History of England from the Accession of James II* (London, 1849), Vol. I, pp. 74–5.
4. [Sir Walter Scott, ed.] *Secret History of the Court of James the First* (Edinburgh, 1811), Vol. I, pp. 301–2 [hereafter *Secret History*].
5. *Secret History*, Vol. II, pp. 75–6.
6. *Dictionary of National Biography* [hereafter *DNB*] *sub* WELDON, Sir Anthony.
7. *DNB sub* WOOD, Anthony.
8. *Secret History*, Vol. I, p. 142.
9. *Secret History*, Vol. I, pp. 143–5.
10. *DNB sub* WILSON, Arthur.
11. David Harris Willson, *King James VI and I* (Jonathan Cape, 1956) [hereafter Willson].
12. Marc L. Schwarz, 'James I and the Historians: Towards a Reconsideration', *Journal of British Studies*, Vol. XIII, 1974.
13. C.H. Carter 'Gondomar: Ambassador to James I', *Historical Journal*, Vol. 7, 1964.

14. Mark Curtis, 'The Hampton Court Conference and its Aftermath', *History*, Vol. 46, 1961; D.E. Kennedy, 'The Jacobean Episcopate', *Historical Journal*, Vol. 5, 1962; S.B. Babbage, *Puritanism and Richard Bancroft* (SPCK for the Church Historical Society, 1962).

15. Kenneth Fincham and Peter Lake, 'The Ecclesiastical Policy of King James I', *Journal of British Studies*, Vol. 24, 1985.

16. Roger Lockyer, *Buckingham: The Life and Political Career of George Villiers, First Duke of Buckingham 1592–1628* (Longman, 1981).

17. Linda Levy Peck, *Northampton: Patronage and Policy at the Court of James I* (George Allen & Unwin, 1982).

18. Linda Levy Peck (ed.), *The Mental World of the Jacobean Court* (Cambridge University Press, 1991).

19. Jenny Wormald, 'James VI & I: Two Kings or One?', *History*, Vol. 68, 1983.

20. Maurice Lee, Jnr., *Government by Pen: Scotland under James VI & I* (University of Illinois Press, 1980).

21. Conrad Russell, *Parliaments and English Politics 1621–1629* (Clarendon Press, 1979).

22. [Sir J.G. Dalyell (ed.)] *Fragments of Scotish [sic] History* (Edinburgh, 1798), p. 83.

23. David Irving, *Memoirs of the Life and Writings of George Buchanan* (Edinburgh, 1817), pp. 160–1 [hereafter Buchanan].

24. Buchanan, p. 160.

25. Francis Osborne, *Advice to a Son*, ed. Edward Abbott Parry (1896), p. 2.

26. *DNB sub* YOUNG, Sir Peter.

27. Quoted in Willson, p. 29.

28. *The Autobiography and Diary of Mr James Melville* ed. Robert Pitcairn, Wodrow Society (Edinburgh, 1842), p. 45 [hereafter Melville].

29. Melville, p. 61.

30. Quoted in Gordon Donaldson, *Scotland: James V to James VII* (Oliver & Boyd, 1965), pp. 168–9.

31. *The Correspondence of Robert Bowes*, Surtees Society (Edinburgh, 1842), pp. 15 and 115 [hereafter Bowes].

32. Bowes, pp. 38 and 117.

33. Bowes, p. 141.

34. Bowes, p. 143.

35. *Letters of King James VI & I* ed. G.P.V. Akrigg (University of California Press, 1984), pp. 44–5 [hereafter *Letters*].

36. *Calendar of Letters and State Papers relating to English Affairs preserved principally in the archives of Simancas*, ed. Martin A.S. Hume, Vol. III *Elizabeth 1580–1586* (1896), pp. 207–8.

37. *The Poems of James VI of Scotland*, ed. James Craigie, Scottish Text Society (William Blackwood, 1958), Vol. II, p. 133.

38. Melville, p. 130.
39. Melville, p. 133.
40. Bowes, p. 134.
41. John Spottiswoode, *The History of the Church of Scotland* (Edinburgh, 1851), Vol. II, p. 290.
42. Bowes, pp. 477 and 479.
43. *Calendar of State Papers relating to Scotland and Mary, Queen of Scots 1547–1603*, ed. William K. Boyd, Vol. VII *1584–1585* (Edinburgh, 1913), p. 271.
44. Melville, p. 142.
45. *The Acts of the Parliaments of Scotland*, Vol. II *1567–1592* (1814), pp. 292–3, 296, 303, 347 [hereafter *APS*].
46. Quoted in David George Mullan, *Episcopacy in Scotland: The History of an Idea, 1560–1638* (John Donald, 1986) p. 61 [hereafter Mullan].
47. Quoted in Willson, p. 102.
48. *King James VI and I: Political Writings* ed. Johann P. Somerville (Cambridge University Press, 1994), p. 23 [hereafter *Political Writings*].
49. Quoted in Willson, p. 105.
50. *Letters*, pp. 120–1.
51. *APS*, pp. 541–2.
52. Quoted in Willson, p. 128.
53. *Letters*, pp. 276 and 421.
54. *Political Writings*, p. 28.
55. Melville, pp. 369–70.
56. *Political Writings*, pp. 26–7.
57. Quoted in Mullan, p. 85.
58. *Political Writings*, p. 27.
59. *Letters*, p. 78.
60. *Letters*, p. 82.
61. *Letters*, pp. 84–5.
62. *DNB sub* JAMES I.

Chapter 2

PHILOSOPHER KING AND LAWGIVER

James VI, now also and at last James I of England, reached London in early May 1603. He had been preceded by his written works, which were reprinted and published in the capital in anticipation of the King's arrival. The most important of these, from James's point of view, was the *Basilicon Doron*, a manual of advice composed for the instruction of his son and heir, Prince Henry. James completed the first version of this, written in Middle Scots, in 1598, but the following year he prepared an English edition, of which, however, only a handful of copies were printed. In other words, the work was originally intended for private circulation among the royal family, but the prospect of James's imminent accession to the English throne created a demand for it among his new subjects, which was met by pirate texts. James therefore issued an authorised version, with a specially composed preface in which he emphasised his commitment to the protestant faith, despite his expressed aversion to "puritans, and rash-heady preachers, that think it their honour to contend with kings and perturb whole kingdoms".[1] He also denied that he held any "vindictive resolution against England" because of the circumstances surrounding his mother's captivity and death.[2] James was at pains to point out that the treatise concerned Scotland. As far as England was concerned he would speak nothing of it, "as a matter wherein I never had experience". In any case there was, at the time when he composed the preface "a lawful Queen there presently reigning, who hath so long, with so great wisdom and felicity, governed her kingdoms as . . . the like hath not been read nor heard of, either in our time or since the days of the Roman Emperor Augustus".[3]

James had chosen his moment well, for the *Basilicon Doron* was already in print when Elizabeth died, and by the time he reached London it had circulated all over the country. It seems likely that the book was widely read as well as purchased, for James's new subjects were eager to have some indication of what lay in store for them. If they read it carefully they would have found few grounds for alarm in the *Basilicon Doron*. James began with God, who had given "this glistering worldly glory" to kings so that they might "glister and shine before their people in all works of sanctification and righteousness, that their persons, as bright lamps of godliness and virtue, may, going in and out before their people, give light to all their steps".[4] It followed that christian kings had a duty to discharge their office with equity and justice, maintaining the rule of law and subjugating their own private appetites to the common good. "Let your own life be a law-book and a mirror to your people", James advised his son, "that therein they may read the practice of their own laws, and therein they may see, by your image, what life they should lead."[5] Kings should maintain a pure and uncorrupt Court and make their choice of counsellors from "men of known wisdom, honesty, and good conscience . . . free of all factions and partialities".[6] In their personal life they should be above reproach, modest in dress and appetite, and models of conjugal fidelity.

James no doubt hoped that by publishing the *Basilicon Doron* he would reassure his English subjects and convince them that they had nothing to fear. It was not as if his belief in the divine authority of monarchs was anything new. It was, on the contrary, a truism, more or less taken for granted. It had been given formal expression as early as 1547, with the publication of an official homily "concerning good order and obedience to rulers and magistrates". This began by declaring that "Almighty God hath created and appointed all things in heaven, earth and waters in a most excellent and perfect order. In heaven he hath appointed distinct orders and states of archangels and angels. In earth he hath assigned kings, princes, with other governors under them, all in good and necessary order."[7] The Elizabethan homily on obedience, published in the wake of the Northern Rising of 1569, was even more explicit: "As God himself, being of an infinite majesty, power and wisdom, ruleth and governeth all things in heaven and in earth as the universal monarch and only king and emperor over all . . . so hath he

constitute, ordained and set earthly princes over particular kingdoms and dominions in earth, both for the avoiding of all confusion which else would be in the world . . . and also that the
princes themselves, in authority, power, wisdom, providence and
righteousness in government . . . should resemble his heavenly
governance". The authors of the homily acknowledged that not
all rulers measured up to the highest standards, but the worst,
no less than the best, were appointed by God. Mere subjects
had no right to judge "which prince is wise and godly and his
government good, and which is otherwise", for such questioning
might result in rebellion, which was never justified. "A rebel is
worse than the worst prince, and rebellion worse than the worst
government of the worst prince . . . Shall the subjects both by
their wickedness provoke God for their deserved punishment
to give them an undiscreet or evil prince, and also rebel against
him, and withal against God, who for the punishment of their
sins did give them such a prince?"[8]

James, in his political writings, stayed within the parameters
set out in the Elizabethan homily, yet the opening years of his
reign were to show that a good deal of apprehension and
misunderstanding remained. One reason for this was the shift
from the religious to the political sphere. Homilies were moral
injunctions with no specific consequences for everyday existence. James's philosopher king, on the other hand, operated in
the political world, and what he said or did was bound to have
an impact upon the lives of his subjects. James prided himself
upon his rectitude and his commitment to the *salus populi*, the
public good, but by defining the boundaries within which he
believed rulers should operate he was calling into question the
relationship between monarch and subject built up in England
over several centuries. James was, after all, a foreigner, a man
who had never set foot in England prior to his accession. The
emphasis in the *Basilicon Doron* was on the authority of the King
and the obedience owed to him. Little or nothing was said
about the rights and liberties of the subject, even though these
were of prime concern to the English political nation.

In his preface to the *Basilicon Doron* James explained that
he wrote it "for exercise of mine own engine [i.e. mind], and
instruction of him who is appointed by God (I hope) to sit on
my throne after me".[9] In the first part of the book, which deals
with religion and the nobility, James shows considerable skill
in arguing his case, but thereafter it becomes little more than a

collection of current commonplaces. There are a few Jamesian touches among these, such as the recommendation of hunting "with running hounds, which is the most honourable and noblest sort thereof", but even on a matter such as this, where James could have spoken out of practical knowledge, he feels the need to buttress his argument with the authority of the classics, calling to his aid "Xenophon, an old and famous writer, who had no mind of flattering you or me in this purpose".[10] There are many other pieces of advice which, far from reflecting James's own experience, run quite counter to it. The injunction to appoint as officers of state only men who were "free of that filthy vice of flattery, the pest of all princes"[11] comes oddly from a ruler who was particularly susceptible to it. And James's notorious addiction to favourites sits strangely with his advice to "employ every man as ye think him qualified, but use not one in all things, lest he wax proud and be envied of his fellows".[12] It could be that James, conscious of his defects in these respects, was warning his son against them, but this would imply a degree of self-knowledge for which there is little or no evidence. James had a defined morality, a coherent view of what was right, but he remained apparently unaware that in his own life he frequently departed from it.

It is significant that James chose to issue an authorised version of the *Basilicon Doron* for the benefit of his English subjects rather than *The True Law of Free Monarchies* which he had composed slightly earlier. In practice it made little difference, since the *True Law* was reprinted and in circulation at the time he reached London, but James had good reasons for wanting to distance himself from it at this particular moment, for it expressed far more forcefully than the *Basilicon Doron* his belief that kings were appointed by God and solely responsible to him. The *True Law* sprang directly from James's experience as King of Scotland, having its origins in his repudiation of the teachings of his tutor, George Buchanan, who has been described as 'by far the most radical of all the Calvinist revolutionaries'.[13] Buchanan was prompted to formulate his theories by the deposition of James's mother, Mary, Queen of Scots, in 1567. He took as his starting point the proposition that human societies are not created by God but by the people who compose them. If the people decide to delegate their authority to a ruler, they do so only under strict conditions and on the understanding that the grant is revocable: 'as Buchanan rather crushingly affirms, the people . . . must not be imagined to make any "transmission" of their original sovereignty, since they simply "prescribe to their king the form of his *Imperium*" with the aim of ensuring that "he acts like a guardian of the public accounts" '.[14] If the ruler failed to keep to the terms of the contract the people had made with him, they had a right to resist. In such circumstances even tyrannicide was justifiable.

Buchanan was not the originator of resistance theory. It was the French protestants, the Huguenots, who had been forced to develop such ideas when confronted with the reality of catholic rulers determined to destroy their faith. In Scotland the ground had been prepared by, among others, John Knox, but it was Buchanan who gave the theory its clearest and fullest exposition. He did so first in a Latin treatise, but followed this up with a vernacular *History of Scotland* which gave the fullest expression to his beliefs. The *History* was published shortly before Buchanan's death in 1582, but no sooner did James come of age than he secured a formal condemnation of it from the Scottish Parliament. Time brought no softening of his attitude, and although in the *Basilicon Doron* he encouraged his son to study the history of his own nation, he warned him against "such infamous invectives as Buchanan's or Knox's *Chronicles*: and if any of these infamous libels remain until your days, use the law upon the keepers thereof".[15]

James was not content with mere condemnation. He set himself to refute Buchanan's theories and put in their place a philosophical defence of kingship. The result was *The True Law of Free Monarchies*, published anonymously, but by the King's printer, in 1598. James explained, by way of introduction, that apart from knowledge of God there was nothing more important for subjects to understand than the constitution of their own state, "especially in a monarchy (which form of government, as resembling the divinity, approacheth nearest to perfection)". Sadly, the virtues of monarchy had been obscured by wilful men who encouraged rebellion and thereby brought about the destruction of the state. "And among others, no commonwealth . . . hath had greater need of the true knowledge of this ground than this our so long disordered and distracted commonwealth hath: the misknowledge hereof being the only spring from whence have flowed so many endless calamities, miseries and confusions." James had decided to provide his subjects with a defence of monarchy, so that they might know "the ground from whence these your many endless troubles have proceeded" and, by rejecting contrary courses, "divert the lamentable effects that ever necessarily follow thereupon".[16]

When James talked of a 'free monarchy' he meant one that was non-elective, one in which the ruler enjoyed full power and was not a mere Doge of Venice. Free kings were unconstrained by any human institution, being responsible only to God who appointed them. However, this did not mean they could rule as they pleased. The very fact that they would be called to account by the Almighty should encourage them to be good rulers, putting the welfare of their people above all other considerations. It was to emphasise this that when James published the *True Law* he gave it as a sub-title *The Reciprock and Mutual Duty betwixt a Free King and his Natural Subjects*. He began, understandably, with an analysis of the authority of the monarch, since this was the basis on which everything else depended. James turned for support to the Old Testament, and reminded his readers that "kings are called gods by the prophetical King David, because they sit upon God his throne in the earth, and have the [ac]count of their administration to give unto him".[17] But they were placed in this high office in order to ensure the worship of God and to administer justice impartially. Moreover, they voluntarily committed themselves to this task by the rite of coronation, in which they "give their oath, first to maintain the religion presently professed within their country . . . and next to maintain all the . . . good laws made by their predecessors". It was "this oath in the coronation", according to James, which was "the clearest civil and fundamental law whereby the King's office is properly defined".[18]

In return for the benefits of royal rule, the subject was required to give unconditional obedience. James was at one with the homily on obedience in believing that there was never any justification for rebellion. This applied even where a ruler was behaving tyrannically, for tyrants were as much the instruments of God as good kings, being sent to chastise a sinful people. The only remedy for subjects confronted by tyranny was prayer, and until God chose to answer their supplications they must patiently endure whatever suffering He chose to inflict upon them. In short, as James summed it up, the people owed allegiance and duty to their sovereign "as to God's lieutenant in earth, obeying his commands in all things, except directly against God, as the commands of God's minister, acknowledging him a judge set by God over them, having power to judge them, but to be judged only by God".[19]

When James turned to consider the origins of kingship he admitted that in "divers commonwealths and societies" it was the people who had, in the first instance, chosen one among themselves to rule over them in order to maintain peace and harmony in the body politic. This was not the case with Scotland, however, for the first King of Scots was an Irishman, Fergus, who came with an army and established his authority by conquest. "The kings therefore in Scotland were before any estates or ranks of men within the same, before any parliaments were holden, or laws made: and by them was the land distributed (which at the first was wholly theirs) . . . And so it follows of necessity that the kings were the authors and makers of the laws, and not the laws of the kings."[20] What was true of Scotland, said James, was also true of England, for William the Conqueror had imposed himself in exactly the same manner as Fergus, and changed the laws to suit his own convenience. It was true that in both countries the people, through their representatives in Parliament, were involved in the making of new laws, but unlike the King they had no power to act alone. "For albeit the King make daily statutes and ordinances, enjoining such pains thereto as he thinks meet, without any advice of Parliament or estates, yet it lies in the power of no Parliament to make any kind of law or statute without his sceptre be to it, for giving it the force of a law."[21] In practice, James conceded, monarchs would usually observe existing laws because they promoted the common good, to which the King was committed. But this was a matter of choice, not obligation, and if the laws were not working satisfactorily the King had the right to suspend or alter them.

Kings, then, according to James, were like fathers to their people, and enjoyed the same authority over their subjects that the law of nature gave to fathers over their families. And just as it would seem "monstrous and unnatural"[22] for sons to rise up against their father, so would it be for subjects to rebel against their sovereign. There were some people, James acknowledged, who claimed that the principal duty of subjects was to the state or society in which they lived. If a tyrannical ruler was doing harm to that state, then they had the right to get rid of him. James countered this with the by now familiar argument that those born to be judged can never become judges; where kings were concerned, the only valid judgment came from God. But he also argued that rebellion, even if it was for the purpose of saving the state, invariably led to its destruction, for a bad king is better than no king at all, and the only alternative to royal rule is anarchy. James appealed to "the divine poet Du Bartas" for confirmation of his belief, quoting his dictum that "better it were to suffer some disorder in the estate, and some spots in the commonwealth, than, in pretending to reform, utterly to overthrow the republic".[23]

If bad rulers, no less than good rulers, could justifiably demand allegiance from their subjects, surely this would imply that "the world were only ordained for kings, and they without controlment to turn it upside down at their pleasure"? Not so, replied James, for they were subject to divine judgment, and God was "the sorest and sharpest schoolmaster that can be devised".[24] The greater the ruler, the greater his responsibility; and the higher his throne is set, the further he will fall when God condemns him for ruling badly. James ended, however, by turning to the positive aspects of kingship and expressing his desire that Kings of Scotland should be loving fathers to their people. While the King should desire "all his earthly felicity and happiness" to be grounded upon his subjects' wellbeing, they in return should demonstrate their "care for his honour and preservation". In such a case, "the land may think themselves blessed with such a king, and the King may think himself most happy in ruling over so loving and obedient subjects".[25]

The *True Law* is a classic defence of divine-right monarchy, but it is important to remember that it was written in the context of Scottish post-Reformation society, for the presbyterian insistence upon the primacy of God's word made reading a virtual necessity for all adherents of the reformed faith. This was a source of strength and authority to authors such as George Buchanan, whose writings were widely disseminated and admired. Buchanan's *History of Scotland* was particularly influential, and its republican message might well have gone unchallenged had not James produced the *True Law*. Given that an intellectual war was raging in Scotland it made sense for James to intervene, and by basing his arguments upon the Bible he appealed to the same audience as his adversaries. It should not be assumed that the *True Law* was a final statement of James's position. It was a propaganda piece, designed to make the case for monarchy in the most forceful fashion, and later on, after his accession to the English throne, James would withdraw from some of his more extreme positions. Yet he never wavered in his belief that monarchy had been ordained by God as the best form of government, and that the authority of sovereigns could never rightfully be called into question by subjects.

The nature of the King's authority, and in particular the relationship between the royal prerogative and the rights of the subject, became a matter of public controversy in 1610 when the House of Commons initiated proceedings against John Cowell, professor of civil law at Cambridge, who, in his law dictionary entitled *The Interpreter*, had stated that the King was "above the law by his absolute power . . . and though at his coronation he take an oath not to alter the laws of the land, yet this oath notwithstanding, he may alter or suspend any particular law that seemeth hurtful to the public estate".[26] A similar view was expressed by Samuel Harsnett, Bishop of Chichester, in a sermon given in March 1610. James moved swiftly to defuse the crisis by issuing a proclamation suppressing *The Interpreter*, not because of what it said but on the grounds that nobody had the right "to wade in all the deepest mysteries that belong to the persons or state of kings or princes, that are gods upon earth".[27] Shortly after this, on 21 March 1610, James appeared before both Houses of Parliament, where, in a long and carefully constructed speech, he defined his position.

James began with an uncompromising assertion of divine-right kingship. "The state of monarchy", he declared, "is the supremest thing upon earth, for kings are not only God's lieutenants upon earth, and sit upon God's throne, but even by God himself they are called gods . . . for that they exercise a manner or resemblance of divine power upon earth".[28] Following the same line of argument that he had already set out in the *True Law*, James likened royal power to that of fathers over their families and compared the King to the head of a natural body, which "hath the power of directing all the members of the body to that use which the judgment of the head thinks most convenient".[29] But he went on to make two important concessions. While approving the substance of what Bishop Harsnett had said, he emphasised that Harsnett had been arguing in the abstract and along theological lines. Had James been in his place he would have pointed out the "difference between the general power of a king in divinity, and the settled and established state of this crown and kingdom".[30]

James expanded upon this difference in his second concession, when he distinguished "between the state of kings in their
first original, and . . . the state of settled kings and monarchs
that do at this time govern in civil kingdoms". While in a primitive society the will of the King would be law, in a settled state
he would be *lex loquens,* the mouthpiece of existing law.[31] James
emphasised that a good king was not merely bound to observe
the law by virtue of his office; he also explicitly contracted
to do so through his coronation oath. Therefore, while James
would never allow the fundamental nature of royal authority to
become a matter for public debate, he accepted that his actual
policies could be called into question. "To dispute what God
may do is blasphemy; but *quid vult Deus* [i.e. what God wishes],
that divines may lawfully and do ordinarily dispute and discuss."
In like manner, he would "not be content that my power be
disputed upon; but I shall ever be willing to make the reason
appear of all my doings, and rule my actions according to my
laws".[32]

James, of course, came from a country which had no common law in the English sense. Scotland, with its close links with
France and European culture in general, had been strongly
influenced by the revival of Roman or civil law that had begun
in the late Middle Ages and accelerated during the Renaissance. While humanists admired Roman law for its coherence
– especially when compared with the patchwork of customs,
enactments and codes that made up the differing legal systems
of European states – rulers were attracted by its legitimation
of their authority. One of the most famous (or notorious) civil-
law maxims was *quod principi placuit legis habet vigorem* – 'the
prince's will has the force of law' – and although there were
other maxims pointing in a different direction they attracted
less attention. James's defence of kingship was in accord with
the principles of civil law, even though he preferred to base
his arguments upon the Old Testament, and there were many
among his English subjects who feared that he would favour
the reception of civil law. James acknowledged as much in his
speech of 21 March 1610: "some had a conceit I disliked [the
common law], and (in respect that I was born where another
form of law was established) that I would have wished the civil
law to have been put in place of the common law for government of this people".[33] But this fear, James protested, was
entirely unjustified. He did indeed esteem the civil law, "the

profession thereof serving more for general learning, and being most necessary for matters of treaty with all foreign nations",[34] but he would only allow it to operate, as was already the case, in the Church courts and Court of Admiralty. Where property rights and "the fundamental laws of this kingdom"[35] were concerned, the common law alone would have jurisdiction. Just in case his listeners doubted his commitment, James assured them that he had "least cause of any man to dislike the common law, for no law can be more favourable and advantageous for a king, and extendeth further his prerogative, than it doth".[36] Not only this: "I am so far from disallowing the common law, as I protest that if it were in my hand to choose a new law for this kingdom, I would not only prefer it before any other national law, but even before the very judicial law of Moses."[37]

James's admiration for the common law – always assuming it was genuine – did not blind him to its deficiencies. As an outsider he could see these more clearly than many of his English subjects, and he noted, in particular, the lack of system in its recording and classification. Despite the Herculean efforts of Sir Edward Coke, the common law had nothing to match Justinian's *Institutes* and *Digest*, on which the study of the civil law was based. As James correctly observed, "our common law hath not a settled text in all cases, being chiefly grounded upon old customs or else upon the Reports and cases of judges". He suggested that Parliament should set on foot the codification of English law, and, at the same time, reduce the statute book to order, "in respect there are divers cross and cuffing statutes, and some so penned as they may be taken in divers, yea contrary, senses". He also proposed that the law should be written in English instead of Norman-French, which he described as "an old, mixt and corrupt language, only understood by lawyers, whereas every subject ought to understand the law under which he lives".[38] Not all lawyers were proponents of reform. They valued the privileged position which their mastery of precedents and law-French gave them, and they believed that Coke's magnificent series of *Reports* came as close as need be to classification. Overlapping and lack of clarity in statutes, on the other hand, were acknowledged weaknesses, and when, in 1621, James appointed commissioners to survey and improve the statute book, Parliament gave the project its blessing. Much of the impetus for this came from Sir Francis Bacon, now Lord Chancellor, but his fall from power, following accusations that he had accepted bribes, caused interest to wane. In any case, by 1621 the European crisis was coming to dominate English politics, and law reform dropped out of sight.

While James acknowledged the pre-eminence of the common law he insisted that it should not go beyond its customary boundaries and invade other jurisdictions. In particular, he upheld the right of the Church courts to deal with matters that properly pertained to them, and not to be inhibited by writs of prohibition from the two principal common-law courts, King's Bench and Common Pleas. This, as will be seen in Chapter 6, brought him into open conflict with Sir Edward Coke, the Chief Justice of King's Bench and one of the greatest lawyers of his day. Coke worshipped at the shrine of common law, which he regarded as the quintessence of human wisdom and the lodestone by which rulers as well as subjects should be guided. He could not accept that a mere king, even one as learned and conscientious as James, should act as arbiter in disputes over the boundaries that divided one jurisdiction from another. Coke was perfectly ready to acknowledge that God had endowed James with great natural gifts, but insisted that matters affecting "the life or inheritance or goods or fortunes of his subjects are not to be decided by natural reason, but by the artificial reason and judgment of law".[39] James would not have disagreed with this, for he acknowledged that property cases were the preserve of the common law, but he would never accept Coke's vision of that law as, in effect, the fundamental law or constitution of England, to which not only the King's subjects but the King himself were subordinate.

For James, the King was the source of law as well as its guardian, and the judges whom he charged with upholding the law acted in his name and on his behalf. He informed the judges in 1616 that "the seat of judgment is properly God's, and kings are God's vicegerents, and . . . judges are deputed under them, to bear the burden of government . . . As kings borrow their power from God, so judges from kings. And as kings are to account to God, so judges unto God and kings."[40] James did not mean to imply by this statement that judges should be mere executants of the royal will. Although he acknowledged his own accountability towards God he did not interpret this as meaning that he was not a free agent when it came to ruling his kingdoms. Similarly with the judges: once he had appointed them, their duty was to act as they saw fit in order to uphold the law. James took pride in the fact that, as he told Parliament in 1621, he had made "the best judges that I knew; judges of learning and integrity". Even more to the point, he had maintained their integrity: "I did neither move them either directly or indirectly to do otherwise than was agreeable to right and equity." This was the function of monarchs. Indeed, "he is not fit to be a king that hath not a care to have the judges under him like unto himself, just and faithful".[41]

The independence of the judges was demonstrated when they decided, quite contrary to James's expressed opinion, that the creation of a new state of Great Britain would automatically annul existing English liberties, yet they were not totally detached from the royal government. Twice a year they set out on assizes which took them the length and breadth of the country, and while their principal function was to deal with cases remitted to them by the Justices of the Peace they also conducted an enquiry into the functioning of local administration and reported back to the King when they returned to Westminster. In the opinion of Sir Francis Bacon – himself, of course, a distinguished lawyer as well as philosopher – no ruler had ever worked so closely with his judges as James did. "He confers regularly with them upon their returns from their visitations and circuits. He gives them liberty both to inform him and to debate matters with him, and in the fall and conclusion commonly relieth on their opinions."[42]

Although the judges were independent in the exercise of their authority, they were expected to consult with the crown when matters directly affecting it were at issue. Sometimes the government itself took the initiative – as in Bate's Case, 1606, when Lord Treasurer Dorset enquired about the attitude of the Exchequer judges towards the validity of Impositions. Similarly, in 1615, the Privy Council asked the judges whether they thought there was sufficient evidence to proceed with the indictment of Edmond Peacham, a clergyman accused of inciting sedition. On this occasion James insisted that the judges should be consulted individually rather than as a body, for he was increasingly distrustful of Sir Edward Coke and feared that his opinionated and uncompromising Lord Chief Justice might induce the bench to hold aloof from giving a reply. The following year saw another case involving the crown, but when Attorney-General Bacon, at James's command, asked the judges to delay any decision on the matter until they had been fully informed of the crown's position, Coke persuaded them to reject this request on the grounds that it was contrary to their oath to delay justice. James was furious, and did not conceal his anger at what he regarded as a totally unwarranted rebuff. He reminded the judges of the care he had taken "to see justice administered to our subjects with all possible expedition, and how far we have ever been from urging the delay thereof in any sort". With respect to the present case, "we are far from crossing or delaying anything which may belong to the interest of any private parties . . . but we cannot be contented to suffer the prerogative royal to be wounded through the sides of a private person".[43]

James summoned the judges to appear before him so that he could explain his position in person, and so impressed were they by what he said – and no doubt also overawed by the display of regal indignation to which they were subjected – that they "fell down upon their knees and acknowledged their error for matter of form, humbly craving His Majesty's gracious favour and pardon for the same".[44] The only exception, as always, was Coke, who continued to maintain, albeit from a kneeling position, that the judges were inviolably bound never to delay justice. James dismissed this assertion as "mere sophistry" and called on Lord Chancellor Ellesmere to give a decision on the point of law which had been raised. Ellesmere "delivered his opinion clearly and plainly that the stay that had been by His Majesty required was not against law, or any breach of a judge's oath". James then instructed the judges to deliver their individual opinions. Eleven of the twelve accepted that in any case "which His Majesty conceived to concern him either in power or profit, and thereupon required to consult with them" they should stay proceedings until consultation had taken place. The odd man out was Coke, who declined to make any decision on an entirely hypothetical case and contented himself with the Delphic utterance that when the time came he would act as a judge ought to do.[45]

Coke

James was not by temperament a patient man, but although he clearly regarded Sir Edward Coke with increasing irritation and suspicion he was not, as yet, ready to take the momentous step of removing him from office. It was Coke himself who precipitated his downfall by threatening in 1616 to bring an action in King's Bench against the Court of Chancery. The common lawyers' suspicion of Chancery was of long standing, for its *raison d'être* consisted in submitting the judgments of other courts to considerations of equity and overriding the letter of the law in favour of the spirit. In short, it stood for common sense over and against common law. Coke had no time for such pretensions. He dismissed Chancery as an upstart, and regarded its attitude towards judgments given in King's Bench and Common Pleas as something approaching blasphemy. By threatening to curtail its independence he was asserting the supremacy of the common law and its institutions. But James regarded all courts as the King's courts and insisted that where there was a clash of jurisdictions it was for him alone to adjudicate. Coke was the equivalent, in the legal sphere, of the Scottish Melvillians, who had claimed an authority co-equal and in some respects superior to the King's. It was a claim that James could never accept, and in June 1616 he suspended Coke from office. Six months later he formally dismissed him.

Coke was undeniably a great lawyer, and there is something appealing about his vision of the judges as independent arbiters between King and people, interpreters of a law that was above all human restraints or considerations. He is sometimes regarded as the archetypal early seventeenth-century lawyer, embodying the profession's view of itself and its role, but in fact he was a maverick. The prevailing attitude was much closer to that expressed by Coke's rival, Sir Francis Bacon, shortly after his appointment as Lord Keeper in 1617. One of his functions was to address the judges before they went on circuit, and he took the opportunity to remind them that although their principal concern must be "by all means with your wisdom and fortitude to maintain the laws of the realm" they should also remember that "the twelve judges of the realm are as the twelve lions under Solomon's throne. They must be lions, but yet lions under the throne. They must show their stoutness in elevating and building up the throne."[46]

James's repeated professions of his commitment to the common law and of his determination to administer justice impartially were not mere word play. As the years passed it became clear to his English subjects that he meant what he said and that they had nothing to fear. He kept alive the study of the civil law and he upheld the authority of those courts – particularly the Church courts – in which it was practised. He also insisted on his right to be consulted by the common-law judges in all matters affecting the royal prerogative, not so that he might bring undue pressure to bear upon them but to ensure that his legitimate interests, as well as those of his subjects, were taken into account. But there was never any threat under James to the supremacy of the common law; nor, despite his dismissal of Sir Edward Coke, was there any threat to the integrity of the judicial bench. Indeed, it was Coke himself who declared, on the title page of Part IX of his *Reports*, that it was published "in the 10th year of the most high and most illustrious James, King of England, France, and Ireland, and of Scotland the 46, the fountain of all piety and justice, and the life of the law". Coke was not above using flattery when he thought it would serve his turn, but on this occasion he was speaking no more than the truth.

. . .

REFERENCES

1. *King James VI and I: Political Writings* ed. Johann P. Somerville (Cambridge University Press, 1994), p. 5 [hereafter *Political Writings*].
2. *Political Writings*, p. 8.
3. *Political Writings*, p. 11.
4. *Political Writings*, p. 13.
5. *Political Writings*, p. 34.
6. *Political Writings*, p. 37.
7. *Certain Sermons or Homilies* (1547) and *A Homily against Disobedience and Wilful Rebellion* (1570) ed. Ronald B. Bond (University of Toronto Press, 1987), p. 161 [hereafter *Certain Sermons*].
8. *Certain Sermons*, pp. 212, 213 and 214.
9. *Political Writings*, p. 4.
10. *Political Writings*, p. 56.
11. *Political Writings*, p. 37.
12. *Political Writings*, p. 38.
13. Quentin Skinner, *The Foundations of Modern Political Thought.* Vol. 2: *The Age of Reformation* (Cambridge University Press, 1978), p. 343, n. 1 [hereafter Skinner].
14. Skinner, p. 342.
15. *Political Writings*, p. 46.
16. *Political Writings*, p. 63.
17. *Political Writings*, p. 64.
18. *Political Writings*, pp. 64–5.
19. *Political Writings*, p. 72.
20. *Political Writings*, pp. 72–3.
21. *Political Writings*, p. 74.
22. *Political Writings*, p. 77.

23. *Political Writings*, p. 79.
24. *Political Writings*, p. 83.
25. *Political Writings*, p. 84.
26. G.W. Prothero (ed.), *Select Statutes and other Constitutional Documents illustrative of the reigns of Elizabeth and James I*, 4th edn (Clarendon Press, 1946), pp. 409–10.
27. J.P. Kenyon (ed.), *The Stuart Constitution 1603–1688*, 2nd edn (Cambridge University Press, 1986), p. 126.
28. *Political Writings*, p. 181.
29. *Political Writings*, p. 182.
30. *Political Writings*, p. 182.
31. *Political Writings*, p. 183.
32. *Political Writings*, p. 184.
33. *Political Writings*, p. 180.
34. *Political Writings*, p. 185.
35. *Political Writings*, p. 185.
36. *Political Writings*, p. 184.
37. *Political Writings*, p. 185.
38. *Political Writings*, pp. 186–7.
39. *The Reports of Sir Edward Coke, Kt.* (1738), Part XII p. 65.
40. *Political Writings*, pp. 205–6.
41. *Commons Debates 1621* ed. Wallace Notestein, Frances Helen Relf and Hartley Simpson (Yale University Press, 1935), Vol, II, p. 11.
42. *The Works of Francis Bacon* ed. James Spedding (1874), Vol. XII, p. 11 [hereafter Bacon].
43. Bacon, Vol. XII, p. 361.
44. Bacon, Vol. XII, p. 365.
45. Bacon, Vol. XII, pp. 365–7.
46. Bacon, Vol. XII, pp. 201–2.

Chapter 3

THE UNION

When James VI of Scotland ascended the English throne as James I he inaugurated a new dynasty. But while we think of James as the first Stuart, this was not his own view of himself. He always emphasised his descent from the Lancastrian Henry VII – whose chapel in Westminster Abbey he selected as his burial place – and also from Henry's wife, Elizabeth of York. He took great pride in the fact that, as he reminded his first Parliament in March 1604, "the union of the two princely roses of the two houses of Lancaster and York" was "reunited and confirmed in me". Henry VII had put an end to the Wars of the Roses; now it was the turn of James VI & I to put an end to the centuries of hostility between Scotland and England. "The union of these two princely houses", he told the assembled members of Parliament, "is nothing comparable to the union of two ancient and famous kingdoms."[1]

To James it was self-evident that he had been divinely chosen as the agent of this supreme achievement. Henry VII had only been able to unite York and Lancaster through marriage, but James was, in his own person, the legitimate ruler of both England and Scotland. Simply by acceding to the English throne he had created a union of crowns. The silver medal minted to celebrate his accession described him, in Latin, as 'Emperor of the whole island of Britain', and the coronation medal of 1604 hailed him as 'Caesar Augustus of Britain'. The new coinage issued in the same year and designed for use in both kingdoms similarly carried James's new title of 'King of Great Britain'. When he made his formal entry into London James passed under a series of elaborately decorated arches on which the figure of Monarchia Britannica welcomed him as the imperial ruler of a united realm.[2] All that was now needed was to turn the union of crowns into a union of states, and this, thought James, should not be difficult, since the way had been prepared by divine providence. "Hath not God first united these two kingdoms both in language, religion, and similitude of manners?" he asked the assembled members of Parliament in March 1604. "Yea, hath He not made us all in one island, compassed with one sea?" And he went on, in language resonant with biblical undertones and deliberately echoing the marriage service, "what God hath conjoined then, let no man separate. I am the husband, and all the whole isle is my lawful wife. I am the head, and it is my body. I am the shepherd, and it is my flock."[3]

James did not anticipate opposition to a project that was so clearly in accord not only with God's will but with the best interests of his subjects in both kingdoms. Even before leaving Edinburgh he had ordered new signets to be prepared, in which the arms of England and Scotland should be joined together, and he also announced that in future the former borderlands should be regarded as "the very heart of the country". A month later, in May 1603, but this time from London, he issued a proclamation commanding all his people "to repute, hold and esteem both the two realms as presently united and as one realm and kingdom, and the subjects of both the realms as one people, brethren and members of one body". He also announced that he had "found in the hearts of all the best disposed subjects of both the realms, of all qualities, a most earnest desire that the said happy union should be perfected".[4] This may have been little more than wishful thinking on James's part, but the merits of union were so transparently obvious to him that he regarded "would-be hinderers of this work" as "either blinded with ignorance, or else transported with malice . . . and only delighting to fish in troubled waters".[5]

James saw no reason, at this stage, to doubt the willingness of his English subjects to go along with him. The first Parliament of the new reign opened in March 1604, and the Commons were initially preoccupied with a dispute over the Buckinghamshire election. One of the candidates was Sir John Fortescue, a Privy Councillor, but he had been defeated at the polls by Sir Francis Goodwin. However, Goodwin was under sentence of outlawry for failure to pay his debts, and the Chancery office, which was responsible for the issue and return of writs, therefore decided that his election was invalid. This did not please the Commons, who, in Elizabeth's reign, had claimed the right to make the final decision upon disputed elections. James, however, was concerned to uphold the traditional rights of the crown, and he therefore instructed the members to confer with the Lords before they took further action. The Commons were always sensitive upon the issue of their privileges, and particularly resented any suggestion that the Lords should have a role in defining their parameters. James therefore intervened again, announcing via the Speaker that "he was now distracted in judgment" and commanding the House "as an absolute King" that they should attend a conference with the judges.[6] Members seem to have been taken aback by James's message, but not, apparently, by his use of the term 'absolute'. All that James meant by this was that his right to the throne was beyond dispute and that he would exercise all the powers that had belonged to his predecessors. The Commons were far more worried by the prospect of having their privileges defined by the judges than they were at James's intervention. Indeed, one member proposed that they should ask James "to be present, to hear, moderate and judge the case himself".[7]

James did in fact preside over the meeting and, after listening to the various points of view, decided that both Fortescue and Goodwin should be disbarred and that a new election should take place. This was the umpiring role that James delighted to play, and although some members of the Commons no doubt resented what they regarded as unwarranted interference in their affairs, the House expressed its satisfaction and sent a delegation to James to give him formal thanks. In his response, James insisted that he had never had any intention of infringing the Commons' privileges. On the contrary, "he carried as great a respect to our privileges as ever any prince did. He was no ground-searcher. He was of the mind that our privileges was his strength." And in case any lingering doubts remained, James assured the delegates that just as they came to give him thanks, "so did he redouble his thanks to us: that he had rather be a king of such subjects than to be a king of many kingdoms".[8]

James took advantage of the goodwill evident at this meeting to urge the Commons to make the Union their main business – "that union which with the loss of much blood could never be brought to pass, as now it is". It was, he told them, his deepest wish to leave behind him at his death "one worship to God, one kingdom entirely governed, one uniformity in laws".[9] Given this order of priorities it came as a shock to James when the Commons, far from hastening towards a statutory union as he had hoped and expected, postponed consideration of it. Opposition was most marked in the Lower House, though it was rumoured that the leading critics had covert support from certain lords. James was anxious to obtain parliamentary authority to assume the title of King of Great Britain, and on 14 April 1604 the Lord Chancellor, speaking on the King's behalf, called on both Houses to give this speedy consideration. He also proposed that the Parliaments of Scotland and England should appoint commissioners "to see what laws are to be taken away, what to be new made, [and] what to be else done for the perfecting of this union".[10] The change of royal title might seem a mere formality, but many members of the Commons feared that the creation of the new state of Great Britain would inevitably entail the end not only of the name of England but also of English political liberties. The summary of speeches given in the *Commons' Journal* for 19 April 1604 reflects these fears: "We cannot make any laws to bind *Britannia* . . . If we take away the name we take away the maxims of the law . . . Let us proceed with a leaden foot. As our predecessors have left us free, so let us leave our successors without prejudice."[11]

James could not understand why there should be any objections to granting him a title which was *de jure* already his: "the isle was Britany, and therefore, being king of the whole island, he would be King of Britany, as Brutus and Arthur were, who had the style and were kings of the whole island". This, said James, was the reason for pressing ahead. Not simply was it a matter of honour for him "to be called that which he was", but the change of title in itself would help bring about closer unity, "because shadows beget substance, and unity in name an unity in affection". As for fears about the loss of traditional liberties and the danger of innovation, what foundation could there be for these when he had made plain his commitment to maintain his subjects' rights as well as the legitimate prerogatives of the crown? "To suspect him to bring in innovation", James declared, "were to slander him."[12]

Because he was so sure of the correctness of his position on this issue, James instructed the judges to consider the matter and "declare the truth". However, his confidence was given a severe jolt when he received their response, for in the words of Robert Cecil, his chief minister, they had "joined with the opinion of three parts of the House, that the first hour wherein the Parliament gives the King the name of Great Britany, there followeth necessarily . . . an utter extinction of all the laws now in force".[13] James's initial reaction to this unexpected verdict was moderate. He instructed Cecil to inform the Commons that he had no intention of assuming his new title until his subjects' liberties were assured; meanwhile, they should press ahead with the appointment of commissioners to treat with the Scottish Parliament. But James's pride had been wounded and he deeply resented the rebuff which the Commons had in effect delivered him. He showed his hurt in a letter to the Speaker, in which he accused members of displaying "jealousy and distrust, either of me the propounder, or of the matter by me propounded. If of me, then do ye both me and yourselves an infinite wrong, my conscience bearing me record that I ever deserved the contrary at your hands." James insisted that there were no valid grounds for the Commons' negative attitude, since nothing could or would be done without their consent. He blamed them for allowing themselves to be "transported with the curiosity of a few giddy heads" and reminded them that they alone had to make the choice, either "by the away-taking of that partition wall which already, by God's providence, in my blood is rent asunder, to establish my throne and your body politic in a perpetual and flourishing peace", or else to spit in God's face by dishonouring their King and sowing the seeds of discord for their posterity.[14]

The Commons were stung by James's accusations, not least because there was so much truth in them. Like many modern politicians they claimed they had been misreported, and therefore proposed sending a deputation to the King, to show "how much we take his late letter to heart".[15] Later they changed their minds, but James sent a message saying that he approved of their original intention, and that "if they had come [he] would have explained himself, and endeavoured to have given them satisfaction".[16] The Commons expressed their thanks for this gracious message, but the bitterness at what they regarded as unfair criticism remained, and expressed itself in an attack on the Bishop of Bristol for daring to publish *A Discourse plainly proving the evident Utility and urgent Necessity of the desired happy Union of England and Scotland* – a work which, according to one member, tended "to the derogation and scandal of the proceedings of the House in the matter of the union" and was described by another as "the greatest scandal that may be remembered to be offered to the House of Parliament".[17] When the attention of the House of Lords was called to this matter, the bishop apologised for inadvertently causing offence, but discontent continued to simmer in the Commons. Members were drawing up a comprehensive defence of their actions and attitudes to present to the King, and in this they described the bishop's book as "injurious and grievous to us, being written expressly with contempt of the Parliament and of both the Houses in the highest degree".[18]

This *pièce justificative*, known as *The Form of Apology and Satisfaction*, was never formally adopted by the House, which presumably wanted to avoid an open confrontation with James, but it almost certainly reflected the opinion of the majority of members. It was prompted in part by the union, by the fear that, as one anti-union pamphlet put it, "the change of style will be, as it were, the erecting of a new kingdom, and so it shall be, as it were, a kingdom conquered, and then may the King add laws and alter laws at his pleasure".[19] It was also a riposte to the version of benevolent royal absolutism propounded by James in his writings and speeches. James saw no alternative, other than anarchy, to the rule of the prince, but insisted that subjects had nothing to fear from such a rule, particularly when, as in his case, the prince was godly and committed to his people's welfare. Such an attitude made sense in the Scottish context, where weak rule had indeed resulted in widespread lawlessness. This had also been the case in England during the Wars of the Roses, but these had been brought to an end soon after the accession of James's forebear, Henry VII, in 1485, and England had thereafter enjoyed more than a century of relative internal peace. There was another difference between the two kingdoms. The common law of England enshrined property-rights in a way that protected them even against the crown, and the statutes which both clarified and amended the common law included the various confirmations of *Magna Carta* that further limited the sovereign's power. It was hardly coincidence, therefore, that the classic statement of English liberties and the English constitution had been provided by a lawyer, Sir John Fortescue, who held office as Chief Justice of the King's Bench under Henry VI. In his *De Laudibus Legum Angliae* ('In Praise of the Laws of England') and *On the Governance of the Kingdom of England* Fortescue distinguished between two types of polity. The first was *dominium regale*, or absolute kingly rule, as epitomised in Valois France. The second was *dominium politicum et regale*, of which England was the shining example. In such a state the authority of the crown was circumscribed and the King "may not rule his people by other laws than such as they assent unto".[20] Fortescue's work was well known in early Stuart England, as indeed was *Magna Carta*, of which an English version had been published in 1524. The lawyers in the House of Commons were among its most prominent members, and because they had daily experience, in their court cases, of the authority of precedent, they were particularly aware of the need to ensure that James did not permanently alter the balance of power between crown and law, King and Parliament, royal prerogative and the rights of the subject. And even if they had little to fear in this respect from James himself, what of his successors? In the words of the *Form of Apology*, "if good kings were immortal as well as kingdoms, to strive so for privilege were but vanity perhaps and folly; but seeing the same God who in his great mercy hath given us a wise King and religious doth also sometimes permit hypocrites and tyrants in his displeasure and for the sins of the people, from hence hath the desire of rights, liberties, and privileges . . . had its just original, by which an harmonical and stable state is framed".[21]

Although the *Apology*, since it had no formal status, was never officially presented to James, he clearly knew of its contents, for when he prorogued Parliament in July 1604 he observed that "the best apology-maker of you all, for all his eloquence, cannot make all good". He also commented on the contrast between his experience in Scotland and that in England. "In my government bypast of Scotland (where I ruled amongst men not of the best temper), I was heard not only as a king, but, suppose I say it, as a counsellor. Contrary, here nothing but curiosity from morning to evening to find faults with my propositions. There, all things warranted that come from me; here all things suspected." He did not accuse members of disloyalty but of being over-inquisitive, looking for possible dangers where in fact there were none, and more concerned to make a name for themselves than to advance the King's and kingdom's business. Worst of all, they had displayed bad manners. "I wish you had kept better form," he told them. "I like form as much as matter. It shows respect, and I expect it, being a king [as] well born (suppose I say it) as any of my progenitors."[22]

The first session of Parliament had not been totally sterile. Commissioners had been nominated to treat with their Scottish counterparts, and they held their first meeting in October 1604. The question of the royal title was not included in the commissioners' remit, but James put an end to further discussion on this matter by issuing a proclamation announcing that "we have thought good to discontinue the divided names of England and Scotland out of our regal style, and do intend and resolve to take and assume unto us . . . the name and style of King of Great Britain".[23] Proclamations, unlike statutes, had no effect upon the common law, so James had not overridden Parliament; rather, he had by-passed it. It is easy to see why he did so, and indeed to sympathise with him. James was undoubted King of England, Ireland and Scotland; he was therefore, *de facto*, King of Great Britain. All he had wanted from Parliament was formal acknowledgment of what God had already given him, but the Commons had declined to consider the new royal title until they fully understood what sort of a state 'Great Britain' would be. James was so convinced of the rightness of his claim that he blamed private interests, malice, and wilful obstruction for the Commons' reluctance. Instead of waiting indefinitely for Parliament to act, he chose "to do by ourself that which justly and safely we may by our absolute power do . . . by force of our kingly power and prerogative".[24]

The issue of the union was not taken up again until 1606, by which time the two Houses had before them the draft Instrument drawn up by the commissioners. James, in his opening speech, called the attention of members to three main issues – the abolition of all laws deriving from the former hostility between England and Scotland; the establishment of free trade between the two kingdoms; and the naturalisation of the *pre-nati*, those Scots who had been born before his accession to the English throne. If James was hoping for swift progress he was once again to be disappointed. A bill abolishing the hostile laws was eventually passed, but nothing was done about free trade. And rather than agree to the naturalisation of the *pre-nati*, the Commons spent many hours discussing whether even the *post-nati*, born after James's accession, should, like their sovereign, be simultaneously English and Scottish – in other words, British. When the Lords called on the judges for their advice on this matter, the judges came down in favour of the *post-nati*, but the Commons remained unconvinced. They were asking for guarantees that the rights of native-born English men and women should not be undermined, but as James pointed out, if they would not trust either the judges or himself they might well find that they finished up in a worse condition than before.

There had been suggestions made by certain members of the Commons that if the House did not receive satisfaction in the matter of the union it should in effect go on strike by refusing to consider any other legislation. James warned the Commons against such a course, and reminded them that although he was their sovereign he was also "a man of flesh and blood, and have my passions and affections as other men. I pray you, do not too far move me to do that which my power may tempt me unto."[25] But rather than end with an implied threat, James appealed directly to the hearts of his listeners. "Let your affection and love to your Prince appear . . . and go forwards so as you may redeem time . . . so as you may rejoice in me, and I glory in you. And tempt not my patience with frivolous discourses and delays, who ever have striven to overcome you in patience."[26]

James was not, by nature, a patient man, but in projects as close to him as the union he displayed a remarkable degree of restraint. Addressing Parliament in March 1607 he said that when he had first broached the topic of the union he thought it would be a mere matter of form, requiring little or no discussion. This, he now admitted, was a misjudgment, caused by over-confidence on his part: "I knew mine own end, but not others' fears." He did not blame the members for their reluctance to trust him, since they had "not yet had so great experience of my behaviour and inclination, in these few years past, as you may peradventure have in a longer time hereafter"; nor had they had "occasion to consult daily with myself, and hear mine own opinion in all those particulars which are debated among you". He now realised that great causes needed long deliberation and he was content that they should "go with leaden feet, so you make still some progress, and that there be no . . . needless delay".[27]

James spoke as if the project for statutory union between his two principal kingdoms was still alive, but in fact it was dead. When a member attempted to revive it in the 1610 session, he was greeted with "interruption and whistling" from his fellow members, who had "no great taste *en ce potage rechauffé* ['for this warmed-up soup']".[28] James accepted defeat since he had no choice, but it came as a severe blow to his self-esteem. The debates on the subject had revealed the depth of anti-Scottish sentiment in the Commons. The new member for Buckinghamshire, Sir Christopher Pigott, was speaking for many when he declared that the Scots were all beggars, rebels and traitors, who made a habit of murdering their rulers: "they have not suffered above two kings to die in their beds these last two hundred years. Our King hath hardly escaped them."[29] This pithy summary of recent Scottish history was all the more wounding in that it was soundly based, but James saw irrational prejudice rather than historical accuracy in Piggott's outburst, and believed that it extended to himself. Far from concealing his emotions, James put them on public display. He alternately cajoled and wooed his audience, and constantly appealed for their trust. When this was not forthcoming, he took it as a personal affront.

James's experience in Scotland had taught him that time could often accomplish what mere human endeavour had failed to achieve. He never abandoned the concept of union, and the Court masques, which were regarded as a means of moulding informed opinion, continued to emphasise what one of them entitled "Triumphs of reunited Britain".[30] His journey to Scotland in 1617, carried out in the face of determined opposition from his English advisers, was another means of forcing public attention to lift its horizon beyond the northernmost English counties. These areas, like their Scottish counterparts, were ceasing to be frontier zones plagued by lawlessness and gradually turning into the 'heart of the country' as James had foreseen. Certainly for the inhabitants of these parts the union of crowns brought positive gains. But there was never any merging of national identities in either England or Scotland, and James seems to have been unique in his acceptance of the fact that he was neither English nor Scots but 'British'. He had set an example and invited his subjects to emulate it, but in this instance there was no response. The failure of James's attempt to reshape the way in which his people thought of themselves was a reminder of the limits on what even a divinely appointed and ordained monarch could achieve.

. . .

REFERENCES

1. *King James VI and I: Political Writings* ed. Johann P. Somerville (Cambridge University Press, 1994), pp. 134–5 [hereafter *Political Writings*].

2. Keith M. Brown, 'The Vanishing Emperor: British Kingship and its Decline 1603–1707' [hereafter Brown] in Roger A. Mason (ed.), *Scots and Britons: Scottish Political Thought and the Union of 1603* (Cambridge University Press, 1994).

3. *Political Writings*, pp. 135–6.

4. Quoted in James F. Larkin and Paul L. Hughes (eds), *Stuart Royal Proclamations. Vol. I: Royal Proclamations of King James I* (Clarendon Press, 1973), p. 19 [hereafter *Proclamations*].

5. *Political Writings*, p. 136.

6. *Journals of the House of Commons 1547–1714*, Vol. I (1742), p. 166 [hereafter *CJ*].

7. *CJ*, p. 166.

8. *CJ*, p. 171.

9. *CJ*, p. 171.

10. Historical Manuscripts Commission, *Report on the Manuscripts of the Duke of Buccleuch & Queensberry*, Vol. III (1926). VI: *The Montagu Papers*, Second Series, p. 86.

11. *CJ*, p. 178.

12. *The Works of Francis Bacon* ed. James Spedding (1874), Vol. X, p. 194 [hereafter Bacon].

13. Bacon, p. 200.

14. *CJ*, pp. 193–4.

15. *CJ*, p. 197.

16. *CJ*, p. 199.

17. *CJ*, p. 226.

18. J.R. Tanner (ed.), *Constitutional Documents of the Reign of James I* (Cambridge University Press, 1930), p. 225 [hereafter Tanner].

19. Quoted in Brian Levack, *The Formation of the British State: England, Scotland, and the Union 1603–1707* (Clarendon Press, 1987), p. 38.

20. Sir John Fortescue, *The Governance of England*, ed. Charles Plummer (1885), p. 109.

21. Tanner, pp. 222–3.

22. J.P. Kenyon (ed.), *The Stuart Constitution 1603–1688*, 2nd edn (Cambridge University Press, 1986), p. 37.

23. *Proclamations*, p. 96.

24. *Proclamations*, pp. 96–7.

25. *CJ*, p. 368.

26. *The Parliamentary Diary of Robert Bowyer 1606–1607* ed. David Harris Willson (University of Minnesota Press, 1931), p. 288.

27. *CJ*, p. 358.

28. John Beaulieu to William Trumbull, 15 February 1610, printed in *Memorials of Affairs of State in the Reigns of Q. Elizabeth and K. James I collected (chiefly) from the Original Papers of the Right Honourable Sir Ralph Winwood, Kt., Sometime one of the Principal Secretaries of State* (1725), Vol. III, p. 119.

29. Quoted in Bruce Galloway, *The Union of England and Scotland 1603–1608* (John Donald, Edinburgh, 1986), p. 4.
30. Brown, p. 73. See also Martin Butler, 'The Invention of Britain and the Early Stuart Masque' in R. Malcolm Smuts (ed.), *The Stuart Court and Europe: Essays in Politics and Political Culture* (Cambridge University Press, 1996).

Chapter 4

PRIVILEGES AND PREROGATIVE

At the beginning of every Parliament the Speaker of the Commons formally requested the sovereign to confirm the House's privileges. The most important of these was the privilege of freedom of speech, but there was no agreement on what exactly this entailed. In the 1590s Elizabeth I had insisted that while every member was free "to say yea or no to bills . . . with some short declaration of his reason therein", he did not have the right "to frame a form of religion or a state of government as to their idle brains shall seem meetest. She saith no king fit for his state will suffer such absurdities."[1] James's attitude was identical. In 1610 he forbade members to "meddle with the main points of government", since "that is my craft".[2] In 1621 he was more explicit, warning the Commons not "to meddle with complaints against your King, nor with the Church, nor with state matters, nor with princes' prerogatives". If there was among the members any "unquiet spirit and busybody" seeking to bring up such forbidden topics, he should be rejected as "a spirit of Satan sent into the House to overthrow the good errand in hand".[3]

Elizabeth had taken it for granted that it was up to her to define the boundaries within which the privileges of the Commons were operative, and had never felt any need to justify her position. But James preferred a more explicit approach. He was, after all, an unknown quantity in his new kingdom, and it therefore made political sense for him to prevent unjustified apprehension by explaining where he stood on such issues, and why. Furthermore, he was a philosopher, with a desire to enlighten. He was also a man of reason, seeking to persuade by argument, particularly since he was certain he was right. He therefore told the members of his first Parliament "that he had no purpose to impeach their privilege, but since they derived all matters of privilege from him, and by his grant, he expected they should not be turned against him".[4]

James can hardly have anticipated that the Commons would be upset by his observation that they derived their privileges from royal grant. What he had written about Scottish kingship – namely, that it existed "before any parliaments were holden, or laws made"[5] – was equally applicable to the English monarchy. Since "kings and kingdoms were before parliaments"[6] it followed that parliamentary privileges must originally have been conferred by the ruler. History, in this instance, was confirmed by current practice, for it was the Commons' Speaker who requested confirmation of the House's privileges, and the sovereign who granted this.

The Commons, however, could not and would not accept that their privileges were dependent upon the King's grant, for this would have implied the King's right to rescind them if he saw fit. The House decided to draw up a defence of its own position, and a committee was appointed to draft what became known as *The Form of Apology and Satisfaction* (see above, p. 56). This began by claiming that the privileges of the Lower House were part and parcel of "the rights and liberties of the whole commons of your realm of England which they and their ancestors from time immemorable have undoubtedly enjoyed". As for the Speaker's request for these privileges to be confirmed, it was "an act only of manners" and had no substantive significance.[7] It was not only freedom of speech which was at stake. Bearing in mind other disputes that had disturbed the wished-for harmony between Commons and crown in the first Parliament of the new reign, the *Form of Apology* affirmed that "our House is a court of record, and so ever esteemed", and that it was also "the sole proper judge" of election returns.[8]

As Geoffrey Elton reminded us more than thirty years ago, the *Apology* is not a revolutionary document, not the first step along the highroad to civil war.[9] The Commons were defending their corner at a time when they perceived their position to be under threat. "What cause we your poor Commons have to watch over our privileges", they declared, "is manifest in itself to all men. The prerogatives of princes may easily and do daily grow; the privileges of the subject are for the most part at an everlasting stand. They may be by good providence and care preserved, but being once lost are not recovered but with much disquiet."[10] The *Apology* was suffused with expressions of loyalty, but also with a sense of indignation that James had either not been truly informed of the Commons' rights and privileges, or had misunderstood them. For this reason, as J.R. Tanner correctly observed, the *Apology* was 'a lecture to a foreign King on the constitutional customs of the realm which he had come to govern, but which he so imperfectly understood'.[11] Yet it should not be assumed that the Commons' analysis of the existing conventions was either impartial or authentic. In the absence of any written constitution or supreme court to resolve fundamental disagreements, both King and Parliament were left with no choice but to make a vigorous defence of what they believed to be their rights. James, no less than the Commons, was determined to preserve his inheritance. Addressing Parliament in 1610 he told members not to "meddle with such ancient rights of mine as I have received from my predecessors . . . All novelties are dangerous as well in a politic as in a natural body, and therefore I would be loth to be quarrelled in my ancient rights and possessions, for that were to judge me unworthy of that which my predecessors had, and left me."[12]

It was because the issue of privileges, and in particular the Commons' privilege of free speech, was of such major importance to both parties that it was never resolved in James's reign. It flared up again in 1621, when the outbreak of the Thirty Years War had brought into question the very survival of protestantism in Europe. The temperature of debate among the populace rose to such a pitch that James issued a proclamation requiring all his subjects, "from the highest to the lowest, to take heed how they intermeddle, by pen or speech, with causes of state and secrets of empire either at home or abroad".[13] When Parliament assembled in January 1621, members of the Commons were apprehensive that the proclamation might inhibit their own discussions, even though the Lord Chancellor, in response to the Speaker's customary request at the opening of the new session, had assured them "that His Majesty did give them free liberty of speech, so as they kept themselves within the compass of dutiful subjects".[14] Sir Robert Phelips, one of the leading members of the Commons, gave his opinion that they had "a duty of care to them that succeed us, to leave our liberty to them in the entire we received it from those that went before us", and recalled, albeit inaccurately, that in 1604 the House had presented a remonstrance to James – i.e. *The Form of Apology*

– "declaring that they had as good right to their liberties of Parliament, principally that of speech, as to their inheritance".[15]

Another echo of the *Apology* came when the House went into committee to consider what to do about the apparent breach of its liberties implicit in the King's proclamation, and "it was said that the prerogatives of princes grow daily, but the liberties of subjects stand at a stay".[16] The House was minded at first to proceed by petition, but subsequently decided in favour of a bill to establish their freedom of speech.[17] The idea of placing the Commons' privileges upon a statutory basis was anathema to James, and he therefore instructed his Secretary of State, George Calvert, to take the heat out of the debate by transmitting a message to the House. In this, James declared that "we neither have by any act or speech of ours heretofore, nor intend by any hereafter, any way to lessen or diminish the lawful and free liberty of speech which appertains unto the House of Commons and hath been heretofore allowed unto them by any of our noble progenitors".[18] Calvert added that up to this point the Commons had behaved in so dutiful and loyal a fashion that James had no reason to expect that any member would "so far transgress the bounds of his duty as to give any cause to be questioned for speaking that which becomes him not in this place". If such a transgression should occur, it was up to the House to pre-empt royal intervention by taking appropriate action itself.[19]

The King's message calmed the House and put an end to the debate on the issue of free speech for that session. But it rose up in an even more acute form when Parliament reassembled in the winter of 1621. In December, the Commons – acting, as they thought, in response to an implied request from the King – presented James with a petition on foreign policy, an area of government that was traditionally reserved to the crown. James, in his reply, accused members – or at least "some fiery and popular spirits" – of debating topics far above their reach, "to our high dishonour and breach of prerogative royal". He therefore commanded them not to "presume henceforth to meddle with anything concerning our government or deep matters of state".[20] The Commons, convinced they had been the victim of misunderstanding because James had given credence to "partial and uncertain reports", sent a further petition protesting that they had never intended "to encroach or intrude upon the sacred bounds of your royal authority, to whom and to whom only we acknowledge it doth belong to resolve of peace and war". They were alarmed, however, by the way in which James seemed "to abridge us of the ancient liberty of Parliament for freedom of speech", for this was "our ancient and undoubted right, and an inheritance received from our ancestors; without which we cannot freely debate nor clearly discern of things in question before us, nor truly inform Your Majesty".[21]

In his response to this second petition, James threw the charge of being misled back in the Commons' face. As "an old and experienced King" he needed no such lessons, since he never gave any attention to "idle reports". It would be better for the Commons if they did the same and ignored the special pleadings of "some tribunitial orators among you". As for their claim that they had never intended to encroach upon the royal prerogative, this was like a thief stealing a man's purse while at the same time insisting that he did not mean to rob him. Whatever the Commons said, their actions implied a "plenipotency . . . [which] invests you in all power upon earth, lacking nothing but the Pope's to have the keys also both of heaven and purgatory". In this respect they were no better than Scottish puritans or catholic controversialists. James could not accept that the privileges of the Commons were theirs by undoubted right and inheritance, since they "were derived from the grace and permission of our ancestors and us (for most of them grow from precedents, which shows rather a toleration than inheritance)". As King, he would be careful to maintain and preserve the liberties of the Commons, so long as they contained themselves within dutiful limits, but if they attempted to "pare his prerogative and flowers of the crown" he would be left with no alternative but "to retrench them of their privileges".[22]

James's forceful reiteration of his position was initially received with some relief, since it ended by committing him to uphold the liberties of the House. But after a day's reflection the mood changed to such an extent that James sent another letter designed to remove all doubts about his attitude. While still insisting that he could not allow the House to use "antimonarchical words . . . concerning their liberties" he assured them that "whatsoever liberties or privileges they enjoy by any law or statute shall be ever inviolably preserved by us . . . Whatsoever privileges they enjoy by long custom and uncontrolled and lawful precedents we will likewise be as careful to preserve them, and transmit the care thereof to our posterity."[23] From the Commons' point of view, the problem with this letter, as with James's position in general, was his continuing insistence that their privileges derived from, and were therefore dependent upon, royal grant. Moreover, there was considerable irritation at the extent to which the daily activities of the House were guided, if not controlled, by royal decree. Sir Nathaniel Rich objected to the way in which they were commanded to "Meddle not with this business!" or to "Go to this business first!" He felt the Commons should be free to choose their own priorities and order their own debates. "When I speak of freedom of speech, I mean not licentiousness and exorbitancy, but speech without servile fear, or, as it were, under the rod."[24]

The House was so preoccupied with the question of its privileges that work on bills had ground to a halt. James regarded this as wasting time – "time . . . which is not theirs but ours"[25] – and warned members that if they did not immediately turn to their principal business he would bring the session to a close. This had the effect of concentrating the Commons' minds, but not on the King's business so much as their own. In the short time that remained to them they – or at least the minority of prominent and regular speakers – were determined to draw up a statement in defence of their privileges, something that could be recorded in the *Commons' Journal* for the guidance of future generations. In the words of William Noy, "Freedom of speech we must have, or else no counsel. It is the life of counsel . . . This we must stand upon."[26] The outcome was *The Commons' Protestation* of 18 December 1621. This began with the unambiguous statement that the liberties of Parliament were "the ancient and undoubted birthright and inheritance of the subjects of England", and that members had the right to discuss "arduous and urgent affairs concerning the King, state, and defence of the realm, and of the Church of England". Moreover, in debating such matters the Commons should have "freedom of speech to propound, treat, reason and bring to conclusion the same". No member should be liable to any censure, other than that of the House, for speeches concerning parliamentary business, nor should the King "give credence to any private information" about individuals without first seeking the declared opinion of the House as a whole.[27]

Although the 1621 *Protestation* was clearly inspired by, and to some extent based upon, *The Form of Apology*, it went well beyond that document in the extent of its claims. And whereas the *Apology* had remained in a sort of limbo, half-way between an unofficial and an official statement of the Commons' position, the *Protestation* was to be given formal sanction by being inscribed in the *Commons' Journal*. The Commons intended thereby to establish it as, in some sense, a legal record, or at any rate a clear precedent for future generations. Since James regarded the Commons' position as usurped and untenable, he could not possibly allow such a record to remain. He therefore summoned his Councillors and the judges to attend him at Whitehall, sent for the *Journal*, and ripped out the offending page. This was a considered act, not a display of bad temper. By removing the *Protestation* from the *Journal* he had removed its quasi-legal status and consigned it to formal oblivion.

James was not content with this symbolic gesture. He believed that the Commons, misled by a handful of "evil and discontented persons", had behaved in a manner which did not accord with the attitude or desires of their constituents. He therefore broke with English precedent by issuing a proclamation in which he gave a detailed account and defence of his proceedings. He was now going over the heads of the Commons and appealing to informed public opinion at large. Beginning with a reminder that "the assembling, continuing and dissolving of parliaments [is] a prerogative so peculiarly belonging to our imperial crown . . . that we need not give account thereof to any", James announced that "according to our continual custom to make our good subjects acquainted with the reasons of all our public resolutions and actions, we have thought it expedient at this time . . . to note some especial proceedings moving us to this resolution". There followed a summary of parliamentary proceedings, in which James emphasised that "it was our intent to have made this the happiest Parliament that ever was in our time" and that in the opening session there had "passed greater and more infallible tokens of love and duty from our subjects to us, their sovereign, and more remarkable testimonies from us of our princely care and zeal of their welfare, than have been in any parliament met in any former age". The harmony between King and Commons would have continued, had it not been for the fact that some "particular members of that House took such inordinate liberty, not only to treat of our high prerogatives . . . but also to speak with less respect of foreign princes, our allies, than were fit for any subject to do of anointed kings". When James warned the Commons to keep within their accustomed bounds, "they either sat silent, or spent the time in disputing of privileges [and] descanting upon the words and syllables of our letters and messages". The last straw came when, "in an unseasonable hour of the day and a very thin House, contrary to their own custom in all matters of weight", they drew up a protestation "in such ambiguous and general words as might serve for future times to invade most of our inseparable rights and prerogatives". This, declared James, was "an usurpation that the majesty of a king can by no means endure".[28]

James was so convinced that members of the political nation would see the justice of his case that in early 1622 he followed up the proclamation with "His Majesty's Declaration touching his proceedings in the late Assembly and Convention of Parliament". He had already assured his subjects that the abrupt end of the 1621 Parliament did not mean that he was out of love with the institution. In order to avoid "all sinister suspicions and jealousies" he declared that it was "our intent and full resolution . . . to govern our people in the same manner as our progenitors and predecessors, kings and queens of this realm of best government, have done . . . and that we shall be as glad to lay hold of the first occasion in due and convenient time, which we hope shall not be long, to call and assemble our Parliament, with confidence of the true and hearty affections of our subjects".[29] No doubt James meant what he said, but if circumstances had permitted him to spend the rest of his reign without a Parliament, he would probably have been quite content. In the event, his hand was forced by the growing pressure for English involvement in the Thirty Years War, and the need to make financial provision for such an eventuality. In February 1624 James opened his fourth, and last, Parliament, expressing the hope that "after the miscarriage of three, this may prove happy".[30] When the Speaker made the customary request for the Commons' privileges, he chose his words with care. He spoke, he said, as a "humble suitor" and he asked James to confirm the House's "ancient privileges . . . with your gracious favour according to ancient precedents".[31] The ensuing weeks were to show that the Commons had no wish to renew the struggle over their liberties. The whole future of English policy was now at stake, and James had, for this once, set aside his prerogative by inviting the Commons to make known their views. "Never king gave more trust to his subjects than to desire their advice in matters of this weight", he informed them, and "I assure you ye may freely advise me, seeing, of my princely fidelity, ye are entreated thereunto".[32] In these circumstances it would have been madness on the part of members to raise an issue certain to provoke the King's anger and lead to an abrupt dissolution. When Sir John Eliot attempted to draw them along this path, they refused to follow, for they "were afraid this motion would have put the House into some such heat as to disturb the great business".[33] James's last Parliament was not without its share of 'misunderstandings', but they did not arise out of disputes over the privilege of free speech. This was a matter on which both parties maintained a *de facto* truce, but neither changed its position. The gap between them was as wide at James's death as it had been at his accession to the English throne.

Freedom of speech was not the only privilege matter to cause dissent between James and the Commons. Freedom from arrest was another, for James, like Elizabeth before him, believed this privilege did not apply to any action taken by the crown. During the bitter exchanges of December 1621 James warned the Commons "that we think ourself very free and able to punish any man's misdemeanours in Parliament, as well during their sitting as after",[34] and he had already given evidence of this. After the bad-tempered and frustrating Addled Parliament of 1614, he ordered the interrogation of nine members, of whom four were imprisoned, and following the dissolution of the 1621 Parliament he sent Sir Edward Coke and Sir Robert Phelips to the Tower. The House did not take kindly to the imprisonment of its members, but since this usually occurred after their meeting was ended it never became a major source of dissension in James's reign.

The language of liberty spoken by the Commons' leaders when they defended their privilege of free speech is very much in tune with the beliefs and assumptions of present-day democratic societies. Conversely, James's assertion of his 'absolute rights' seems to smack of tyranny and dictatorship. But this is to confuse 'absolute' with 'arbitrary' rule. When James spoke of being an 'absolute king' he meant one who was in full possession of those powers which customarily belonged to monarchs, but who would rule in a traditional manner, putting the welfare of his subjects above all other considerations. Divine right, far from being a licence for tyranny, was a restraint on arbitrariness. Yet kings had a duty to God to rule, as well as to rule well: they were under an obligation to uphold both the powers and the duties associated with their high office. James was undoubtedly correct in stating that the privileges of the Commons derived from royal grant, and although the Commons might affirm, and indeed believe, that they were doing no more than defend their ancient privileges, they were in fact making new claims. As James's Lord Chancellor, Lord Ellesmere, observed in 1611, "the popular state, ever since the beginning of His Majesty's gracious and sweet government, hath grown big and audacious, and in every session of Parliament swelled more and more. And if way be still given unto it (as of late hath been) it is to be doubted what the end will be." He went on to warn that it was the duty of wise and skilful pilots, when they saw a storm approaching, to take appropriate measures. "Great and dangerous inundations happen, for the most part, by reason that small breaches are neglected and not looked unto and stopped in the beginning."[35]

James was convinced that among the most active members of the Commons were a handful of what he called "tribunes of the people".[36] These were the persons whom the Speaker described as "our seedmen of . . . sedition", members who deliberately disrupted the crown's programme by diverting the attention of the House into issues calculated to provoke heated discussion and ill feeling. James would have agreed with the Speaker's judgment "that two such fiery spirits will enflame more than many discreet minds will cool or temperate again".[37] In 1610 the King warned the Lower House that obstructive behaviour on their part would disincline him to further meetings. Parliaments were a convenient way of transacting the business of the kingdom, but only if they worked properly. "Many things I may do without Parliament which I will do in Parliament, for good kings are helped by Parliament, not for power but for convenience . . . But . . . the more wayward you shall be, I shall be the more unwilling to call you to Parliament, for such behaviour will make me call you the seldomer to council."[38]

James's first Parliament ended in 1610 with bad feeling all round. When he gave the opening address to the second, in 1614, James said that one of the reasons for calling it was "that I might take away the misunderstanding between you and me which was in the last Parliament" and expressed the hope that it would become known as "the Parliament of love".[39] The King's advisers had suggested that he should prepare the ground for a harmonious meeting by taking into his confidence a number of Commons' members who could be relied on to promote government business. James, who had reservations about the project, gave it only half-hearted support, but rumours of a secret 'undertaking' began to circulate and had precisely the opposite effect to what had been intended. The 'Parliament of love' turned out to be even more fractious than its predecessor, and acquired the nickname of the Addled Parliament, because it accomplished nothing of substance. James brought it to an abrupt end, much as he had done with its predecessor. The use of dissolution, or the threat of dissolution, to punish Parliament for its unco-operative behaviour was unprecedented, and the addition of this weapon to the royal armoury is an indication that James either faced new problems or needed novel means of dealing with old ones.

There followed a period of seven years in which no parliament met, and fears were expressed that James would in future do without such a body. It was the deteriorating situation abroad which drove him to summon Parliament again in 1621, but, as before, he began with an appeal for mutual understanding. When he first came into England, said James, he had been an apprentice, inexperienced in such assemblies. "I was led by the old counsellors that I found, which the old Queen had left; it may be there was a misleading and misunderstanding between us, which bred an abruption [i.e. a breaking off]."[40] His second Parliament had been ruined by "a foul beast called Undertakers, which . . . would undertake to guide the whole House – an opinion albeit some believed in, yet by himself was ever misliked. He had therefore now called this, trusting himself upon the good affections of his people."[41] James's trust seemed to be well grounded during the first session of the 1621 Parliament, but when discussion turned to foreign affairs later in the year it led to increasing dissension and bitterness, culminating in the *Commons' Protestation.* James's last Parliament, which met in 1624, was far more harmonious, but only because the Court was split, with Prince Charles and the Duke of Buckingham in league with the unofficial leaders of the Commons.

One of the problems that confronted James when he dealt with his English parliaments was the degree of formality that constrained him. The Scottish Parliament had been a far easier body to deal with (see above, pp. 16–17), and James had built up personal contacts with its members. He would have liked to do the same with the House of Commons, but it was simply not possible to establish an informal relationship with an institution that contained close on 470 representatives. At the end of the 1610 Parliament, when the key question of the royal finances was under discussion, James tried to break the deadlock by inviting thirty members to come and confer with him, not "as parliament men, but as private men". The meeting was apparently successful, and one parliamentary diarist noted that "they departed exceedingly well and graciously used by the King to every man's contentment".[42] But when the Commons learned of the way in which James had short-circuited time-honoured procedures, members made their reservations plain. One was afraid that the King "might by thirty, twenty or as he please, send for and so know the opinion of the whole House – which is a great infringing of our privileges".[43] The House agreed with him and gave its collective view that "such private conferences . . . do very much tend to the weakening and infringing of the ancient liberty and freedom of this council and may in future times become very prejudicial as well to the King as to the subject".[44] Members were henceforth forbidden to act in this informal manner, and James never repeated the experiment.

When James addressed the two Houses in January 1621 he outlined his vision of what Parliament should be. "Here the King is to open himself in his wants and the people to supply them. For this I minister . . . justice and mercy unto my people. And where this is done on my part (which shall not fail) and on yours (which should not) the harmony will be sweet between Prince and people, and . . . a happy King and happy kingdom shall that be."[45] No doubt this is what James longed for, but he rarely found it. After the bitter experience of the Addled Parliament he told the Spanish ambassador that the House of Commons consisted of five hundred men who "voted without order, nothing being heard but cries, shouts, and confusion". He was astonished, James added, "that the kings his predecessors had consented to such a thing".[46] Nothing angered James more than the way in which the Commons wasted time, as he saw it, by neglecting government business and focussing upon grievances and privileges. As early as June 1604 he was complaining about "the continuance of the Parliament and little done, and so much time spent in privilege . . . and not that haste in some matters which he looked for".[47] The situation was no better six years later, when James declared that despite a long session "the delay and lingering was so great" that "only eight or ten days were spent in the business".[48]

James never entirely abandoned his hope of achieving a satisfactory relationship with Parliament, and above all the Commons. He could not believe that a good king and his loyal subjects should be doomed to perpetual disharmony. As late as 1624, when he gave the opening speech at what was to be his last Parliament, James declared that "never man in a dry and sandy wilderness, where no water is, did thirst more in hot weather for drink than I do now for a happy conclusion of this Parliament. And now I hope, after the miscarriage of three, this may prove happy."[49] He had already explained that he desired "to be your husband and ye should be my spouse; and therefore, as it is the husband's part to cherish his wife, to entreat her kindly, and reconcile himself towards her, and procure her love by all means, so it is my part to do the like to my people". After reminding his audience "that spending of time is spoiling of business" he called on them to open their hearts to him, "for you know in your consciences that of all the kings that ever were, I dare say, never king was better beloved of his people than I am".[50]

There is no reason to doubt James's frequently expressed desire to be a good ruler, but it would be mistaken to focus on his goodness at the expense of his rulership. James was, after all, the governor of his three kingdoms, and unlike Parliament he was in permanent session. His reign in England lasted for more than twenty-one years, during which time Parliament met for a total of 154 weeks, which gives an average of 7.3 weeks per regnal year. This was considerably higher than the comparative figure for Elizabeth's reign, of 2.7 weeks, but minuscule compared with modern practice. Parliament was indeed, as James himself stated, a convenience, not a necessity. Certain matters, particularly taxation, were better done with Parliament than without, but the monarch had an inherent authority which enabled him to continue ruling whether or not Parliament performed its traditional functions. It was awareness of the latent power of princes that alarmed the Commons, made them fearful for their continued existence, and prompted them to defend their privileges in an uncompromising and assertive manner. It was fear also, more perhaps for the future than the present, that inhibited their response to James's repeated appeals for co-operation in carrying through the King's and kingdom's business. James could have eased tension by underplaying his prerogative and allowing elements of it to slip away, but this would have been, for him, a dereliction of a God-given duty. His relationship with his parliaments therefore never matched his ideal, yet he managed to maintain a *modus vivendi* that kept the institution alive and with it the *dominium politicum et regale* that James's subjects regarded as the key feature of their inheritance.

．　．　．

REFERENCES

1. G.R. Elton (ed.), *The Tudor Constitution*, 2nd edn (Cambridge University Press, 1982), p. 274.
2. *King James VI and I: Political Writings* ed. Johann P. Somerville (Cambridge University Press, 1994), p. 190 [hereafter *Political Writings*].
3. *Commons Debates 1621* ed. Wallace Notestein, Frances Helen Relf and Hartley Simpson (Yale University Press, 1935), Vol. VI, p. 272 [hereafter *1621 Debates*].
4. *Journals of the House of Commons 1547–1714*, Vol. I (1742), p. 158 [hereafter *CJ*].
5. *Political Writings*, p. 73.
6. *1621 Debates*, Vol. II, p. 3.
7. J.P. Kenyon (ed.), *The Stuart Constitution 1603–1688*, 2nd edn (Cambridge University Press, 1968), p. 31 [hereafter Kenyon].
8. Kenyon, pp. 31–2.
9. G.R. Elton, *Studies in Tudor and Stuart Politics and Government*, Vol. II (Cambridge University Press, 1974).
10. Kenyon, p. 32.
11. J.R. Tanner (ed.), *Constitutional Documents of the Reign of James I* (Cambridge University Press, 1930), p. 202 [hereafter Tanner].
12. *Political Writings*, p. 191.
13. James F. Larkin and Paul L. Hughes (eds), *Stuart Royal Proclamations*. Vol. I: *Royal Proclamations of King James I* (Clarendon Press, 1973), p. 496 [hereafter *Proclamations*].
14. *1621 Debates*, Vol. V, p. 431.
15. *1621 Debates*, Vol. V, p. 433.
16. *1621 Debates*, Vol. V, p. 438.
17. *1621 Debates*, Vol. II, pp. 83–5.
18. Public Record Office, *SP14* 119, 96.
19. *1621 Debates*, Vol. V, pp. 462–3.
20. Tanner, p. 279.
21. Tanner, pp. 280–3.

22. Tanner, pp. 284–7.
23. Tanner, pp. 287–8.
24. *1621 Debates*, Vol. V, pp. 242–3.
25. *1621 Debates*, Vol. VI, p. 425.
26. *1621 Debates*, Vol. V, p. 244.
27. Kenyon, pp. 42–3.
28. *Proclamations*, pp. 527–33.
29. *Proclamations*, p. 534.
30. Kenyon, p. 44.
31. Quoted in Robert E. Ruigh, *The Parliament of 1624* (Harvard University Press, 1971), p. 159 [hereafter Ruigh].
32. Kenyon, p. 44.
33. Quoted in Ruigh, p. 173.
34. Tanner, p. 279.
35. Louis A. Knafla, *Law and Politics in Jacobean England: The Tracts of Lord Chancellor Ellesmere* (Cambridge University Press, 1977), pp. 254–5.
36. *CJ*, p. 314.
37. *The Parliamentary Diary of Robert Bowyer 1606–1607*, ed. David Harris Willson (Octagon Books, New York, 1971), p. 54, n. 1.
38. *Proceedings in Parliament 1610* ed. Elizabeth Read Foster (Yale University Press, 1966), Vol. 2, p. 105 [hereafter *1610 Proceedings*].
39. *Proceedings in Parliament 1614 (House of Commons)* ed. Maija Jansson (American Philosophical Society, Philadelphia, 1988), pp. 18–19.
40. *1621 Debates*, Vol. II, p. 12, n. 21.
41. *1621 Debates*, Vol. V, p. 429.
42. *1610 Proceedings*, p. 338.
43. *1610 Proceedings*, p. 342, n. 7.
44. *1610 Proceedings*, p. 391.
45. *1621 Debates*, Vol. VI, p. 366.
46. Francisco de Jesus, *El Hecho de los Tratados del Matrimonio Pretendido por El Principe de Gales con La Serenissima Infanta de España Maria* ed. S.R. Gardiner (Camden Society, 1869), p. 288.
47. Historical Manuscripts Commission, *Report on the Manuscripts of the Duke of Buccleuch & Queensberry*, Vol. III (1926). VI: *The Montagu Papers*, Second Series, p. 89.
48. *1610 Proceedings*, p. 309.
49. Kenyon, p. 44.
50. Kenyon, pp. 43–5.

Chapter 5

A SPENDTHRIFT KING?

Although Scotland was in the mainstream of European culture, in economic terms it was a backwater. It had limited natural resources, and its public finances were in disorder. Many crown lands had been alienated to the nobility in the disturbed years preceding James's birth, and the machinery of government was so weak and inefficient that those revenues which still belonged to the crown were collected only in part and with difficulty. In addition, corruption was widespread. There was not a great deal James could do about this, particularly during his long minority, nor was he fitted by temperament for such a task. Finance was virtually a closed book to him, and he confessed to the English Parliament in 1610 that "I am less naturally eloquent, and have greater cause to distrust mine elocution in matters of this nature, than in any other thing".[1]

There *were* monarchs who kept a close watch upon their finances. Henry VII of England, the first Tudor sovereign and James's great-great-grandfather, was outstanding in this respect and acquired a justified reputation for tight-fistedness. His example was followed by the last Tudor, his granddaughter, Elizabeth, who was pastmaster – or, rather, pastmistress – in the art of maintaining magnificence on the cheap. Not so James. He was far more typical of monarchs in spending freely and leaving it to his treasurers and comptrollers somehow to produce the money. Fontenay had commented in 1584 on the King's "ignorance and lack of knowledge of his poverty",[2] but James did realise he was extravagant, and confessed to Chancellor Maitland in 1591 that he had "offended the whole country . . . for prodigal giving".[3] Following the costly ceremonies attendant upon the baptism of his eldest son, Prince Henry, in 1594, the royal finances were under even greater strain, and James, who blamed his "extreme want" on "the mishandling of my rents by my careless and greedy officers", called on his close friend, the Earl of Mar, to head a commission "for putting me in some better estate". With all the fervour of a repentant sinner he announced that "I apprehend deeply the straits I am cast in and am resolved to follow constantly their counsel [and] back their conclusions".[4] This was the first of a number of occasions on which James turned to his advisers to pull him out of the slough of debt into which he was in constant danger of sinking.

James assumed that his longed-for accession to the throne of England would put an end to his financial problems. When the good news came at last, he said he felt like "a poor man wandering about forty years in a wilderness and barren soil, and now arrived at the land of promise".[5] His belief that England was possessed of limitless wealth can only have been confirmed by the lavish entertainment he received in the palaces of the aristocracy as he made his way south towards London. England was indeed much richer than Scotland, and the public finances were in better order, but even under the frugal Elizabeth the royal revenue had been insufficient for the demands made on it. Robert Cecil, who was to be James's chief minister, had served under Elizabeth and had told a friend in 1602 that "all the receipts are so short of the issue, as my hairs stand upright to think of it".[6] James's euphoria quickly disappeared as he became aware of the true situation. In October 1605 he told Cecil "that it is a horror to me to think upon the height of my place, the greatness of my debts, and the smallness of my means", and he called on his Councillors to let him know "how my estate may be made able to subsist with honour and credit".[7]

One of the conventions of the English constitution – to use a phrase that would have been incomprehensible to James I and his subjects – was that 'the King should live of his own', in other words off the crown's resources. But galloping inflation during the sixteenth century had created such havoc with the royal revenue that it was now insufficient to meet even the ordinary costs of government. The twin pillars of the revenue were the crown lands and the Customs duties, but these had not kept pace with rising prices. The yield from crown lands was falling as they were sold off during the second half of the sixteenth century in an attempt to make ends meet. This produced capital, but only at the cost of diminishing future income.

Those lands which remained were scattered all over the country, which meant they could not be efficiently administered as a single unit. In any case, the crown could hardly turn into an exploiting landlord when it was trying to set an example and restrain the unprincipled greed of other landowners. This was one of many instances in which the crown's public role was at odds with its economic interests. Unlike the crown lands, the Customs duties – Tonnage and Poundage – were not hereditary but were voted to the sovereign for life by the first Parliament of every reign. The value of the items on which Customs duties were levied was laid down in the Book of Rates, but this had not been updated since the reign of Mary Tudor. James's first Lord Treasurer, whom he inherited from Elizabeth, was Thomas Sackville, Earl of Dorset, and it was he who, in 1604, issued a new Book of Rates which took account of inflation. He also privatised the administration of the Customs by farming it out to a group of wealthy merchants and financiers at a fixed rent. As a consequence, over the course of James's reign the income from Customs went up by nearly 50 per cent.

The crown also benefited from duties on trade which were levied not by parliamentary grant but prerogative action. These duties, known as Impositions, originated in the reign of Mary Tudor but had been continued on a small scale by Elizabeth. They were deeply resented because they were in effect non-parliamentary taxes, and the accession of a new monarch aroused hopes that they might be done away with altogether. One of the Elizabethan Impositions had been levied on currants, and it was this which John Bate, a merchant who traded with the Levant, decided to challenge in 1606 by refusing to pay it. James could have stood firm on his prerogative rights, but as a newcomer to the throne, and one, moreover, who was unfamiliar with English law, he remitted the matter to the judges. The case came to trial in the Court of the Exchequer, whose judges were known as barons. Dorset, as Lord Treasurer, was the nominal head of this court and he made known to the Chief Baron, Sir Thomas Fleming, his opinion that a favourable verdict would establish "an assured foundation for the King's Impositions for ever".[8] Whether or not Fleming was swayed by Dorset's intervention, he and his fellow judges found for the crown.

The barons, as was usual in such matters, made their decision on narrow, technical grounds, but in delivering judgment Chief Baron Fleming, with an eye to resolving the issue once and for all, expounded the theory that the King's prerogative was two-fold, ordinary and absolute. The ordinary prerogative operated through customary legal channels and procedures, but the absolute prerogative was not "guided by the rules which direct only at the common law". Its operation was left to the King's discretion, and varied according to his view of what would be best for the general good. Fleming acknowledged that the monarch's capacity to levy Impositions by virtue of the absolute prerogative might appear limitless, but "this is to be referred to the wisdom of the King, who guideth all under God by his wisdom, and this is not to be disputed by a subject; and many things are left to his wisdom for the ordering of his power, rather than his power shall be restrained".[9] The victory of the crown in Bate's Case opened the way to a substantial increase in the number and range of Impositions. James was not the initiator of this policy but he went along with it because he was convinced that Impositions provided "almost the only sure hope that is left for increase of my rent".[10] He was right, in the sense that they brought him in some £70,000, the equivalent of a parliamentary subsidy, every year, and could be increased if need arose. Other sources of revenue were far less fruitful or elastic, particularly after 1609, when Salisbury persuaded James to agree that the remaining crown lands should be entailed and thereby made inalienable.

Despite the increase in his revenue brought about through the extension of Impositions, James was still unable to make ends meet. This was partly because, as a married monarch, he had to maintain two households apart from his own – one for the Queen, Anne of Denmark, and one for Prince Henry, the heir to the throne. His journey south from Edinburgh entailed expenditure on an appropriately regal scale, and once in London he had to meet the costs of Queen Elizabeth's funeral and his own coronation. High spending was not confined to the opening years of the reign. James lavished money on Court entertainments, particularly masques, and he spent large sums on jewels, which he loved. He also broke with recent precedent by reviving the fortunes and activities of the royal masons. As Howard Colvin, the historian of the King's Works, explains, 'Elizabeth herself built no palaces. Not only did she inherit rather more than she needed but her sense of economy ran against extravagant building. James I had no such prejudice but he also found his palatial heritage more than adequate and contented himself with a few costly rebuildings, the provision of minor royal residences for hunting and the erection of a few very special and expensive buildings in existing palace precincts.'[11] These special buildings included the Banqueting House in Whitehall, whose magnificent painted ceiling by Rubens is a glorification of the first Stuart sovereign and creator of Great Britain. Elizabeth had been content with a temporary structure, but James wanted something more in keeping with his majesty. The first building he commissioned burnt down, but he immediately instructed Inigo Jones to design its successor, at a cost of over £15,000.

Expenditure designed to uphold or increase the royal dignity might have been accepted by James's new subjects, however grudgingly; not so, however, the lavish grants of crown lands and money which James made in the opening years of his reign. By 1610 he had given away to his Scottish followers some £90,000 in gifts and more than £10,000 a year in pensions. Such generosity could be justified on the grounds that the Scots, as well as the English, needed to be won over to the union, and since James had promised not to grant them offices in England he was obliged to give them money instead. When addressing Parliament in 1610 James acknowledged that "it may be thought that I have given much amongst Scottishmen" but he argued that "if I had not been liberal in rewarding some of my old servants of that nation, ye could never have had reason to expect my thankfulness towards any of you that are lately become my subjects".[12] In any case, he added, the English had received twice as much as the Scots. This may be true if titles and offices are put into the scales, but it did not alter the received opinion among the King's new subjects, particularly members of Parliament, that James was pouring English money into Scottish pockets. In the words of one of many scurrilous tracts or 'libels' circulating at this time:

The Scotchmen are but beggars yet,
Although their begging was not small.
But now a Parliament doth sit,
A subsidy shall pay for all.[13]

Parliament was, indeed, the traditional recourse for English monarchs who were unable to live of their own. In theory, James had a good case to argue, for the costs of government were undoubtedly increasing much faster than the crown's income. Since traditional sources were inadequate, James's Treasurers had to borrow money, but interest payments meant a further erosion of net government income. By 1608 the accumulated public debt had risen to over a million pounds and was increasing at the rate of £140,000 a year. There was no way of closing the gap between income and expenditure without parliamentary assistance, but James's undoubted extravagance created a climate of opinion in which such assistance was likely to be half-hearted – if it was forthcoming at all. Extravagance was not easy to define, especially in the institution of monarchy, which functioned as a system of rewards. James was entirely correct in stating that "a King's liberality must never be dried up altogether, for then he can never maintain nor oblige his servants and well-deserving subjects".[14] Robert Cecil, now Earl of Salisbury, made the same point in 1610. "For a king not to be bountiful were a fault, for that duty is best and surest tried where it is rewarded, which is the cause and makes men the willinger to do service."[15] He reminded a conference of Lords and Commons that royal generosity was "a disease that few complained of in the late Queen's days, and I think there is not many in both Houses that will be hasty to give back anything they have received. Bounty is inseparable from a king."[16]

However, Salisbury recognised that there must be limits on the King's bounty, and despite his habitually deferential manner towards his sovereign he went so far as to advise James to restrain his generosity. "Though the liberality and goodness that lieth in you are virtues", he wrote, "yet they are somewhat improper for this kingdom, which being compared with other monarchies may certainly be counted potent, but not opulent." He reminded James that even Elizabeth had felt "the dangerous effects of want", and gave his considered opinion "that it is not possible for a king of England, much less of Great Britain . . . to be rich or safe, but by frugality".[17] Financial prudence would not simply improve the King's position in the short run; it would also strengthen the hand of his ministers when they called on Parliament to vote supply. The general assumption on which English financial and political attitudes were based was that subjects should come to the aid of their sovereign only in exceptional circumstances, of which war was the most obvious. They accepted no responsibility for freeing him from debts, especially when these were incurred by his own extravagance.

One of James's first actions after coming to the English throne was to put a formal end to the war with Spain which had dominated the last two decades of Elizabeth's reign. The war had not been unpopular – England was, after all, defending both itself and the protestant faith – and Elizabethan parliaments had voted subsidies in every session. The subsidy had been invented by Henry VIII's chief minister, Cardinal Wolsey, in an attempt to tap the wealth of the country more efficiently than the existing system of Fifteenths and Tenths. These had originally been closely related to actual levels of wealth, but they were not regularly updated and had gradually ossified into a standard grant worth some £30,000. Early subsidies showed just how much the state could raise and the country could afford, for one subsidy might bring in as much as £120,000. However, subsidies, like Fifteenths and Tenths, quickly became arthritic, because the local gentry who were charged with making an accurate assessment of the tax liability of themselves and their neighbours were remarkably skilful in evading their responsibilities. Little or no account was taken of changes in landownership or fluctuations in fortunes, and as a consequence the value of the subsidy steadily declined. At the beginning of Elizabeth's reign a single subsidy was worth about £130,000, but by the middle of James I's reign this figure had dropped to a little over £70,000.

When inflation is taken into account the decline in the value of the subsidy becomes even more marked. During the course of the sixteenth century prices rose some four or five times, and if Parliament had adjusted its grants in line with inflation, then one subsidy would have produced well over £500,000 by James's reign. The actual figure of £70,000 meant that in real terms the value of a subsidy to the crown had decreased by 87 per cent since Henry VIII's reign. The Commons reacted to this situation not by increasing the yield of individual subsidies but by voting two, three, or even four at a time. Elizabeth's last Parliament voted her four subsidies and eight Fifteenths and Tenths, worth well over half a million pounds, and even though these went only part of the way towards meeting the crown's extra costs – particularly those of suppressing the Irish rebellion (see below, p. 188) – there was a widespread feeling that the fiscal limits had been reached. In the public perception it was the number of subsidies and their frequency that mattered, rather than the total amount raised. Not long after James's accession to the English throne, Robert Cecil warned him about the consequences of this attitude: "Your Majesty may . . . please to remember first that you found a people worn with great and heavy burdens, which they endured the better in hope of the change of your blessed government, which in matter of payment continues yet not a little burdenous to those that expected ease in contributions, feeling the weight of so many in the days of peace."[18] In other words, the end of the war with Spain implied a return to 'normality', and this, in turn, implied an end to taxation.

However, the financial situation confronting the new ruler of England was so grave that a plea to his subjects for assistance was inevitable. There was no question of a grant in 1604 since the taxes voted in the last year of Elizabeth's reign were still being collected, but in 1606 the Commons decided to offer three subsidies and six Fifteenths and Tenths, worth in all nearly £400,000. This was untypically generous and owed much to the reaction in the King's favour generated by the discovery of the Gunpowder Plot in November 1605. In some ways the Commons' action had an unfortunate effect, for it encouraged James to believe that his financial problems could be solved without undue stringency on his part. With a carefree open-handedness that marked a reversion to type, he gave away £44,000, the equivalent of more than half a subsidy, to three of his Scottish followers to help them pay their debts. It is hardly surprising, given these circumstances, that complaints about the King's profligacy continued to be voiced. One Commons' member expressed doubts whether replenishing the King's coffers was worth while, "for if the bottoms be out, then can they not be filled", while another reminded the House that "a subsidy is a public contribution, not to be employed to private uses, bounties [and] expenses".[19] When, in 1610, James decided to appeal once again to his subjects and ask for their assistance in solving his financial problems, he assured them that the bad old days really were over. The opening years of his reign, he admitted, had been marked by the "vastness of my expense", but "that Christmas and open tide is ended" and he was not minded "to live in any wasteful sort hereafter".[20]

What turned out to be the last session of James's first Parliament was dominated by the issue of the Great Contract – an imaginative proposal put forward by Robert Cecil, Earl of Salisbury (who had succeeded Dorset as Lord Treasurer), whereby

Parliament would be invited to re-endow the crown. Salisbury, who took office in 1608, had managed to reduce both the debt and the annual deficit by a further bout of land sales combined with stringent economy measures, but he realised that such short-term remedies were no more than stop gaps. In 1610, therefore, he offered, with James's approval, to surrender the crown's feudal 'incidents', or prerogatives, in return for permanent funding from Parliament. The most important, as well as unpopular, of the prerogatives on offer was purveyance – the right to buy goods and services for the royal household at a lower than market price. However, the Commons insisted that a much more onerous prerogative should be included in the negotiations – namely, wardship.

The principal landowners in England were technically tenants-in-chief of the crown, and held their estates in return for providing it with 'knight service' or military assistance when called on to do so. Under-age inheritors could not provide knight service themselves; moreover, on account of their youth, they might come under the malign influence of the King's enemies. In order to prevent such an occurrence, the Kings of England had long exercised the prerogative right of taking the young heir into their guardianship and assuming temporary custody of his estates. The protection of both the ward and his property was a noble ideal, but the practice of wardship fell far short of it. The King – or rather the Master of Wards whom he appointed to deal with such matters – would sell the wardship, usually to the highest bidder, and the purchaser was left to recoup his outlay by despoiling the unfortunate ward's inheritance. Wardship, in short, was a form of land tax which was deeply resented because it entailed no element of consent. It operated in a haphazard and highly arbitrary fashion, and two or more wardships in a row could leave a family impoverished. It is hardly surprising that a Parliament made up largely of landowners and their representatives should have been keen to abolish this hated feudal incident.

Under pressure from Salisbury, James agreed that wardship should be included in the proposed Contract. Salisbury had originally asked for a lump sum of £600,000 to pay off the King's debts and provide a contingency fund, and £200,000 a year in perpetuity. The Commons never even considered the lump sum, although they eventually agreed to the annual grant of £200,000 it was unclear whether they had also accepted the

principle of compensating James for the revenues he was sur-
rendering: purveyance and wardship, for instance, were each
worth some £40,000 a year. Contact with their constituents
during the summer recess of 1610 apparently hardened the
resolve of many Commons' members to drive the hardest possible bargain, and although a draft of the Contract had been
drawn up before they left Westminster they were in no hurry to
put it into effect upon their return. Not only was the idea of
permanent taxation unpopular; many people felt it made no
sense to subsidise a spendthrift monarch, particularly a Scottish
King who was bound to divert part of his extra revenue into
the pockets of his own countrymen. In the words of one of Secretary Winwood's correspondents, "I conceive by the common
discourse that the Parliament could be content to replenish
the royal cistern (as they call it) of His Majesty's Treasury, were
they assured that His Majesty's largess to the Scots' prodigality
would not cause a continual and remedy-less leak therein."[21]

Negotiations over the Great Contract had been made even
more difficult by the continuing dispute over Impositions,
which the Commons insisted on regarding as illegal despite
the judgment in Bate's Case. In fact, Chief Baron Fleming's
exegesis on the crown's absolute prerogative had hardened
attitudes. Fleming's views were very close to James's own, especially his emphasis on the need to trust the King, but the
cumulative experience of several centuries of English history
provided grounds for believing that trust was not enough.
Monarchical power needed to be restrained, above all where
the subjects' money and property were at stake. Impositions,
then, remained a bone of contention between King and Parliament, and did much to embitter their relationship. In the 1610
session the Commons mounted an attack upon their validity,
but James promptly intervened, ordering them not to take into
"consideration any disputation touching the prerogative of
the King in the case of Impositions, for that was determined
by judgment in the proper court". This was not well received,
so ten days later James sent for the two Houses and explained
that he had never meant to debar the Commons from complaining about specific Impositions on grounds of "heaviness,
inequality, disproportion or disorder in matter of trade", for
this was something they were entitled to do. But he warned
them against using the pretext of specific Impositions to "go to
the root and dispute my prerogative . . . Leave to the King that

which is in his power, and do you take into your consideration the inconveniences."[22]

James's refusal to allow Parliament to consider the general question of Impositions raised once again the issue of free speech. The Commons therefore drew up a petition in which they declared it "an ancient, general, and undoubted right of Parliament to debate freely all matters which do properly concern the subject and his right or state; which freedom of debate being once foreclosed, the essence of the liberty of Parliament is withal dissolved". As for Impositions, they denied that they wished to challenge the judges' decision in Bate's Case, but they wanted to know the reasons for it, since they were fearful that the judgment might be "extended much farther, even to the utter ruin of the ancient liberty of this kingdom and of your subjects' right of propriety [i.e. property] of their lands and goods".[23] In his reply to this petition, James gave an assurance that he would never interfere with property rights and that he wanted no more than "that which other virtuous and good Kings of England had".[24] This did not stop the Commons from launching into a two-week debate upon Impositions, in which constitutional issues held centre ground. James resented the time given to this matter, particularly since he wished to see progress upon the Great Contract, but he was also anxious to heal the breach between him and the Commons. He therefore made a significant concession by agreeing to accept an Act making it a legal requirement in future for Impositions to have parliamentary consent. He made it known that he was also prepared to surrender existing Impositions, as long as he was given adequate compensation. A bill to this effect was drawn up in 1610 and passed through the Commons before the summer recess. But when members returned to Westminster in the autumn their time was taken up with the question of whether or not to go ahead with the Great Contract.

In fact, many members delayed their return, presumably in the hope that the unpopular project would somehow disappear from the scene. Those who were present were equally unenthusiastic, but reluctant to provoke an open breach with James by an outright refusal. They took refuge, therefore, in other topics, and spun out time as much as they could. James chided the Commons for their dilatoriness, complaining that "as his estate lay a-bleeding so his honour lay a-bleeding; for to require help of his people and be denied were a disgrace both to him and his people". He regarded the lack of response on the part of the Commons as all the more unwarranted in view of the fact that he had not simply asked them for assistance; he had also offered them "retribution" (i.e. concessions) "which was without example of any king before".[25] In the end, as James had probably foreseen, the Commons refused to conclude the Contract and he therefore dissolved Parliament. Not only was the Contract at an end, so also was the Impositions bill, which might have solved a problem which, in the event, was to prove intractable. All James gained from the session was a grant of one subsidy and one Fifteenth, worth a total of £100,000, but to set against this was the searing experience of public humiliation. James was resolved never again to endure "such taunts and disgraces as have been uttered of him", not even if the Commons at their next meeting changed their minds and offered him a substantial grant – "nay, though it were another kingdom".[26]

What angered James most of all was the way in which he had been persuaded to bargain with the Commons and to auction off bits of the prerogative. This was not only an undignified procedure; it ran counter to his deepest beliefs about the nature of kingly rule. In James's view the Commons, as the elected representatives of the people, were in duty bound to aid and assist their King when he made his needs plain. They also had the right to present grievances to the sovereign, who might otherwise be unaware of them, and a good king would welcome the opportunity to implement appropriate remedial action. Obviously there was an implied link between the granting of supply and the redress of grievances, but James did not want this made explicit. He preferred a relationship based upon mutual trust, in which a faithful Commons and a loving King worked harmoniously for the common good. There could be no mutual trust, there could not even be mutual respect, if both sides were engaged in haggling over the price to be paid for their co-operation. This merely produced the situation described by Winwood's correspondent, who reported that "since His Majesty hath spoken of the Great Contract, the Lower House hath been very farouche and untractable, flatly refusing to yield any contribution without an equivalent retribution".[27] Sir Francis Bacon, in a letter of advice which he later penned for James's benefit, said that the collapse of the Great Contract had come as no surprise to him, for when men were "possessed with a bargain . . . it bred in them an indisposition to give". In future, James should "put off the person of a merchant and contractor, and rest upon the person of a king".[28]

This advice coincided with James's own feelings, but for the time being he planned to live without Parliament. This left the problem of what to do about the debt, now amounting to half a million pounds. If his subjects would not aid him, then James must look abroad, and he was pinning his hopes on a French marriage for Prince Charles, who was now – following the death of his brother, Henry, in November 1612 – heir to the throne. It was no coincidence that during the protracted negotiations the English made plain that they expected at least half a million pounds by way of dowry, and had the marriage actually taken place it would have removed the burden of James's debt at one fell swoop. By the beginning of 1614 it seemed that everything was settled, with only a few formalities to conclude, but a sudden transformation in the political situation in France (see below, p. 142) removed any prospect of an immediate marriage. This did not displease the so-called protestant group among James's advisers, who did not want their future King to have a popish wife. They urged James to put his trust in his faithful people rather than foreign princes, and Sir Henry Neville, who was one of the authors of the 'undertaking' proposal (see above, p. 73), "gave me encouragement", as James recalled, "that my subjects did not hate me".[29] The King eventually agreed to try the parliamentary alternative once again, but Neville's optimism was not shared by James's Privy Council, which gave formal approval to the decision only "upon those grounds of hope which we received from Your Majesty's own mouth". The Councillors added that "if there were possibility of repairing or supporting the King's estate by any other mean, the greater part of us would hold this time worse fitted and the means less well prepared than we could wish".[30]

When he opened the 1614 Parliament, James rejected the idea of any haggling over the prerogative, such as had marred the 1610 session. "I will not now deal with you by way of a bargain as at our last meeting but will tell you what I will grant you, the which things shall be such fruits as appertain unto a just prince. For if I should, like a merchant, treat with you, where a contract begins affection ceases."[31] James was appealing, as always, for a relationship based on goodwill and trust, but there was no possibility of meaningful dialogue unless and until the

Commons accepted that the shortfall in the royal finances had causes that went far deeper than royal extravagance. This they were unable to do, despite James's solemn promise to "so husband and govern my revenue that I will not be burdensome to you". Nicholas Hyde, a future Chief Justice, gave his opinion that "there was no apparent cause of the King's wants, [and] that we had many promises that hereafter it should not be, which now we have small hope of". In 1610, according to Hyde, James's debt was £700,000, but this had now doubled. Yet the King was spending two million pounds a year and had given away to one or two men "more than Queen Elizabeth gave to all her servants and favourites in all her reign. If these excesses continue, it is impossible for the kingdom to subsist, or us to help it."[32]

The King's extravagance was not the only cause of dispute between James and the Lower House. There was also the festering topic of Impositions. Many of the old arguments about the threat to property implicit in Impositions were brought up again, and the Commons gave consideration to "An act concerning taxes and impositions upon merchants and other subjects of the realm and upon their wares, goods, and chattels".[33] James tried to clear the air by restating his attitude. He reminded the Commons that when he came to the throne he had not changed his Councillors. On the contrary, he retained those who had previously served under Elizabeth, and it was they who informed him "that the laying of Impositions was my right . . . I was not like Rehoboam that took young and new counsellors and rejected the old. I took the same counsel that I found here. When I had this from the counsel of state I thought I did no wrong." James put the blame for the extension of Impositions upon the dead Salisbury, who had acted "without my consent and knowledge . . . I never offered it. I never projected it. I was ignorant of it, as I hope you will think."[34] The Commons were far from satisfied and went ahead with their bill, but the abrupt termination of the session put an end to the proposed measure.

The significance of the Addled Parliament of 1614 consists in the fact that it was a dialogue of the deaf. Since the Commons, in the words of Conrad Russell, 'believed James did not need the money, they believed that if he had it, he would not need to call Parliaments. In this way they were wrong, but they were the prisoners of their own analysis. Equally, since James knew he did need the money, and believed they knew it too, he believed their motive for denying it to him must be one of settled hostility to his authority or his person. In this too he was wrong, but he equally was the prisoner of his own analysis ... Because both parties were the prisoners of their financial analyses, no constructive debate could take place between them.'[35]

James had hoped that the 1614 Parliament would wipe out the unhappy memory of the 1610 session. In fact it created even more bitterness, as was shown by the interrogation and imprisonment of a number of members who were accused of deliberately wrecking the session by fomenting opposition to the King's proposals. The financial situation had become worse rather than better, and there was no clear way of dealing with it. James acknowledged the dilemma confronting him when he told the Privy Council in 1615 that "as on the one side he would not avoid a Parliament if he might see likelihood of comfort by it, knowing it to be anciently the way of his progenitors; so on the other side he would rather suffer any extremity than have another meeting with his people and take an affront".[36] In the short term, at any rate, he preferred to manage without Parliament and therefore set about reducing his household expenditure. In 1617 he wrote to his Councillors, requiring them to "abate superfluities in all things, and multitudes of unnecessary officers wherever they be placed". They were to "cut and carve" items such as wardrobe expenditure and pensions, and bring the cost of his household down to £50,000 a year: "If you can make it less, I will account it for good service."[37]

James left such matters to his Councillors because he had neither the time nor the inclination to deal with them himself. Following Salisbury's death in 1612 he had put the Treasury in commission, but the experiment was not a success, and after the failure of the Addled Parliament to make any grant, he appointed Thomas Howard, Earl of Suffolk, as Lord Treasurer. It was not a good choice. Suffolk had had a distinguished career in Elizabeth's navy, but in financial matters his expertise was confined to his own enrichment. Admittedly, it was widely assumed in early Stuart England that public office was a way of making money quickly, and Treasurers were particularly well placed to do so. Salisbury had profited from his tenure of the office, partly through shady deals with the Customs farmers, but his intelligence and ability, not to mention his genuine devotion to the crown's service, were totally lacking in his successor. Suffolk's principal achievement consisted in the construction of a palace for himself at Audley End in Essex, but while his private finances flourished the public ones were in an ever worsening condition. From this point of view it was no loss to James when Suffolk, who had been caught up in the power struggle which led to the overthrow of the King's favourite, Robert Carr (see below, p. 170), was suspended from office in 1618. In the following year he was summoned before Star Chamber, where he was found guilty of corruption.

James once again put the Treasury into commission, but his new favourite, George Villiers (later Duke of Buckingham), brought to his attention a man whom he could trust and who would make the reformation of the royal finances his constant care. This was Lionel Cranfield, who had demonstrated his talents by making a fortune for himself out of trade and then setting up as a financier in the City of London. James instructed Cranfield to carry out a searching enquiry into the entire royal administration, and Cranfield immediately set to work on the major spending departments. He established a reputation for ruthless efficiency, and one alarmed government servant wrote in September 1618 that the "scourging and dreadful commission that hath done such wonders in the Lord Treasurer's office is now in hand with the office of the Ordnance, from which it is said they will post to examine the secrets of the Navy".[38] By the following year Cranfield was able to inform the King that his ordinary income and expenditure were now in balance, and James might have continued ruling without Parliament had it not been for the worsening situation in Europe and the strong possibility that Britain might become involved in war. In 1621, therefore, James decided to summon Parliament, but when he opened it he took the precaution of listing all the economies he had made as proof that if the Commons voted him supply "they should not put their money into a broken purse, but might be right well assured to have it well and husbandly disposed of".[39] The Commons responded, for once, in a positive manner, and made a grant of two subsidies. This was nowhere near enough for the King's needs, but James welcomed it as a gesture of goodwill, particularly since it had been made at the beginning of the session, with no hint of bargaining. When he thanked the Commons for "their free, noble and no merchantlike dealing"[40] he was speaking from the heart. The Lower House asked for an audience at which to express their thanks to the King for showing himself "to be tenderly sensible of the

grievances of your people . . . to which you have given remedy",
and the Speaker said what a "comfort [it is] to us all, and to
everyone joy and great rejoicing of heart, to see those mists that
in the other parliaments darkened the sun of our sovereign
. . . so to break up to us that we can . . . behold nothing in Your
Majesty but a very fair heaven and wonderful grace".[41] This was
music to James's ears, and he responded to it in like vein.
"Nothing is better nor better beseeming both King and Parliament than concord", he declared, "so nothing should be more
joyous; and to tell you my mind, nothing more rejoiceth me."
He publicly acknowledged that "no King hath been obliged to
both the Houses of Parliament as I to these", and to show his
pleasure with the Commons he announced that " 'I mean to
kill your Speaker in remembrance of this day's work'. And
therewith drew out my Lord Haddington's sword, and dubbed [i.e. knighted] him."[42]

The Commons' reference to the grievances which James
had remedied applied to monopolies, a topic which dominated
the first session of the 1621 Parliament. Such was the poverty
of the crown in the late sixteenth century that it had resorted
to the sale or grant of monopoly rights over the manufacture
of, or trade in, specified articles. Monopolies could be very profitable, since, in the absence of competition, the grantee could
set the price of the commodity at whatever level he thought fit,
and there was no shortage of takers. Monopoly grants could
only be made after referees, usually the law officers of the crown,
had examined them and certified that they were not against
the public interest, but this system was open to abuse. Monopolists were a sort of mafia, unscrupulous operators, often with
good connections at Court, and by 1620 they were virtually out
of control. It was not therefore surprising that when Parliament
assembled in 1621 the Commons opened a campaign against
the abusers of monopolies, who included a number of their
own members. They were careful to divert all blame from the
King and pin it on the monopolists themselves, as well as on
the referees. Partly for this reason they secured James's co-
operation. Monopolies were admittedly a prerogative matter,
but unlike Impositions they did not have a legal judgment in
their favour. Moreover, there was clear evidence that the system had been wantonly abused, and as this came to light James
expressed his genuine revulsion. He told the Lords he was

"ashamed (and it makes my hair stand upright) to consider how in this time my people have been vexed and polled by the vile execution of projects, patents . . . and such like; which besides the trouble of my people, have more exhausted their purses than subsidies would have done".[43] He confessed his shame also to the Speaker of the Commons, and expressed his regret that it had been left to Parliament to inform him of the true state of affairs. Had he discovered the offenders himself, James assured the members, he would have dealt severely with them. As matters stood, however, "I that give life to the law will concur gladly with you in these your just proceedings."[44]

James was as good as his word, and during the summer of 1621, when Parliament was in recess, he cancelled or revoked many monopoly grants and announced that the validity of others could be tested in the law courts. This was a major concession, since monopolies were granted by virtue of the royal prerogative, which in normal circumstances was not subject to judicial review. But James had been prepared to go farther and accept a Commons' bill severely restricting monopolies. Only the refusal of the Lords to co-operate with the Commons prevented this measure from becoming law, but when the next Parliament met in 1624 a Monopolies Act finally reached the statute book.

During the interval between the two sessions of the 1621 Parliament James had shown his approval of Cranfield by appointing him Lord Treasurer and creating him Earl of Middlesex. Cranfield had gone as far as was possible within the limits of the existing regime towards making the King solvent, but he was no miracle worker. He could not significantly reduce the debt, still hovering around one million pounds, nor could he prevent the drift towards war, which would leave his work in ruins. His cost-cutting won him few friends but many enemies, and when he was forced into the political wilderness in 1624 (see below, p. 195) he attracted little sympathy. James pronounced an appropriate epitaph on him. "All Treasurers", he said, "if they do good service to their master, must be generally hated."[45]

James's commitment to peace, like his foreign policy as a whole, had its financial aspect. As already mentioned, one of the big attractions of marrying the heir to the throne to a French or Spanish princess was that the bride would bring with her a substantial dowry: the figure mentioned in the negotiations for the Spanish match was £600,000, which would have wiped out much if not all of the accumulated debt. As for the general easing of tensions which James hoped to bring about by acting as the peacemaker of Europe, this meant spending money on diplomatic initiatives involving special ambassadors, but it held out the prospect of avoiding war, which would cost far more than the royal government could possibly afford. This was one of the reasons why James had stood out against the war fever that reached a peak in the 1621 Parliament, but in 1624 he was confronted with a bellicose alliance between the leaders of the Commons on the one hand and his son and favourite, Prince Charles and the Duke of Buckingham, on the other.

James was prepared to move some way in their direction, but he insisted that the problem of the royal debt should be dealt with, as well as the costs of the war which seemed inevitable. His initial proposal of five subsidies and ten Fifteenths for the war and an annual grant of one subsidy and two Fifteenths to eliminate the debt was met with a mixture of astonishment and incredulity, but the Commons did eventually agree to offer three subsidies and three Fifteenths for the war. However, this was only on condition that the money should be appropriated to specific uses and its expenditure supervised by a commission of their own choosing. James accepted the grant with good grace but made it plain that he regarded it as sufficient only "to make a good beginning of the war. For what the end will be, God knows."[46] James's obvious pessimism about the costs and consequences of the policy to which his son and favourite were committed turned out to be well justified, but death spared him this particular revelation.

James was undoubtedly extravagant. He could not bear to say 'No', yet so many were the demands made upon him that he could never hope to satisfy them all. There were inevitably more disappointed suitors than satisfied ones, so his generosity was, in this respect, self-defeating; it weakened the bonds between the King and the political nation, rather than strengthening them. Yet the warm welcome James received at his accession reflected discontent with the parsimonious Elizabeth. She had given away too little, not only in pensions but also in titles, and it was hoped that the advent of a new sovereign would be followed by a relaxation of the stringency which had marked the last decade of the Queen's reign. What was unexpected was the suddenness and scale of the change, from drought to flood, from scarcity to abundance. Christmas, to use James's own image, came too quickly and lasted too long. But James was not incorrigible. He learned to control his generous impulses, though with frequent relapses, and he chose men like Cranfield not only to save him from himself but also to carry out necessary but unpopular measures – and, of course, to take the blame for them.

James's extravagance gave the Commons a good reason for withholding supply, and it rendered even more unlikely the re-endowment of the crown by schemes such as the Great Contract. If James had been a model of financial rectitude there might have been a better prospect of fundamental reform, but parliament would still have had difficulty accepting the need for structural change, particularly since public opinion was against any increase in the tax burden. The Commons' lack of vision is attributable to their ignorance of the true facts of the situation. The public finances were a mystery that only a handful of initiates understood, and the sums of money involved were beyond the comprehension of most of the gentlemen who sat in the Lower House. Not only did they believe that the crown's requests for financial assistance were unjustified; they also feared that by making grants on the scale requested they would remove the necessity for further parliaments. Yet by refusing to co-operate they forced the crown to develop prerogative taxation which could have been a real threat to the continued existence of Parliament. During the entire course of his reign in England, James received just over £900,000 from parliamentary grants, which averages out at £41,000 a year. This represented about 8 per cent of the ordinary revenue, and was likely to fall rather than increase in amount. By contrast, Impositions levied by virtue of the prerogative were bringing in £70,000 a year and were capable of indefinite expansion: by the eve of the Civil War they were worth about a quarter of a million pounds annually. In some ways, what is remarkable about the first two Stuart monarchs is not their addiction to absolutist methods but their reluctance to abandon traditional ways of doing things. James had a high view of the royal authority, but in the financial as in the constitutional sphere he preferred to operate within conventional limits.

REFERENCES

1. *King James VI and I: Political Writings* ed. Johann P. Somerville (Cambridge University Press, 1994), pp. 192–3 [hereafter *Political Writings*].

2. *Calendar of State Papers relating to Scotland and Mary, Queen of Scots 1547–1603* ed. William K. Boyd, Vol. VII: *1584–1585* (Edinburgh, 1913) p. 274.

3. *Letters of King James VI & I* ed. G.P.V. Akrigg (University of California Press, 1984), p. 113 [hereafter *Letters*].

4. *Letters*, p. 137.

5. Quoted in David Harris Willson, *King James VI and I* (Jonathan Cape, 1956), p. 171.

6. Quoted in Pauline Croft (ed.), 'A Collection of Several Speeches and Treatises of the Late Lord Treasurer Cecil', Camden Miscellany, Vol. XXIX, Camden Fourth Series Vol. 34 (Royal Historical Society, 1987), p. 255, n. 23 [hereafter *A Collection of Several Speeches*].

7. *Letters*, p. 261.

8. Pauline Croft, 'Fresh Light on Bate's Case', *Historical Journal*, Vol. 30, 1987, p. 536 [hereafter Croft].

9. J.P. Kenyon (ed.), *The Stuart Constitution 1603–1688*, 2nd edn (Cambridge University Press, 1986), pp. 54–5.

10. Croft, p. 536.

11. *The History of the King's Works* ed. H.M. Colvin, Vol. IV: *1485–1660 (Part II)* (1982), p. 28.

12. *Political Writings*, p. 197.

13. Quoted in Pauline Croft, 'Libels, Popular Literacy and Public Opinion in Early Modern England', *Historical Research*, Vol. 68 (1995), p. 277.

14. *Political Writings*, p. 197.

15. *Proceedings in Parliament 1610* ed. Elizabeth Read Foster (Yale University Press, 1966), Vol. 1, p. 6 [hereafter *1610 Proceedings*].

16. *1610 Proceedings*, Vol. 2, p. 23, n. 52.

17. *A Collection of Several Speeches*, pp. 284 and 285.

18. *A Collection of Several Speeches*, p. 289.

19. *Journals of the House of Commons 1547–1714*, Vol. I (1742), pp. 282 and 284.

20. *Political Writings*, pp. 197–8.

21. John More to Secretary Winwood, 1 December 1610, printed in *Memorials of Affairs of State in the Reigns of Q. Elizabeth and K. James I collected (chiefly) from the Original Papers of the Right Honourable Sir Ralph Winwood, Kt., Sometime one of the Principal Secretaries of State* (1725), Vol. III, p. 236 [hereafter Winwood].

22. *1610 Proceedings*, Vol. 2, pp. 82 and 102.

23. J.R. Tanner (ed.), *Constitutional Documents of the Reign of James I* (Cambridge University Press, 1930), pp. 246–7.

24. *1610 Proceedings*, Vol. 2, p. 115.

25. *1610 Proceedings*, Vol. 2, p. 309.

26. Quoted in *The Works of Francis Bacon* ed. James Spedding (1874), Vol. XI, pp. 236–7 [hereafter Bacon].

27. Winwood, p. 235.

28. Bacon, Vol. XI, pp. 370–1.

29. *Proceedings in Parliament 1614 (House of Commons)* ed. Maija Jansson (American Philosophical Society, Philadelphia, 1988), p. 143 [hereafter *1614 Proceedings*].

30. Quoted in Conrad Russell, *The Addled Parliament of 1614: The Limits of Revision*, The Stenton Lecture 1991 (University of Reading, 1992), p. 15 [hereafter Russell].

31. *1614 Proceedings*, p. 17.

32. *1614 Proceedings*, pp. 423–4.

33. *1614 Proceedings*, p. 79.

34. *1614 Proceedings*, pp. 141–2.

35. Russell, p. 18.

36. Quoted in J.D. Alsop, 'The Privy Council Debate and Committees for Fiscal Reform, September 1615', *Historical Research*, Vol. 166 (1995), p. 192.

37. *Letters*, p. 361.

38. British Library *Trumbull MSS*, 18, 26.

39. *Commons Debates 1621* ed. Wallace Notestein, Frances Helen Relf and Hartley Simpson (Yale University Press, 1935), Vol. V, p. 428 [hereafter *1621 Debates*].

40. *1621 Debates*, Vol. V, p. 466.

41. *1621 Debates*, Vol. VI, p. 388.

42. *1621 Debates*, Vol. VI, pp. 389–90.

43. John Rushworth, *Historical Collections* (1682), Vol. I, p. 26 [hereafter Rushworth].

44. *1621 Debates*, Vol. VI, pp. 388–9.

45. Menna Prestwich, *Cranfield: Politics and Profits under the Early Stuarts* (Clarendon Press, 1966), p. 448.

46. Rushworth, p. 138.

Chapter 6

A GODLY PRINCE

. . .

THE CHURCH OF ENGLAND AND THE PURITANS

The accession of a new ruler had become, during the Tudor period, an occasion for redefining the nature of the ecclesiastical settlement. While Henry VIII had broken the links with Rome and turned the Church of England into an autonomous body under royal headship, he had prevented it from becoming protestant. The formal shift to protestantism took place only after Henry's death, when his young son, Edward VI, gave rein to the reformers. The doctrine of the English Church was defined by two Prayer Books. The first, issued in 1549, was relatively conservative, but the second, of 1552, was far less compromising in its commitment to 'reformed' beliefs and practices. Edward's sudden death in 1553 meant that the throne passed to his catholic half-sister, Mary Tudor, who put the whole process into reverse by restoring papal supremacy and bringing back at least the outward forms of the old faith. Unfortunately for Mary and catholicism, she was given even less time to carry through her programme than Edward VI, for she died childless in 1558 and it was her half-sister, Elizabeth, who now became Queen and held the future of the Church of England in her hands. Elizabeth was a moderate protestant, opposed to radical change, not least because it would alienate that section of her people – no one knew how large or significant it was – which still adhered to catholicism. She did not, however, operate in a political vacuum. She had to take account of the views of the political nation and, in particular, of the men she chose as her Councillors. In general, these were far more committed to reformed ideals than she was, and wanted an uncompromisingly protestant religious settlement.

The tensions between the Queen and her advisers were reflected in the Church of England, as re-established by statute in 1559. In its theology it was close to Calvin, but in its form of service, set out in the 1559 Prayer Book, and in its discipline and ritual, as defined by the Act of Uniformity and subsequent royal injunctions, it was far removed from Genevan practice. The most obvious differences were the retention by the Elizabethan Church of an episcopal hierarchy and of distinctive garments for the clergy. These were anathema to many of the protestants whose faith meant so much to them that they had gone into exile in Mary's reign rather than live under a catholic sovereign. They now flocked back to England, looking forward to the task of building a new Jerusalem – or at any rate a replica of Geneva – in their native country. On their return, however, they were faced with a difficult choice. Should they refuse to take an active part in a Church that was still disfigured with Romish practices? If they did so they would merely leave the way open for time-servers and closet papists to assume control. If, on the other hand, they joined the anglican ministry, they would be committing themselves to act in ways that they found deeply repugnant. This was a dilemma that the exiles and their spiritual descendants, the puritans, never fully resolved. Apart from a handful of separatists – who, under Elizabethan legislation, were at constant risk of imprisonment or even death – the puritans remained within the Church of England. Some conformed fully; others modified, omitted or ignored those sections of the Prayer Book and implementing legislation that they found unacceptable. Puritanism, then, was a spectrum rather than a single attitude. What all puritans had in common was the desire for a truly reformed Church, one from which the last vestiges of catholicism had been eradicated. They spent much of Elizabeth's reign trying to achieve this with the aid of their sympathisers in Parliament – for puritanism was as much a lay as a clerical movement – but they were always blocked by the Queen. Furthermore, as the reign went on, the Elizabethan Church began to put down deep roots and satisfy the religious needs of an increasing number of the Queen's subjects. While puritans might continue to think of it as an unhappy compromise, merely half reformed, other people, both within the ministry and outside, were coming to regard it as not simply a valid Church in its own right but one that came closer to the ideal than any of its counterparts.

It is often assumed that by the last decade of Elizabeth's reign the puritan movement had been defeated, but this is not really true. Admittedly, many of its leaders had died or retired from the scene, and there were no more overt challenges to the established Church from campaigns focussed on Parliament. But puritans as such had not ceased to exist. Even if they accepted that they would never be able to achieve their aims while Elizabeth was alive, there was always the accession of James to look forward to, since he came from a country which had an established presbyterian Church of the sort that many English puritans longed for. No sooner had news of Elizabeth's death been announced than the puritan movement went into action. James was still on his way south from Scotland when he was presented with the Millenary Petition, so called because it was said to be signed by a thousand ministers "desiring reformation of certain ceremonies and abuses of the Church [of England]".[1] This was a carefully phrased document. Since its compilers referred to James's writings they were presumably familiar with the *Basilicon Doron*, in which he described puritans as "very pests in the Church and commonweal".[2] But James was thinking of Scottish presbyterians, whose language and actions had connotations of egalitarianism and republicanism. The Millenary Petition, by contrast, emphasised that its signatories accepted James's "just title to the peaceable government of this Church and commonwealth" and that they were neither "factious men affecting a popular parity in the Church" nor "schismatics aiming at the dissolution of the state ecclesiastical". All they wanted was to be relieved of the "burthen of human rites and ceremonies" under which they were groaning.[3] These included signing with the cross in baptism, using the ring in the marriage service, bowing at the name of Jesus, and wearing "the cap and surplice". They asked that in future only "able and sufficient men" should be admitted into the ministry and that they should either preach regularly or pay somebody else to do so. They wanted an end to non-residence and a return to the Church of some of the wealth that had been taken from it. They also wanted Church courts to be more sparing of the sentence of excommunication, which at present, they complained, was imposed for "trifles and twelve-penny matters".[4]

The petitioners claimed that all the abuses which they had listed, as well as a number of others, could be shown to be contrary to what was laid down in the scriptures, and they suggested that James should give them the opportunity to develop their case either in writing "or by conference among the learned".[5] The prospect of presiding over a gathering of divines and thereby opening the way to unity within the Church was something that appealed to James. He planned to do this before the end of the year, but an outbreak of plague forced the postponement of the conference to early 1604. In the proclamation announcing his decision, James began by stating his belief that the constitution and doctrine of the Church of England were "agreeable to God's word and near to the condition of the primitive Church". But human imperfection could lead to corruption, and he therefore welcomed the opportunity which the conference would provide to obtain a fuller understanding of the state of the Church "and receive thereby light to judge whether there be indeed any such enormities as are pretended, and know how to proceed to the redress".[6] Until such time as the conference took place, however, his subjects should "repose themselves and leave to our conscience that which to us only appertaineth; avoiding all unlawful and factious manner of proceeding". In particular, they should refrain from promoting further petitions, undermining ecclesiastical authority, or railing against the existing structure of the Church. Those who did so, declared James, were promoting "novelty, and so confusion, in all estates". This was quite contrary to his own intention, which "ever was, and now is, to preserve the estate, as well ecclesiastical as politic, in such form as we have found it established by the laws here".[7]

James had clearly been taken aback by the speed with which the puritan campaign developed after his accession to the English throne. Its leaders sent out instructions urging puritan ministers to "stir up the people to a desire or a liking of reformation" by preaching against "the superstitious ceremonies and tyranny of bishops",[8] and recommended the drawing up of local petitions, addressed to the King, calling for further reform of the Church. Northamptonshire took the lead in this, but its example was followed in nearby counties, and champions of orthodoxy such as the heads of Oxford colleges complained of the way in which radical puritans, "to bolster out their stale objections

103

and false calumniations, have trudged up and down divers shires to get the consent, they care not of whom, so they may make up a tale and pretend a number".[9] In July a gathering of puritan ministers in London decided to put these local initiatives on a national basis by drawing up a standard form of petition, asking that "the present state of the Church may be farther reformed in all things needful, according to the rule of God's holy word, and as agreeable to the example of other reformed churches which have restored both the doctrine and discipline".[10] In the same month the puritans in Northamptonshire appointed two of their number to move to London so that they could keep up the pressure on local representatives to advance the cause of further reformation.

The bishops were understandably alarmed by the increasing evidence of the puritans' activities, especially since they were not sure, at this stage, what to expect from James. Even before he reached London he had upset them by his decision to give up impropriate tithes in possession of the crown. During the Middle Ages the right of presentation to some third of all livings had been donated by lay patrons to monasteries, along with the tithes which provided a maintenance for the minister. These 'impropriate' tithes were financially beneficial to the monasteries, which kept the major part and paid only a small stipend to the incumbents they appointed. After the dissolution of the monasteries by Henry VIII they were initially acquired by the crown, but as and when monastic lands were sold off or given away the impropriate tithes were transferred to the new owners, who treated them as simply another source of income. James was determined not merely to put an end to the plunder of the Church, which had been a feature of the Tudor period, but to restore its finances and thereby eliminate evils such as pluralism and non-residence. It was the lack of adequate maintenance at the parish level which had forced the ecclesiastical authorities to give ministers more than one benefice, but this was harmful since pluralists could only set up home in one of their parishes; the others were left without a resident priest to give them spiritual succour and guidance. Since impropriate tithes had, in effect, been stolen from the Church it made sense for a godly King to set an example by returning them, and he called on the universities and bishops to do likewise. What James did not appreciate was that impropriate tithes had become an integral part of the financial structure of bishoprics and colleges, which would be unable to function without them. Furthermore, the re-endowment of the Church could not be carried out unless the lay owners who held by far the greater part of impropriate tithes were willing to follow the King's lead by returning them, but of this there was no sign.

When he eventually reached London and met his bishops, James came to appreciate the complexity of the situation and refrained from implementing his initiative. But despite the bishops' forebodings he insisted on going ahead with a conference at which they and the puritan representatives should meet on equal terms. This took place at Hampton Court Palace in January 1604, and the items listed in the Millenary Petition provided the agenda. At an initial meeting with a number of bishops and Privy Councillors, James made what James Montagu – a future bishop, but at this time only a dean, in attendance on the King – described as "a very admirable speech of an hour long at least; for learning, piety and prudency I never before heard the like".[11] James began in retrospective mood, observing that he was better placed than his Tudor predecessors, for whereas their principal concern had been to change the existing order in the Church, his aim was to "confirm that which he found well settled already". He gave thanks to God for his good fortune in this respect, and in particular "for bringing him into the promised land, where religion was purely professed, where he sat among grave, learned, and reverend men, not as before elsewhere, a King without state, without honour, without order, where beardless boys would brave him to his face".[12] The speech ended with "a most excellent prayer", after which James listed the topics to be discussed and promised that if, on any issue, there was scriptural proof that he was wrong, he would give way. But the bishops, he insisted, must accept a similar obligation: "if they erred, they must yield to him; for he would ever submit both sceptre and crown to Christ's, to be guided by His word".[13]

Debate started with those sections of the Prayer Book which the puritans considered smacked of popery, among them general absolution and the confirmation of children. In order to remove any misconceptions it was agreed that in future the first would be styled "absolution or general confession of sins" and the second "confirmation or further examination of the children's faith". The puritans had also objected to the carrying out of baptism in private houses, particularly when it was done by women – usually midwives, in those instances when a new-born baby was thought unlikely to survive long enough for a priest to be summoned. Discussion of this issue took up a good three hours, and the King, in Montagu's opinion, argued "so wisely, wittedly and learnedly, with that pretty patience as I think never man living ever heard the like".[14] It was eventually decided that private baptism should still be permitted, but that only ministers and curates should have the right to perform it. The conference then turned to consider the delicate problem of episcopal juris-diction, especially the abuses complained of by the puritans in diocesan courts presided over by the bishops' commissaries. It was resolved that this and cognate issues should be referred for appropriate action to the Lord Chancellor and the Lord Chief Justice. As for the imposition of excommunication for mere trifles, this was to be "taken away both in name and nature"; anyone refusing to accept the verdict of a Church court should henceforth be dealt with by the Court of Chancery. The pur-itans had also argued that in the exercise of their disciplinary functions the bishops should not act alone. James pressed this point, and managed to win assent to the proposal that episcopal jurisdiction should be "somewhat limited" and that bishops should have "either the Dean and Chapter or some grave min-isters assistant to them in ordination, suspension, degrading, etc."[15] The last topic to be considered was the lamentable state of the Church in Ireland, after which the meeting concluded with the King propounding "matters whereabout he hoped there would be no controversy, as to have a learned ministry, and maintenance for them as far as might be, and for pluralities and non-residencies to be taken away, or at least made so few as possibly might be".[16]

On the following day James conferred with the puritan rep-resentatives, beginning once again with "an excellent oration".[17] There was general agreement on the need to maintain the purity of the Church's doctrine and to appoint worthy ministers – the first two points on the agenda. The third, however, concerned the government of the Church, and here, if the official account of the proceedings (written by a bishop) is to be believed, a misunderstanding occurred. John Reynolds, the principal pur-itan representative, interpreted the concession James had already obtained from the bishops on the exercise of their disciplinary powers to mean that "the bishop, with his presbytery, should determine all such points as before could not be decided". The use of the term "presbytery" brought back unhappy memories of James's encounters with Melville and other leaders of the Kirk, and he reacted strongly. A Scottish presbytery, he declared, "as well agreeth with a monarchy as God and the Devil. Then Jack and Tom and Will and Dick shall meet, and at their pleasures censure me and my Council and all our proceedings . . . Stay, I pray you, for one seven years before you demand that of me, and if then you find me pursy [i.e. short-winded] and fat and my wind-pipes stuffed, I will perhaps hearken to you."[18]

James's outburst did not dampen the proceedings, nor did it affect his good humour. When discussion turned to passages in the Prayer Book that puritans found difficulty in accepting, Reynolds instanced the words from the marriage service, 'With my body I thee worship'. James agreed that at first sight it seemed strange to diminish the term 'worship', which he had assumed to be reserved to God, but he had discovered that this was not uncommon in England, where people spoke, for instance, of "a gentleman of worship". And turning to Reynolds with a smile, he added that "if you had a good wife yourself, you would think all the honour and worship you could do her were well bestowed".[19] On ceremonies in general, James took the position that they should be retained unless it could be demonstrated that "they had either the word of God against them or good authority".[20] He applied this test to all those practices sanctioned by the Prayer Book but objected to by puritans, citing the relevant passages from scripture and the Church fathers. In so doing he became convinced that the puritan complaints were unfounded and that the ceremonies should remain.

This was no doubt a disappointment to the puritan representatives – though according to Montagu they had argued their case very weakly – but they could take comfort from James's acceptance of the need for a new translation of the Bible. The puritans felt that existing versions "were corrupt and not answerable to the truth of the original", and James agreed with them: he had never seen an English translation of which he approved, and as for the Geneva version, used by Scottish presbyterians and favoured by English puritans, it was "the worst of all". He therefore ordered that "the best learned in both the universities" should set to work on a fresh translation, "to be reviewed by the bishops and the chief learned of the Church; from them to be presented to the Privy Council; and lastly, to be ratified by his royal authority; and so this whole Church to be bound unto it and none other". James added the caveat that the new, authorised version should be without marginal annotations, having found that those which were printed in the Geneva translation were "very partial, untrue, seditious, and savouring too much of dangerous and traitorous conceits".[21]

The first two days of the Hampton Court conference had produced a surprising degree of harmony, with at least fifteen of the points at issue resolved. It now remained to put the decisions into execution, and this was the business of the third and last day. It began with a meeting between the King, attended by his Councillors, and the bishops, at which James summarised the reform programme and expressed the hope that "it might not be . . . as smoke out of a tunnel, but substantially done; to remain for ever". It was decided that joint committees of bishops and Councillors should be set up, each charged with implementing a particular section, including the drafting of bills where statutory sanction was needed. The puritan representatives were then called in and told what had been decided. If Montagu's account can be trusted, "they were all exceedingly well satisfied". Their only reservation concerned those ministers of puritan inclination who had long declined to use ceremonies repugnant to their conscience, and who should not, they thought, be abruptly compelled to do so. The King, addressing himself to the bishops, replied that "his end being peace, his meaning was not that any man should be cruel in imposing those matters, but by time and moderation win all men unto them: those they found peaceable, to give some connivency to such, and to use their brethren as he had used them, with meekness and gentleness, and do all things to the edification of God and His Church".[22]

James clearly regarded the conference as a success. Indeed he said as much in a proclamation issued at the beginning of March 1604, even though he admitted that the great expectations aroused beforehand had produced small effects. This was because the "mighty and vehement" puritan charges were "supported with so weak and slender proofs, as it appeared unto us and our Council that there was no cause why any change should have been at all in that which was most impugned, the Book of Common Prayer . . . neither in the doctrine, which appeared to be sincere, nor in the forms and rites, which were justified out of the practice of the primitive Church". Nevertheless, in order to remove any lingering doubts, James had instructed the Archbishop of Canterbury to make a number of explications and alterations. These were to be printed in a new and final edition of the Prayer Book which would in future be "the only public form of serving God established and allowed to be in this realm". James gave notice that he would allow no further alterations, for it was dangerous to permit "innovation in things once settled by mature deliberation".[23]

James's view of the conference was not shared by many puritans. It is not clear how their representatives at Hampton Court had been chosen, but it may well be that the King himself selected them, after consultation with the bishops. Reynolds and his three or four companions were well respected, but they spoke only for the moderate, conforming puritans; they were out of sympathy, if not out of touch, with their more radical brethren, who regarded their conduct at Hampton Court as a betrayal and the conference itself as a lost opportunity. Since there was clearly nothing more to be hoped for from James I the radical puritans pinned their hopes on Parliament, and no sooner did it meet than there were demands for further changes in the Prayer Book, notwithstanding the royal proclamation. James therefore issued another proclamation, condemning "certain ministers who under pretended zeal of reformation are the chief authors of divisions and sects among our people", and warning that "what untractable men do not perform upon admonition they must be compelled unto by authority". He was still ready to give time to non-conforming ministers to try and reconcile their consciences with their Prayer-Book obligations, but he would not wait beyond the end of November 1604. The bishops were to do their utmost, "by conferences, arguments, persuasions, and by all other ways of love and gentleness to reclaim all that be in the ministry to the obedience of our Church laws", but if these measures failed, the non-conformists would be deprived of their livings and replaced by men who were willing to accept the legal requirements of their profession.[24]

Unfortunately, it was not clear exactly what these legal requirements were. The canon law of the Church of England had originally derived from Rome, but ever since the break with the papacy under Henry VIII it had remained in limbo. James therefore instructed the bishops to draw up a new code of canon law, and this was done with such rapidity that he was able to promulgate it, by virtue of his authority as supreme governor of the Church, in September 1604. Among many provisions which aroused little contention, it included Canon 36 forbidding

acceptance into the ministry of any person who would not subscribe in writing to the statement "that the Book of Common
Prayer . . . containeth in it nothing contrary to the Word of God,
and that it may lawfully so be used; and that he himself will
use the form in the said Book prescribed in public prayer and
administration of the sacraments, and none other".[25] Although
this provision applied only to ordinands, and not to existing
ministers, it became one of the tests, along with willingness to
wear the prescribed vestments, used to bring pressure to bear
upon non-conformists.

After the opening of James's first Parliament in March 1604,
puritan sympathisers in the House of Commons took up the
defence of their co-religionists. There were proposals "that
the bishops' canons may be looked into, by authority whereof
the subject is sued and much grieved" and "to draw [up] a petition to beg mercy for the ministers threatened by the bishops,
and inhibited to preach, for not using fruitless ceremonies".[26]
The Commons eventually adopted a petition, in June 1604, listing their grievances in ecclesiastical matters. These included "the
pressing the use of certain rites and ceremonies in this Church,
[such] as the cross in baptism, the wearing of the surplice in
ordinary parish churches, and the subscription required of the
ministers, further than is commanded by the laws of the realm".[27]
Insistence upon such formalities, the Commons argued, led to
the silencing of many good ministers, and put off potential
ordinands who would otherwise have been a source of strength
to the Church. The only people who gained from such provisions
were "ignorant and unable men" who brought the ministry into
discredit.

James, as he made plain in the proclamation issued in July,
would not reopen discussion on issues which, in his opinion, had
been fully considered and finally resolved at Hampton Court.
He pressed the Commons to consult with the bishops, in the
hope that they could agree on the implementation of the reform
programme drawn up by the conference, but many members
of the Lower House regarded the bishops as obstacles to reform
rather than proponents of it. The Commons therefore pursued
their own course, and bills were passed to put an end to pluralism and to provide "a learned and godly ministry".[28] No one
could doubt the Commons' commitment to ecclesiastical reform,
but they chose to ignore the unpalatable fact that many of
the abuses of which they complained, especially pluralism and

non-residence, were the consequence of poverty, and could not be removed unless and until the Church was re-endowed. The return of impropriate tithes, as James had seen, was the key to success, but when a bill was introduced into the Commons "for a convenient portion to be assigned out of every impropriation for the maintenance of a preaching minister" it was not even given a second reading.[29]

The Commons' refusal to accept James's clear message that he would contemplate no further changes in the doctrine or discipline of the established Church seems to have hardened his resolve to drive out the non-conformists. In December 1604 he instructed the bishops to initiate proceedings against recalcitrant ministers, and later complained that they seemed to "have stood as men at a gaze, and have done nothing".[30] This heavy pressure from the King drove the bishops into action, and one informed observer described how "the poor puritan ministers have been ferreted out in all corners, and some of them suspended, others deprived of their livings".[31] This campaign aroused resentment in many areas, particularly those like Northamptonshire in which the gentry tended to be puritan. Sir Edward Montagu was a leading Northamptonshire gentleman, and like his father before him he was very devout. 'On weekdays he prescribed for his household reading of scriptures and also singing of psalms in the hall after supper. On Sundays the family attended church twice, once promptly at nine in the morning and once at one, and after evening prayer one of the servants repeated notes of the sermon in the hall, a chaplain catechized the family, and all joined in psalms and prayers.'[32]

Montagu was one of the signatories of a petition drawn up by the Northamptonshire gentry and presented to James in February 1605. In it they asked for the moderation of the proceedings against puritan clergy, who, "by their conscionable and sincere teaching . . . have proved lights of great comfort and furtherance to us and all others Your Majesty's subjects". They did so because they feared "the loss of many a learned, painful [i.e. diligent] and profitable minister if the execution of this late decree for subscription and conformity should proceed (as in part it is begun) to the deprivation and suspension of many of our most learned and profitable teachers".[33] This was not the first evidence James had been given of the discontent aroused by his hard-line policy. In the winter of 1604, while he was hunting in Northamptonshire, he had received a number of petitions on behalf of the puritan ministers which provided clear, and un-welcome, proof of the extent and degree of organisation of the puritan movement in the county. Fearing that a conspiracy was being organised, he now took firm action against its potential leaders. Montagu and other prominent signatories were sum-moned before the Council, which interrogated them and ordered their dismissal from their offices as Deputy-Lieutenants and Justices of the Peace.

James took part in these proceedings, and made the revealing comment that the revolt in the Netherlands and the troubles in Scotland had begun in just this manner. He clearly equated English puritans with Scottish presbyterians, and had he con-tinued along the same lines he might well have provoked even more widespread dissent. But during the course of long discus-sions in Council, James revised his opinions, for he came to realise that English puritans were basically loyal subjects and upholders of the royal supremacy. What they resented was the apparent lenience shown by James towards Roman Catholics, since they took this as an indication of his lack of commitment to the protestant faith. They also wanted to protect ministers whose reluctance to conform was prompted by the same scruples of conscience that made them beacons of religious and moral guidance within their parishes. Once James became aware of the nature of the puritans' suspicions, he took immediate steps to provide assurance. He publicly declared that he had been "born, bred, schooled [and] brought up" in the protestant reli-gion, that he had "maintained it with the danger of his life, and he will spend his life and best blood for the same and will die in it". To drive the point home, he added that if his son, Prince Henry, showed signs of wanting to alter the established religion "and set up popery, he would disinherit him".[34] As for the puritans, he now realised that they were "good and loving subjects, rather blinded . . . with indiscreet zeal than otherwise carried by any disloyal intentions". He regarded them as being "in another rank than the papists, and he would go half way to meet them".[35]

James gave proof of his good intentions by restoring Sir Edward Montagu to his offices and continuing to honour him with his presence when the hunting season provided the oppor-tunity. James's passion for the chase frequently caused his min-isters to despair, for they had to formulate and execute policy at one remove, communicating with the vagrant monarch only by messengers who spent hours, and sometimes days, spurring their horses down dusty roads and across muddy fields in search of him. They would have preferred a King who remained at Whitehall, or at least went no further away than Greenwich in one direction or Hampton Court in the other. James claimed, as he had earlier done in Scotland, that he could work as efficiently while he was chasing the deer or reposing in one of the royal hunting lodges as when he was resident in his capital city. This may or may not have been true, but James's forays into the countryside of southern England had positive advantages. They enabled him to meet his subjects in a relatively informal manner and, by displaying his royal person, foster their loyalty. They also brought him into close touch with the rulers of the localities, upon whose dedication to the royal service the early Stuart monarchy, like its Tudor predecessor, was dependent.

In the end, some eighty ministers – less than one per cent of the total number – were deprived of their livings for refusing either to subscribe to the articles laid down in the 1604 canons or to conform in matters of dress and ceremonies. The puritans claimed that the true figure was three hundred, and since they had so many sympathisers in the Commons the issue of the deprived ministers became another bone of contention between James and the Lower House. In 1606 Sir Francis Hastings, who had been prominent in organising the petition of the Northamptonshire gentry, introduced a bill, which passed through all its stages in the Commons, giving suspended and deprived ministers the right of appeal. The following year the House included in its proposed petition on religion a plea that "the late deprived, suspended, and silenced ministers . . . may be restored to the use of their ministry" on the grounds that "their refusal of these ceremonies proceedeth only from conscience, and fear to offend God, and not from any contradictious or malignant humour".[36] There was no let-up in the pressure on James and the bishops, for even in the last session of his first Parliament, in 1610, the Lower House included the case of the deprived ministers in its petition of ecclesiastical grievances.

The Commons would never accept James's assumption that the government of the Church was a matter for him alone, acting in concert with the bishops. There were few sessions without some discussion on pluralism and non-residence or the need to provide learned clergy and to punish those who were scandalous and unworthy. But James stood firm. He was as concerned as any member of Parliament to see clerical abuses rooted out, but he preferred a pragmatic approach: the Commons were strong on indignation but weak on practical measures. One of James's principal aims was to improve the standing of the clergy, so that they should acquire self-confidence and be able thereby to give moral guidance to their flocks. He complained in 1616 that "churchmen [are] too much had in contempt. I must speak truth. Great men, lords, judges, and people of all degrees from the highest to the lowest, have too much contemned them." In James's eyes there was no excuse for indiscriminate criticism of the clergy, nor of the Church of England, "which I say in my conscience, of any Church that ever I read or knew of, present or past, is most pure, and nearest the primitive and apostolical Church in doctrine and discipline, and is sureliest founded upon the word of God of any church in christendom".[37]

One of the ways in which the authority of the Church had been undermined was through 'prohibitions'. These emanated from the two principal common-law courts of King's Bench and Common Pleas, and limited the jurisdiction of Church courts by forbidding them to proceed in the case in question. The clergy had complained about prohibitions in the closing years of Elizabeth's reign, and Archbishop Bancroft raised the matter with James in 1605. The King welcomed the opportunity to decide an issue of disputed jurisdictions, particularly if it would strengthen the authority of the Church and diminish that of the common lawyers, whom he was already beginning to distrust. However, he came up against the opposition of the judicial bench, led by Sir Edward Coke, who argued that although the King was the fountain of justice he could not act of his own volition in legal matters, but only through the courts and the judges. Coke was not always representative of public opinion, but fear that the King might override the common law at the behest of the bishops was widespread. John Chamberlain, the London letter writer, reported in November 1608 that "the King hath had two or three conferences of late with the judges about prohibitions . . . which . . . he would fain cut off, and stretch his prerogative to the uttermost".[38] James was made aware of these fears, and dealt with them directly when he addressed Parliament in March 1610. "I am not ignorant", he said, "that I have been thought to be an enemy to all prohibitions, and an utter stayer of them", but in fact he approved of their use in cases where a court was exceeding its jurisdiction, for their true function was "to keep every river within his own banks and channels". What alarmed him was "the swelling and overflowing of prohibitions in a far greater abundance than ever before" as every court strove to attract business to itself. The ultimate responsibility for ensuring that the legal system functioned properly was the King's, and James had therefore spent a lot of time in consultation with the judges, who agreed with him that prohibitions should only be granted after careful consideration. There was no point, James emphasised, in bringing a case to court if the sentence could not be enforced. "A poor minister with much labour and expense having exhausted his poor means . . . obtains a sentence, and then, when he looks to enjoy the fruits thereof, he is defrauded of all by a prohibition . . . And so is he tortured like Tantalus, who when he hath the apple at his mouth, and that he is gaping and opening his mouth to receive it, then must it be pulled from him by a prohibition, and he not suffered to taste thereof." James had resolved the problem, or so he hoped, by giving instructions to the Church courts "to contain themselves within the bounds of their own jurisdictions; and to the courts of common law, that they should not be so forward and prodigal in multiplying their prohibitions".[39]

By controlling the abuse of prohibitions, James helped preserve the canon law and the ecclesiastical courts which enforced it. The bishops were grateful not only for this but for the many other benefits which the accession of a truly godly prince had brought to them and the established Church. Elizabeth had regarded bishops as agents of the royal will, deriving their authority solely from the crown; she had no time for the argument put forward by Richard Bancroft and others that the episcopal office was *jure divino*, of divine origin, and that the sovereign only mediated a spiritual authority which was granted directly by God. James, however, accepted this elevated view of episcopacy. "That bishops ought to be in the Church", he declared, "I ever maintained it, as an apostolic institution and so the ordinance of God".[40] As something of a theologian himself, and a lover of theological discussion, James welcomed bishops to Court. In the closing years of Elizabeth there had never been more than four bishops in attendance, but under James this figure rose initially to six and, by the end of the reign, to ten.[41] He also made greater use of them in secular administration. Elizabeth, in a reign that lasted forty-five years, had appointed only one bishop to the Privy Council, but James, who ruled in

England for less than half that time, had a total of seven episcopal Councillors.

There was a further contrast between James and his predecessor when it came to filling vacant bishoprics. Elizabeth had taken her time over this, since during a vacancy a substantial part of the revenues of the see went to the crown. She had left the diocese of Oxford without a bishop for more than forty years, Ely for nineteen and Bristol for fourteen. Moreover, when bishops were eventually appointed they were often required to exchange valuable lands for a handful of scattered royal manors, which could not be efficiently managed, or impropriate tithes, which were a source of endless conflict with the laity. James began his reign with a statute forbidding the alienation of episcopal property to the crown, and he moved rapidly to fill vacant bishoprics. Thereafter it was very rare for a diocese to be without a bishop for more than a few months.

Most of the bishops whom James appointed were known to him personally by virtue of the fact that they had been royal chaplains. He did not favour either Calvinists or anti-Calvinists, for in the Church as in the state he made it his objective to maintain a balance between the various factions. In a celebrated article published in 1957 Hugh Trevor-Roper characterised the Jacobean episcopate as, for the most part, 'indifferent, negligent [and] secular', and accused these 'worldly, courtly, talented [and] place-hunting *dilettanti*' of being 'the ornamental betrayers of the Church'.[42] Such a damning verdict is no longer acceptable. All but one of the bishops appointed by James had doctorates in divinity, and many had earlier served as heads of Oxford or Cambridge colleges and had thereby acquired valuable administrative experience. A few bishops – most notably Richard Bancroft, Archbishop of Canterbury from 1604 until his death in 1610, and John Williams, Bishop of Lincoln from 1621 – rarely if ever visited their sees. However, Bancroft was an assiduous attender at Privy Council meetings and also took a prominent part in House of Lords debates, defending the Church's interests. As for Williams, he was appointed Lord Keeper of the Great Seal in 1621, which meant that he was one of the principal figures in the royal government, with a heavy burden of administrative and judicial duties. The vast majority of bishops spent part of every year in their dioceses, and by leading the triennial visitations in person they acquired first-hand knowledge of the clergy and their problems. They also,

with James's active encouragement, revived the practice of
confirmation, which had virtually died out in post-Reformation
England. The 1604 canons had made confirmation obligatory
for bishops, but there is every indication that they carried it out
willingly, and evoked a positive response; the number of candidates for confirmation in any diocese often ran into hundreds.
The bishops were also, with one or two exceptions, committed
preachers, much to James's satisfaction. Toby Matthew, whom
James translated from Durham to York in 1606, had a justified
reputation as a Court wit and a constant seeker after prefer-
ment, yet he gave well over five hundred sermons as Bishop of
Durham and more than seven hundred in the first fifteen years
of his archiepiscopate.[43]

When James arrived in England, the seventy-year-old John
Whitgift, appointed Archbishop of Canterbury by Queen Elizabeth in 1583, was still alive. He died in 1604, and James chose
Richard Bancroft, Bishop of London, to succeed him. There
was nothing unexpected about this, for Bancroft had formerly
been Whitgift's chaplain and had taken over many of the archbishop's duties as old age rendered Whitgift increasingly incapable. Bancroft, a passionate advocate of divine-right episcopacy,
was a disciplinarian very much in Whitgift's style. He had no
time for non-conformists and little patience with the conscientious scruples of English puritans, whom he tended to identify
with Scottish presbyterians. It was Bancroft who drew up the
canons of 1604 and pushed them through Convocation, but
he did not share James's initial determination to drive non-
conforming puritans out of the Church. Despite his abrasive
manner, Bancroft preferred to persuade rather than compel,
and he saw the greatest danger to the Church coming not so
much from refractory clergy as from their allies among the
gentry who were strongly ensconced in the House of Commons.
There, in Bancroft's opinion, they indulged in constant and
unjustified criticism of the established Church while refusing
to restore the lands and tithes which they and their predecessors
had, in effect, stolen from it.

Bancroft died in 1610 and many people assumed that James
would appoint Lancelot Andrewes, one of his favourite preachers,
to Canterbury. Andrewes, whose sermons, in the estimation of
T.S. Eliot, 'rank with the finest English prose of their time, of
any time',[44] was Bishop of Ely and royal almoner. He was also
an outstanding scholar and theologian of the first rank, who

took a leading part in preparing the new translation of the Bible authorised by the Hampton Court Conference. Clarendon, in his great *History of the Rebellion,* was later to regret that Andrewes had not succeeded Bancroft, for he might have kept out what Clarendon regarded as the infection of radical puritanism which subsequently poisoned the Church. However, Andrewes was a high churchman, whose chapel, in the words of his first biographer, was 'devoutly and reverently adorned, and God served there with . . . holy and reverend behaviour'.[45] His love of ceremony and his insistence that the Church of England was the lineal descendant of the catholic Church, albeit purged of the impurities which had come to mar that institution, made him the spiritual father of those who came to be known as Arminians. The name derived from Jacob Arminius, who led a movement of revolt in the Netherlands against the extreme Calvinism of the Dutch Church, but the English high-church movement was home grown. Andrewes made no secret of his beliefs, but he was irenic by temperament and quite content to follow James's orders and avoid public controversy. However, this did not make him any more acceptable to the strong puritan element within the Church, which would have been alienated by his elevation to the see of Canterbury.

Puritans admired the low-church George Abbot, whose parents had suffered for their protestant faith under Queen Mary, and it was Abbot whom James appointed. Abbot was not an outsider; in fact he had been the preferred choice of Bancroft, and he had already made a name for himself as a staunch defender of the protestant faith against its catholic adversary. He had been chaplain to James's close friend, the Scottish Earl of Dunbar, and in 1608, when Dunbar attended a general assembly of the Kirk in order to promote the cause of episcopacy in Scotland, Abbot went with him and won praise not only for the quality of his preaching but also for the skilful manner in which he reconciled conflicting factions and thereby opened the way to the restoration of the Scottish episcopate. This delighted James, who had long planned such an outcome, and stood Abbot in good stead when the time came to replace Bancroft. His appointment to Canterbury helped reconcile wavering puritans to the established Church and dampened down the fires which had been stoked by the petitioning campaign at the beginning of James's reign in England. Abbot believed that the greatest threat to the Church came from the catholics, not the puritans, and although he would not tolerate ostentatious non-conformity he was reluctant to drive good ministers out of the Church. Fortunately for him, James was now of the same mind, and for the next decade the King and his archbishop worked in harmony.

The Jacobean Church was not a homogeneous body. At the parish level there was still a considerable variety of practice, even within the Prayer-Book framework, and much depended on the attitude of the minister and also, of course, of the leading members of his congregation. Diversity was likewise a feature of the episcopate, which covered the whole range of the spectrum from low-church to high-church, Calvinist to Arminian, time-server to committed evangelist. James's principal concern was to maintain the maximum degree of unity, even if this meant taking a soft line on uniformity. The Prayer Book and 1604 Canons had, between them, laid down the minimum requirements, and James, at any rate after the opening years of his reign, did not press for more. Ministers who subscribed to the oaths required by the Canons but refused to conform were usually tolerated, as were those who conformed but refused to subscribe. Suspension and deprivation were held in reserve and only employed against ministers who deliberately put their heads above the parapet. 'Martyrdom', in this limited sense, was an option which puritan ministers could either choose or reject. The vast majority rejected it.

Although diversity remained a feature of the Church at the parish level, a distinctive pattern of Jacobean worship gradually established itself in many places. While James condemned an over-emphasis on preaching, he acknowledged its essential role in the instruction of the laity. The 1604 Canons required that pulpits should be "provided and set in a convenient place" in every church and "seemly kept for the preaching of God's Word". They also made it obligatory for a seat to be provided for the minister from which he could conduct the service, which included, of course, selected readings from the scriptures. This trinity of reading, preaching and conducting, around which the service was structured, led to the creation of three-decker pulpits, of which the earliest surviving example in England dates from 1610. When the holy communion was administered, this usually took place at a table placed in the centre of the chancel, behind the screen which separated it from the nave. The table was surrounded by stalls or benches on which the communicants sat, though they were under a formal requirement to kneel when they actually received the sacrament. This arrangement satisfied James's insistence that the administration of the sacraments should be conducted with reverence and dignity. It was also acceptable to those of puritan inclination, for the placing of the table away from the east wall made it apparent that it was not a popish-style altar.[46]

Puritans found it easier to conform to the established Church because its supreme governor was a committed protestant and theologically a Calvinist. James took a keen interest in the dispute that broke out in the Netherlands between the Arminians and the hard-line Calvinists, and when an international synod was convened at Dort (i.e. Dordrecht) to resolve it, he instructed the British delegates to take an anti-Arminian line. This was not solely for religious reasons. The Arminians were disturbing the *status quo*, an action which James regarded as dangerous. They were also setting a bad example by provoking public controversy on topics that were best left to experts: it was wrong, in James's eyes, for ministers to "deliver in the pulpit to the people these things for ordinary doctrines which are the highest points of schools [i.e. universities], and not fit for vulgar capacity".[47]

One of the four British delegates selected by James to go to Dort was George Carleton. At the time he was bishop of the poor Welsh see of Llandaff, but as a reward for his spirited defence of episcopacy at the synod he was soon after translated to the much richer see of Chichester. Carleton, described by Anthony à Wood as a 'severe Calvinist',[48] had published a book in 1610 in which he defended the anglican episcopate against its catholic detractors. Dismissing the claim that bishops in the Church of England were mere pawns of the royal governor, Carleton declared that they were, on the contrary, the guardians of true doctrine. "Herein they are authorised by God. If princes withstand them in these things, they have warrant not to obey princes, because with these things Christ hath put them in trust."[49] Needless to say, Carleton was not inciting rebellion against the King. He was putting forward a hypothetical case, and even then was thinking only in terms of passive non-resistance rather than active disobedience. Yet conforming puritans within the Church were always faced with a potential conflict between the dictates of conscience and the instructions of the supreme governor, and the dilemma became more difficult to resolve after the outbreak of the Thirty Years War in 1618. This was seen by many people, among them Archbishop Abbot, as a war of religion, possibly Armageddon, the last great struggle between the powers of darkness, represented by the papacy and its secular allies, and the champions of true godliness who were defending the protestant cause.

James was undoubtedly a protestant, but he was also a peace-maker, temperamentally averse to the whole idea of war. More-over, he was an ecumenist who longed to narrow the divisions within the christian Church rather than enlarge them. Having married his daughter to the Calvinist Elector Palatine he was now trying to arrange a balancing match between his surviving son, Prince Charles, and the daughter of Philip III of Spain. For many of James's subjects – especially, but not solely, those of puritan inclination – this was equivalent to supping with the Devil, and risked undermining the entire protestant cause. Archbishop Abbot was on the verge of open opposition to the Spanish match, and his views were widely known. He hated catholicism and he feared that the Arminians within the English Church were subtly moving it closer to Rome. Soon after his appointment to Canterbury he had tried to block the appoint-ment of the high-church William Laud as president of St John's College, Oxford, on the grounds that he was a papist, and by 1620, if not earlier, he had extended his suspicions to Arminians in general. As the tide of anti-catholicism mounted, James struggled to contain it, and he found ready support among the Arminians. They had long recognised that, as an unpopular minority, their future prospects depended upon the attitude of the King. They did not share the widespread belief that every-thing associated with Rome was evil, and their lack of fanaticism mirrored James's own. In other words, in the last few years of James's reign the pressure of external events fractured the unity that James had managed to maintain within his Church and drove him into a *de facto* alliance with the Arminians.

As late as 1622 James was still trying to keep religious passions under control. In that year he issued "Directions to Preachers", forbidding anyone under the degree of bishop or dean to give public sermons on disputed points of theology, or to discuss "the power, prerogative, and jurisdiction, authority, or duty of sov-ereign princes, or otherwise meddle with . . . matters of state and the differences betwixt princes and the people". In an unavailing attempt to preserve at least the outward form of unity he also decreed that preachers should not "fall into bitter invectives

and indecent railing speeches against the persons of either
papists or puritans, but modestly and gravely . . . free both the
doctrine and discipline of the Church of England from the
aspersions of either adversary, especially where the auditory is
suspected to be tainted with the one or the other infection".[50]
This attempt to diminish controversy by royal command stood
little chance of success as religious differences became ever more
acute. Puritan fears of an Arminian–catholic takeover of the
established Church were matched by the Arminians' fear that
their very existence was threatened. While it had been possible,
during the first half of James's reign, for an Arminian like
Lancelot Andrewes to remain a relatively uncontroversial figure,
this was not the case with the next generation. Many Arminians
were now convinced that the puritans, far from being the back-
bone of the Church of England, were a fifth column within it,
potential traitors who needed to be driven out. This view was
expressed in a particularly assertive manner by an Essex minister, Richard Montagu, in 1624. He had been alarmed by the
activities of catholic missionaries in his neighbourhood who
claimed that the established Church was essentially Calvinist.
In response to their tract, *The Gag for the New Gospel*, he wrote *A
New Gag for an Old Goose*, in which he emphasised the catholic
elements within the Church while disparaging the Calvinist ones.
Moreover, in a letter to his friend, the Arminian John Cosin,
he said how pleased he would be if the King would "take strict
order that these Allobrogical dormice [i.e. the Calvinists] should
not so much peep out in corners or by owl-light. This riff-
raff rascals make us liable to the lash unto our other adversaries of the Church of Rome, who impute the frantic fits and
froth of every puritan paroxysm to the received doctrine of
our Church."[51]

Puritan ministers and their lay sympathisers were outraged
by Montagu's book, since his argument, if accepted, would out-
law them from the Church. When James's last Parliament met
in 1624 the Commons took up the matter and called on Archbishop Abbot to curb the errant clergyman. Abbot, nothing loth,
summoned Montagu to appear before him and instructed him
to think carefully about the offence he had given and then
write another, less controversial, tract, designed to reassure his
critics. Abbot acted only after consulting the King, but he could
no longer count on his wholehearted support, for the King
had also sent for Montagu and asked him to explain his views.

When he heard these, James was said to have exclaimed "If thou be a papist, I am a papist".[52] Perhaps for this reason, Montagu's second book, significantly titled *Appello Caesarem* (i.e. 'I appeal to the King'), was even more rebarbative than his first. James gave it to Francis White, at that time Dean of Carlisle, to see if it contained anything heterodox, but White, who probably had Arminian sympathies, found nothing in it which was contrary to anglican doctrine. James therefore allowed the book to be published, even though it was calculated to enflame passions rather than dampen them. His attitude towards Montagu puzzled many of his subjects who had previously regarded him as sound on such matters. Sir John Eliot, summarising a debate on the Montagu case in the Commons, said "it seemed strange to some that King James should so affect him, his doctrines being opposed to the decisions made at Dort, and that Synod being so honoured by the King, of which he assumed the patronage and so much gloried in it. This man being opposite, *ex diametro*, to that . . . many did wonder how these things could agree.'[53]

The answer to Eliot's question would seem to be that James was moving away from Calvinist beliefs during the last year or two of his life. It may be that he no longer regarded them as consonant with spiritual truths, but his attitude must have been hardened by the puritans' criticism of his peacemaking efforts and their implied rejection of his prerogative right to determine his own foreign-policy objectives. Nevertheless, the puritans had good reason to be puzzled by James's apparent support for Montagu, for he had previously made clear his dislike for extremists. Admittedly, in 1621 he had appointed William Laud, one of the most prominent and uncompromising of the Arminians, to a bishopric. But this was only in response to heavy pressure from his favourite, Buckingham, who had taken Laud under his wing, and St David's, which was the chosen see, was hardly a glittering prize. James was suspicious of Laud because, as he told Buckingham, "he hath a restless spirit and cannot see when matters are well, but loves to toss and change and bring things to a pitch of reformation floating in his own brain".[54] This was not merely an acute and perceptive judgment; it also cast light on James's own principles. The men he valued were those who were content to work within the *status quo*, those who willingly accepted the royal supremacy as a guarantee of both continuity and change. James never wavered in his view that the Church and state were, or ought to be, mutually reinforcing, and that disturbance in the one threatened the stability of the other. In yet another acute – and this time, sadly, prophetic – judgment, James declared that "whensoever the ecclesiastical dignity, together with the King's government thereof, shall be turned in contempt and begin to vanish in this kingdom, the kings hereof shall not long after prosper in their government, and the monarchy shall fall to ruin; which I pray God I may never live to see".[55]

· · ·

THE ROMAN CATHOLICS

The cement that held James and the vast majority of his subjects together in religious matters was anti-catholicism. As the son of a catholic martyr, and as a child who had rebelled against his presbyterian upbringing, James might be thought to have been well disposed to the old faith. But he was first and foremost a king, and he could never accept that the Pope had a right to depose earthly monarchs and dispose of their thrones as he thought fit. James was also a theologian, whose study of scripture convinced him that the Roman Church had drifted a long way from its primitive state. One of his earliest prose works, written when he was about eighteen, contained "a short compend [i.e. summary] of the history of the Church, the grounds and antiquity of our religion, and the special times when the grossest popish errors were introduced",[56] and although he later told Robert Cecil that he reverenced the catholic Church "as our mother church", he added that it was "clogged with many infirmities and corruptions".[57]

There was no question, at least in James's mind, that after he ascended the English throne he would uphold the established Church and keep it firmly protestant. But he was by nature tolerant, and believed that "persecution [was] one of the infallible notes of a false church".[58] He knew that, in the second half of Elizabeth's reign, catholics had been tarred with the brush of treachery and made the object of punitive legislation, but he hoped to put an end to this. His aim, as with the puritans, was to drive a wedge between the minority of fanatics and the harmless majority. Writing to a correspondent in England on the very day that Elizabeth died, James gave a promise that "as for the catholics, I will neither persecute any that will be quiet and give but an outward obedience to the law, neither will I spare to advance any of them that by good service worthily deserve it".[59] When James offered catholics a quiet life, he did so in the hope that they would ultimately come to accept the validity of the Church of England, or, at worst, slump into a state of suspended animation. He had no intention of presiding over a catholic revival; he informed Cecil that although he could "never allow in my conscience that the blood of any man shall be shed for diversity of opinions in religion", he "would be sorry that catholics should so multiply as they might be able to practise their old principles upon us".[60]

Prior to his accession to the English throne, James had smoothed the way by establishing contact with the papacy. Clement VIII had promised his support, no doubt anticipating the relaxation and eventual abolition of the penal laws against catholics, and encouraged by the knowledge that James's wife, Anne of Denmark, had been converted to catholicism in or around 1600. The papacy had hopes that James himself might be won over, and the King employed his noted duplicity by letting it be understood that this was not beyond the bounds of possibility. James was reported to have said that he would be "gladly reunited with the Roman church and would take three steps in that direction if only the church would take one".[61] But there could be no question, for James, of ever accepting papal supremacy while the Pope claimed the right to depose monarchs. Indeed, as he stated in a proclamation issued in February 1604, "when we consider the course and claim of that see, we have no reason to imagine that princes of our religion and profession can expect any assurance long to continue". James recognised that religion was one of the principal elements in the civil wars and conflicts between states that had marked the bloody course of European history during his lifetime. He therefore proposed that "some good course might be taken (by a general council free and lawfully called) to pluck up those roots of dangers and jealousies which arise for cause of religion, as well between princes and princes as between them and their subjects". Papal power was, by implication, one of these roots, and James declared that the council should "make it manifest that no state or potentate either hath, or can challenge [i.e. claim], power to dispose of earthly kingdoms or monarchies, or to dispense with subjects' obedience to their natural sovereigns".[62]

The main purpose of the 1604 proclamation was to order the immediate departure from Britain of all Jesuits and seminary priests. In the nine months following Elizabeth's death some 140 catholic missionaries had arrived in England,[63] including many Jesuits, whom James regarded as "venomed wasps and firebrands of sedition".[64] He hoped that by expelling them he would make it possible for the non-militant majority of catholics to live quietly and peaceably within his kingdoms. To this end he reduced the rate at which recusancy fines – paid for non-attendance at anglican services – were levied, even though this meant a loss to the Exchequer as the yield dropped from close on £8,000 a year to around £2,000. In March 1604 James told Parliament that he abhorred persecution "or thralling of my subjects in matters of conscience". As far as the penal laws were concerned, he hoped to put forward some proposals for clarifying them "in case they have been in times past further or more rigorously extended by judges than the meaning of the law was, or might tend to the hurt as well of the innocent as of guilty persons".[65] James made it plain that he did not intend any concession to the catholics on religious grounds: "I will never cease, as far as I can, to tread down their errors and wrong opinions. For I could not permit the increase and growing of their religion without first betraying of myself and mine own conscience." But he wanted to make it possible for catholic lay men and women to live without fear, and he gave an assurance that he would be "a friend to their persons if they be good subjects".[66]

Members of Parliament did not share James's belief that the catholics could be won over by leniency. Their views were given expression in an Act of 1604 requiring the penal laws to be "put in due and exact execution",[67] and they objected strongly to the contrast between the lax treatment of catholics and the punitive campaign against the puritans. The Archbishop of York felt the same, and told Robert Cecil in late 1604 that papists and recusants, "partly by this round dealing against puritans and partly by reason of some extraordinary favour, have grown mightily in number, courage and influence . . . Some are come down to this country in great jollity, almost triumphantly."[68] Another observer confirmed "in what jollity they now live". The catholics, he said, had no doubt that they would be granted toleration, and were hopeful in due course of bringing about "an alteration of religion". Because of this prospect, "many who before did dutifully frequent the Church are of late become recusants".[69]

James was alarmed by these reports of widespread triumphalism on the part of the catholics, not least because it imperilled his relations with Parliament. In February he declared before a meeting of the Privy Council that he had never intended toleration for catholics, and that "if he thought his sons would condescend to any such course, he could wish the kingdom translated to his daughter". He had only reduced recusancy fines "in consideration that not any one of them [i.e. the catholics] had lift up his hand against his coming in", but now that he saw his leniency abused and producing the opposite result to what he had intended, he had given orders that the penal laws should once again be put into full effect.[70] The King was as good as his word, for in that same month one observer reported that "the sword now begins to cut on the other edge, and to fall heavily on the papists' side, whereof there were 28 indicted at the last sessions at Newgate".[71]

The abrupt transformation from the velvet glove to the iron hand was too much for some of the younger and more hot-headed catholics, who were already planning rebellion. They had been shocked that the ending of the war with Spain had been achieved at their cost, for Philip III, to whom English catholics looked for protection, had accepted the Treaty of London which made no provision for their better treatment. The message was clear. English catholics must work out their own salvation. While the majority might be prepared to wait patiently for better times, Guy Fawkes and his associates believed in hastening the process. By blowing up Parliament at the very moment when the King was opening it, they would remove the entire protestant establishment and leave the way clear for a catholic takeover.

The Gunpowder Plot of November 1605, even though it was discovered before it could be put into effect, was a setback for James's policy of increasing toleration, for it seemed to confirm the truth of what many Englishmen had long believed – namely, that all catholics were potential traitors and could only be held on a leash by constant repression. The 1606 Parliament gave voice to this belief. The preface to the "Act for the better discovering and repressing of popish recusants" affirmed that many of the King's subjects "that adhere in their hearts to the popish religion, by the infection drawn from thence, and by the wicked and devilish counsel of Jesuits, seminaries and other like persons dangerous to the Church and state, are so far perverted in the point of their loyalties and due allegiance unto the King's Majesty and the crown of England, as they are ready to entertain and execute any treasonable conspiracies and practices".[72] Catholics were now forbidden to live in or near London, to practise the law, or to hold any public office. They were also required to take an oath of allegiance which James himself had drawn up. His purpose, as he later explained, was to "make a separation between so many of my subjects who, although they were otherwise popishly affected, yet retained in their hearts the print of their natural duty to their sovereign; and those who, being carried away with the like fanatical zeal that the Powder-traitors were, could not contain themselves within the bounds of their natural allegiance, but thought diversity of religion a safe pretext for all kind of treasons and rebellions against their sovereign".[73]

The oath of allegiance required suspected recusants to swear not simply that "our sovereign lord King James is lawful and rightful King of this realm" but also that the Pope did not have "any power or authority to depose the King . . . or to discharge any of his subjects of their allegiance and obedience to His Majesty". In addition, everyone taking the oath had to swear "that I do from my heart abhor, detest and abjure as impious and heretical this damnable doctrine and position, that princes which be excommunicated and deprived by the Pope may be deposed or murdered by their subjects or any other whatsoever. And I do believe, and in my conscience am resolved, that neither the Pope nor any person whatsoever hath power to absolve me of this oath or any part thereof."[74] It was the latter provision which caused problems, for although catholics were in general only too happy to acknowledge that James was King and that the Pope had no right to depose him, they found difficulty in accepting the proposition that the papal position in this respect was "impious and heretical" or that the Pope had no power to absolve anyone from an oath. As with his defence of absolutism, this was another example of James, in a laudable attempt to avoid ambiguity, expressing himself so clearly that he provoked a hostile response. Had he been content with less, he might have obtained more. Even so, many catholics initially took the oath. Only after the papacy condemned it did opposition mount.

The most formidable broadside against the oath was fired by the distinguished catholic theologian, Cardinal Bellarmine, in a treatise published in Rome in 1607. James responded in kind, with *Triplici Nodo, Triplex Cuneus, or an Apology for the Oath of Allegiance,* issued early in 1608, and thereby launched a pamphlet war which brought him into European prominence. In a subsequent work, the *Premonition* of 1609, James attempted to prove by scriptural exegesis that the Pope was Antichrist. It is unlikely that his polemical tracts produced many converts, but they increased his prestige at home and confirmed his protestant credentials. However, after 1605 such confirmation was hardly needed, for Guy Fawkes had done for James what James alone could never have achieved. By attempting to assassinate the King, the Gunpowder plotters had given the clearest possible demonstration that they regarded him as an enemy. This gave James, in the eyes of his protestant subjects, a reserve of credit on which he was able to draw for the rest of his reign.

Although the Gunpowder Plot had harmed the catholic cause and set back James's policy of reconciliation, he continued to be far less bloodthirsty than many of his subjects, particularly members of the Commons, would have wished. He could not prevent the execution of priests who fell foul of the penal laws, and nineteen were put to death during his reign. This was, however, a big reduction from the 124 executed under Elizabeth, and James preferred exiling priests to killing them. He made this plain in a proclamation of June 1606 commanding all catholic priests to quit his dominions: "we do heartily protest that this is done with no other purpose but to avoid the effusion of blood, and by banishing them presently . . . to remove all cause of such severity as we shall otherwise be constrained to use".[75] The following year James addressed the judges and told them to show as much leniency towards captured priests as the law would permit. Bacon, who was present, recorded the King as saying that no priest should be executed "that would confer, or showed not arrogance and violence, [and] even of them sparingly. The King's word was 'No torrent of blood'."[76] However, James had always to take account of public opinion, which was far more hard-line than he was. When he addressed the 1610 session of Parliament he blamed the judges and the clergy for failing to enforce the laws, and told them to "take care . . . that the papists be from time to time strictly presented and, according to the statutes already made, duly punished". But he drew a distinction, as he did on a number of occasions, between recent converts and "ancient papists". As far as the latter were concerned, there were "divers of them so honest and so fair-conditioned men as if I were a subject I could be contented to live and spend my time with them".[77]

There was never a real meeting of minds between James and his parliaments on the question of popery. On the contrary, it became another of those issues which prevented the establishment of harmonious relations. All parties to the debate agreed that catholic numbers were going up, but they differed on how to reverse this trend. Members of the Commons believed that nothing effective would be accomplished unless catholic priests were expelled from Britain and the remaining catholic community was driven into conformity by the rigid application of the penal laws. James professed his willingness to see the laws enforced, but he doubted whether this would solve the problem, for, as he told the 1614 Parliament, "I never saw either true or false religion ever bettered by prosecution."[78] James was so secure in his protestant faith that he could not doubt its ultimate victory: in his own words, "if this be the true religion, popery will fall".[79] Whereas the Commons objected to catholicism for its own sake, James saw it as a danger only when it was combined with disloyalty – which was why he had devised the oath of allegiance. When he addressed the judges in Star Chamber in 1616 James confessed that he was "loth to hang a priest only for religion sake and saying mass; but if he refuse the oath of allegiance (which, let the Pope and all the devils in hell say what they will . . . is merely civil) those that so refuse the oath, and are polypragmatic recusants, I leave them to the law. It is no persecution, but good justice."[80]

Where the catholics were concerned there was always a gap between James's public pronouncements and the facts on the ground. Despite his assurance "that if he thought any of his Council were popish, or did favour the papists, or countenance them, or hinder the proceedings of the law against them, he would remove them from his Council",[81] James retained a number of catholics or crypto-catholics among his advisers. At the beginning of his reign the most notorious of these was the Lord Privy Seal, the Earl of Northampton, while at the end of the reign there were a number of prominent catholic converts to be found in the circle of the King's favourite and principal adviser, the Duke of Buckingham. Apprehension about the spread of popery at Court was not unfounded, therefore, but James seemed either unable or unwilling to prevent it. From the point of view of his subjects, matters were likely to get much worse if James succeeded in his aim of securing a Spanish catholic wife for his son, Prince Charles. In secular terms there was much to be said for the Spanish match. It would show that the British monarchy was accepted as being in the first rank; it would also produce a dowry that would go a long way towards wiping out James's accumulated debt. But the principal objective was religious. James had married his daughter, Elizabeth, to a leading protestant prince. If he could now link himself through marriage to the greatest catholic power he would be in a position to reconcile religious differences and heal the deep wound in christendom – or so he hoped.

The outbreak of the Thirty Years War in 1618 affected James and his subjects in diametrically opposed ways. The King was now more than ever convinced of the need for a negotiated settlement, of which the Spanish marriage would form an integral part. But public opinion in England, as reflected in Parliament, was in favour of armed intervention to advance the protestant cause and defend its champion, Frederick, Elector Palatine, now King of Bohemia, who was married to James's daughter, Elizabeth. James did not rule out the use of force – or at least the threat of it – but he could not possibly afford armed intervention without assistance from his subjects. He therefore summoned Parliament in 1621, after an intermission of seven years. In his opening speech he admitted that "some of his subjects, by reason of the treaty [i.e. negotiations] which he had long held with Spain, thought he grew cold in religion; which he much marvelled at, seeing he had taken so much pains, both with his pen and otherwise, for the defence thereof . . . and therefore his subjects ought to repose themselves upon the integrity and piety of their King, protesting that he would do nothing that should either be dishonourable to the state or prejudicial to religion".[82] The Commons, however, were not prepared to leave matters solely to the King, who had shown himself, as they thought, far too conciliatory towards the catholics. They pressed for an intensification of the penal laws, but once again they were frustrated. James pointed out that there were enough laws already, and if they were not enforced it was through no fault of his. In any case, "it was against his nature to be too rigorous in matters of conscience".[83]

The abrupt ending of the 1621 Parliament left James with no alternative to diplomacy if he was to secure the restoration to his son-in-law of the hereditary Palatinate lands which had been occupied by Spanish and imperial troops. But there was no question of achieving the Spanish marriage – which would require a papal dispensation for the Infanta – without concessions to English catholics. The King had no real choice in this matter, for in 1623 Prince Charles, accompanied by Buckingham, rode off to Madrid to claim his bride. Although he was treated as an honoured guest, he had put himself in the power of the King of Spain, who demanded the suspension of the penal laws as the price for the marriage. James duly complied, and John Chamberlain reported in July 1623 that "the judges, before they went on circuit, were admonished by the King to deal favourably with the papists, except they found them turbulent and seditious".[84] This change of course on the part of the government encouraged the catholics to come out of internal exile and make their presence felt once again. The regius professor of divinity at Oxford declared that "the papists here and everywhere assault and insult upon our brethren in the ministry", and Chamberlain, writing from London, reported that "the priests and Jesuits swarm here extraordinarily".[85]

It was fortunate for James that Parliament was not in session in 1623, because the issue of toleration for the catholics would undoubtedly have dominated it. When Parliament did meet, in February 1624, the Spanish match had been abandoned, and all the talk now was of war. The Commons took the view that the campaign against the Pope and his secular allies should begin at home, and drew up a petition calling for all catholics to be brought once again under legal restraint. Also, bearing in mind the events of the previous year, they demanded that in any further marriage negotiations the King should never agree to "take away or slacken the execution of his laws against the Popish recusants".[86] James resented being dictated to, especially on what he regarded as prerogative matters, and a confrontation with Parliament was only avoided when Prince Charles made a formal declaration in the House of Lords "that whensoever it should please God to bestow upon him any lady that were popish, she should have no further liberty but for her own family [i.e. household] and no advantage to the recusants at home".[87]

It was one thing to make such a promise; it was quite another to fulfil it. When negotiations were opened for a marriage between Charles and Henrietta Maria, sister of the King of France, the French quickly made it plain that they, no less than the Spaniards, would insist on a suspension of the penal laws. James, however, made it equally plain that he would accept no such condition in the marriage treaty. The whole project might have been stillborn had not a compromise been reached whereby James would give a written promise to free his catholic subjects from persecution, but only in what was called an *Ecrit Particulier*, which would not be included in the marriage articles. In practice, of course, it made little difference, since the King had to instruct his ministers and judges to put an end to all proceedings against catholics on grounds of their religion. "This", in the words of James's old friend, the Earl of Kellie, "makes men believe that the same course goes on now with the French that was concluded with the Spaniard", and he added that such a development was unlikely to be pleasing to Parliament when it reassembled.[88]

It was fortunate for James that he died a few months later, before reconvening the two Houses. It was left to his son to deal with the consequences of a catholic French marriage and the growth of popery at Court. James had not, as his subjects wished, eradicated catholicism from his dominions. The main reason for this was that he did not really wish to do so. He believed that persecution would merely serve to harden catholics in their faith, whereas a light-handed approach might win them over initially to outward conformity and thereby prepare the ground for their ultimate conversion. James did make sporadic efforts to enforce the penal laws, but only in order to reassure Parliament. The moment a session was over, the impetus behind enforcement declined. This was not entirely James's doing. Anti-catholicism bordering on fanaticism seemed to be a characteristic of seventeenth-century English men and women, but while they genuinely detested what they labelled 'popery' and feared its malign influence, in practice they usually tolerated individual catholics as their neighbours and kinsfolk. There was a big difference in temperature between the heated atmosphere at Westminster and the temperate climate of provincial society: fiery potions distilled at the centre of government all too often turned into pale and harmless liquids when they were eventually consumed in the local communities.

James, then, was not merely shifting the buck when he declared that failure to enforce the penal laws was not his responsibility but that of the judges, Justices of the Peace and clergy. He gave the orders; it was up to his subordinates and agents to see that they were carried out. But James gave the orders only sporadically; there was never any sustained campaign of repression during his reign. With the catholics as with the puritans, his bark was worse than his bite, and he preferred unity to uniformity. This makes him, by twentieth-century liberal standards, a far more appealing figure than many of his critics, yet any government puts itself at risk if it gets too far out of touch with public opinion. James may well have been approaching that point by the end of his reign.

· · ·

REFERENCES

1. G.W. Prothero (ed.), *Select Statutes and other Constitutional Documents illustrative of the Reigns of Elizabeth and James I*, 4th edn (Clarendon Press, 1946), p. 413 [hereafter Prothero].
2. *King James VI and I: Political Writings* ed. Johann P. Somerville (Cambridge University Press, 1994), p. 26 [hereafter *Political Writings*].
3. Prothero, p. 413.
4. Prothero, pp. 413–15.
5. Prothero, p. 415.
6. James F. Larkin and Paul L. Hughes (eds), *Stuart Royal Proclamations.* Vol. I: *Royal Proclamations of King James I* (Clarendon Press, 1973), p. 62 [hereafter *Proclamations*].
7. *Proclamations*, p. 63.
8. Roland G. Usher, *The Reconstruction of the English Church*, Vol. I (1910), p. 295 [hereafter Usher].
9. Usher, p. 296.
10. Usher, p. 296.
11. James Montagu to his mother, 18 January 1604, printed in *Memorials of Affairs of State in the Reigns of Q. Elizabeth and K. James I collected (chiefly) from the Original Papers of the Right Honourable Sir Ralph Winwood, Kt., Sometime one of the Principal Secretaries of State* (1725), Vol. II, p. 13 [hereafter Winwood].
12. J.R. Tanner (ed.), *Constitutional Documents of the Reign of James I* (Cambridge University Press, 1930), p. 60 [hereafter Tanner].
13. Winwood, p. 13.
14. Winwood, p. 14.
15. Winwood, p. 15.
16. Winwood, p. 14.
17. Winwood, p. 14.
18. Tanner, p. 67.
19. Tanner, p. 67.
20. Winwood, p. 14.
21. Tanner, pp. 63–4.

22. Winwood, p. 15.
23. *Proclamations*, pp. 75–6.
24. *Proclamations*, pp. 89–90.
25. J.P. Kenyon (ed.), *The Stuart Constitution 1603–1688*, 2nd edn (Cambridge University Press, 1986), p. 123 [hereafter Kenyon].
26. *Journals of the House of Commons 1547–1714*, Vol. I (1742), p. 235 [hereafter *CJ*].
27. *CJ*, p. 238.
28. *CJ*, p. 235.
29. *CJ*, p. 244.
30. Usher, p. 414.
31. Winwood, p. 48.
32. Esther S. Cope, *The Life of a Public Man: Edward, First Baron Montagu of Boughton, 1562–1644* (American Philosophical Society, Philadelphia, 1981), p. 37.
33. W.J. Sheils, *The Puritans in the Diocese of Peterborough 1558–1610*, Northamptonshire Record Society, Vol. XXX (1979), p. 110.
34. W.P. Baildon (ed.), *Les Reportes del Cases in Camera Stellata 1594–1609* (1894), p. 189 [hereafter *Cases in Camera Stellata*].
35. B.W. Quintrell, 'The Royal Hunt and the Puritans, 1604–1605', *Journal of Ecclesiastical History*, Vol. 31, 1980.
36. *CJ*, p. 385.
37. *Political Writings*, p. 210.
38. *The Letters of John Chamberlain* ed. Norman Egbert McClure (American Philosophical Society, Philadelphia, 1939), Vol. I, p. 269 [hereafter Chamberlain].
39. *Political Writings*, pp. 187–8.
40. Quoted in Kenneth Fincham, *Prelate as Pastor: The Episcopate of James I* (Clarendon Press, 1990), p. 10 [hereafter Fincham].
41. Fincham, p. 35.
42. Hugh Trevor-Roper, *Historical Essays* (Macmillan, 1957). pp. 136, 145.
43. Patrick Collinson, *The Religion of Protestants: The Church in English Society 1559–1625* (Clarendon Press, 1982), p. 48 [hereafter Collinson]; Fincham, p. 89.
44. T.S. Eliot, *Selected Essays* (Faber & Faber, 1949), p. 331.
45. *Dictionary of National Biography* [hereafter *DNB*] *sub* ANDREWES, Lancelot.
46. George Yule, 'James VI and I: Furnishing the Churches in his Two Kingdoms' in Anthony Fletcher and Peter Roberts (eds), *Religion, Culture and Society in Early Modern Britain: Essays in Honour of Patrick Collinson* (Cambridge University Press, 1994).
47. John Platt, 'Eirenical Anglicans at the Synod of Dort' in Derek Baker (ed.), *Reform and Reformation: England and the Continent c.1500–c.1750*, Ecclesiastical History Society, Studies in Church History (Blackwell, 1979), p. 223.

48. *DNB sub* CARLETON, George.
49. Quoted in Collinson, p. 14.
50. Kenyon, pp. 129–30.
51. *The Correspondence of John Cosin, Lord Bishop of Durham* ed. G. Ornsby (1869), Vol. I, p. 32.
52. *Proceedings in Parliament 1625* ed. Maija Jansson and William B. Bidwell (Yale University Press, 1987), p. 325 [hereafter *1625 Proceedings*].
53. *1625 Proceedings*, p. 509.
54. H.R. Trevor-Roper, *Archbishop Laud 1573–1645* 2nd edn (Macmillan, 1962), p. 56.
55. *Letters of King James VI & I* ed. G.P.V. Akrigg (University of California Press, 1984), p. 295 [hereafter *Letters*].
56. *Letters*, p. 259.
57. *Letters*, p. 205.
58. *Letters*, p. 205.
59. *Letters*, p. 205.
60. *Letters*, p. 204.
61. W.B. Patterson, 'King James's Call for an Ecumenical Council' in G.J. Cuming and Derek Baker (eds), *Councils and Assemblies*, Ecclesiastical History Society, Studies in Church History (Cambridge University Press, 1971), p. 273.
62. *Proclamations*, p. 73.
63. Samuel R. Gardiner, *History of England from the Accession of James I to the Outbreak of the Civil War 1603–1642* (1883), Vol. I, p. 143.
64. *Letters*, p. 205.
65. *Political Writings*, p. 139.
66. *Political Writings*, p. 141.
67. Tanner, p. 84.
68. Winwood, p. 40.
69. Quoted in David Harris Willson, *King James VI and I* (Jonathan Cape, 1956), p. 222.
70. Chamberlain, p. 204.
71. Winwood, p. 48.
72. Kenyon, p. 168.
73. *Political Writings*, p. 86.
74. Kenyon, p. 168.
75. *Proclamations*, p. 145.
76. *The Works of Francis Bacon* ed. James Spedding (1874), Vol. XI, p. 91.
77. *Proceedings in Parliament 1610* ed. Elizabeth Read Foster (Yale University Press, 1966), Vol. 1, p. 51.
78. *Proceedings in Parliament 1614 (House of Commons)* ed. Maija Jansson (American Philosophical Society, Philadelphia, 1988), p. 15 [hereafter *1614 Proceedings*].

79. *1614 Proceedings*, p. 14.
80. *Political Writings*, p. 224.
81. *Cases in Camera Stellata*, p. 190.
82. *Commons Debates 1621* ed. Wallace Notestein, Frances Helen Relf and Hartley Simpson (Yale University Press, 1935), Vol. V, p. 426.
83. Chamberlain, p. 345.
84. Chamberlain, p. 508.
85. *The Court and Times of James the First* [ed. Thomas Birch] (1848), Vol. II, p. 418; Chamberlain, p. 531.
86. *Journals of the House of Lords 1578–1714* (1767), Vol. I, p. 289.
87. *CJ*, p. 756.
88. Historical Manuscripts Commission, *Supplementary Report on the Manuscripts of the Earl of Mar & Kellie* (1930), p. 216.

Chapter 7

BLESSED ARE THE PEACEMAKERS

As ruler of a small and relatively insignificant state, James VI of Scotland had been merely an observer of the bitter conflicts – the French wars of religion, the revolt of the Netherlands, and the contest for power between France and Spain – that convulsed western Europe in the late sixteenth century. Queen Elizabeth was not so fortunate, and the war with Spain into which she had been drawn in the early 1580s was still dragging on and consuming her revenues at the time of her death in 1603. James, now King of England, had no interest in continuing the struggle, and since the Spaniards were also tired of it, negotiations for a settlement were quickly set on foot.

The Treaty of London, which brought the war to an official close, was not signed till August 1604, but in March of that year, at the opening of his first English Parliament, James announced with pride that the first of the blessings which he was bringing to his new kingdom was "outward peace: that is, peace abroad with all foreign neighbours". James gloried in the fact that he had been a man of peace from the beginning of his reign in Scotland: "I have ever, I praise God, yet kept peace and amity with all, which hath been so far tied to my person as at my coming here, you are witnesses, I found the state embarked in a great and tedious war, and only by mine arrival here, and by the peace in my person, is now amity kept where war was before." James acknowledged that the keeping of peace was not a matter for him alone, but he gave his promise "in the word of a king . . . that I shall never give the first occasion of the breach thereof, neither shall I ever be moved for any particular or private passion of mind to interrupt your public peace, except I be forced thereunto either for reparation of the honour of the kingdom or else by necessity for the weal and preservation of the same". If such circumstances should arise, said James, "a secure and honourable war must be preferred to an unsecure and dishonourable peace. Yet do I hope by my experience of the by-past blessings of peace, which God hath so long, ever since my birth, bestowed upon me, that he will not be weary to continue the same."[1]

One of the obstacles in the way of ending the Spanish war was the reluctance of England's allies, the Dutch, to abandon their struggle for independence from Spain. At the very beginning of his reign in England James had renewed the agreement with France, whereby both states committed themselves to uphold the Dutch, but fortunately he was not called upon to honour his commitment, for in 1609 the United Provinces signed a twelve-year truce with Spain. Now, for the first time in many years, there was no major war in Europe, but peace looked unlikely to endure because of the bellicose intentions of Henri IV, the charismatic ruler of France. Henri had been born and brought up a protestant, but had changed his faith in order to win the French throne. Nevertheless, he was quite prepared to ally with the protestant princes of Germany so as to counteract the expansion of the power and influence of the Habsburg House of Austria, of which the two major representatives were the Holy Roman Emperor – Rudolph II until 1612, and then Matthias – and his cousin, Philip III, King of Spain.

Although an uneasy peace had descended upon Germany, the religious tensions between catholic and protestant states had not diminished. The latter had come together in the Protestant Union, set up in 1608 under the leadership of Frederick IV, the Calvinist ruler of the Palatinate. A year later the catholic princes, led by Maximilian of Bavaria, followed suit with the Catholic League. Germany, then, was a tinder-box. All that was needed was a spark to set it alight. Although James had agreed, in concert with the Dutch, to provide several thousand troops to support the Protestant Union, he intended them only to maintain the *status quo*. But Henri IV seemed intent on upsetting this. He was convinced that the peace treaty between France and Spain signed at Vervins in 1598 was the result of exhaustion, and that the struggle for supremacy between the two states would break out again as soon as each side had recovered its breath. Henri had laid his plans accordingly, and support for the German protestant princes was an integral part of his strategy. When, in 1609, a dispute broke out over who should succeed to the Rhine principality of Cleves-Julich, and the protestant princes appealed to Henri for help, he was only too willing to give it. Whether James knew of Henri's plans, or suspected them, is unclear, but he might well have found himself involved in a major war in Germany had it not been for the assassination of Henri in May 1610.

The French throne now passed to Henri's son, Louis XIII, but as he was only nine years old the government of the state was in the hands of his mother, Marie de Médicis, who shared James's love of peace. However, she was not prepared to ditch the German protestants completely, and authorised the despatch of a French expeditionary force to Julich. James, not to be outdone, did the same, and English troops helped secure possession of Julich for the Union of Protestant Princes. Following the abrupt removal of Henri IV from the scene, James was now of greater significance in European affairs, and in November 1610 the German protestant princes urged him to take them under his protection. The King was prepared to do so, but only on condition that the aims of the Union should be defensive, not aggressive. He wanted to dampen down religious passions rather than inflame them, and he was determined not to be dragged into a war from which he would have little to gain and a great deal to lose. His immediate concern was to strengthen the protestant cause by bringing an end to the struggle between the major protestant states of Sweden and Denmark. Two English agents were despatched for this purpose, and in January 1613 they were able to report that, thanks to their endeavours, peace had been brought about.

James obviously relished his self-appointed role as international mediator. It satisfied his vanity at the same time as it helped bring about the conditions for peace in Europe. The greatest potential source of conflict was, as always, religion, and James set himself the task of building a bridge between the protestant and catholic states. He began by concluding a defensive alliance with the Protestant Union in March 1612. He had already proposed that his daughter, Elizabeth, should be married to its leader, Frederick V, who had succeeded his father as Elector Palatine in September 1610, and now the negotiations were set on foot. Frederick seemed the ideal son-in-law from James's point of view, for not only was he one of the most important of German protestant princes; he was also the grandson of William the Silent, the hero of the Dutch struggle against Spain, and connected by marriage with the King of Sweden, the Elector of Brandenburg, and the Huguenot Duke of Bouillon, all of them major figures in the protestant world. Since James was the brother-in-law of the King of Denmark, another leading protestant, the Palatine match would put him at the centre of the web of family connections linking the protestant states of Europe. Frederick himself arrived in England in September 1612, and in February of the following year he married Elizabeth.

While James was well placed to speak for the protestants, he had no privileged access to the catholic powers. If, however, he could marry his son to a catholic princess, he would immediately acquire this. As early as 1604, when the Constable of Castile had been in London for the signing of the peace treaty with Spain, there had been a suggestion that Prince Henry should marry a Spanish infanta. It apparently came from Queen Anne, herself a catholic, but may well have been prompted by the Constable, for he needed to give some reassurance to English catholics that Spain had not totally abandoned their cause. What better means could there be for improving their condition than the setting on foot of negotiations for a Spanish match? The Spaniards would insist upon relaxation of the penal laws as the price for their agreement. There was also a strong possibility that the children of such a marriage, who would be heirs to the English throne, would be brought up in the old faith and might, in due course, undo the damage done by Henry VIII and his protestant successors.

Although the idea of a Spanish marriage had been broached, it was not followed up at that time. There was no urgency so far as the main participants were concerned, for Prince Henry was only ten years old, and the Infanta Anna three. Moreover, the situation in Europe was relatively peaceful, and remained so despite – or, rather, because of – the assassination of Henri IV. Marie de Médicis had neither the temperament nor the political will to carry through her late husband's grandiose plans for humbling the House of Austria. On the contrary, she was determined to pursue a policy of peace and reconciliation with Spain, at least while her son remained a minor. Given the ambitions of the French princes of the blood and the resentment felt by the Huguenots, the French protestants, it made sense in Marie's eyes to enlist the support of the greatest military power

141

on the Continent. In August 1612, therefore, she signed treaties which provided for the marriage of her son, Louis XIII, to the Infanta Anna, and of her daughter, Elizabeth, to the heir to the Spanish throne. If the marriages actually took place it seemed likely that France would become a Spanish satellite.

James recognised the dangers inherent in this development, and moved to bolster his own influence in France by a marriage between his son, Prince Henry, and Princess Christina, the younger daughter of Marie de Médicis. This plan came to naught, because of the sudden death of Henry in November 1612, but after the period of mourning was over the French marriage proposal was revived, this time on behalf of James's sole surviving son, Prince Charles. James hoped to use this match to abort the double marriage treaties between France and Spain. In his opposition to this aspect of Marie de Médicis' policy he had the support of the Huguenots, who feared that an alliance between the two principal catholic sovereigns would pose a threat not simply to their freedom of worship but to their very existence. He was also backed by the princes of the blood, who resented the fact that control over the destiny of France had come to be vested in Marie de Médicis, a foreigner, and her clique of Italian favourites. As for the Queen Regent herself, she may well have thought that an English match for her younger daughter would free her from the charge of being in Spanish leading strings. In other words, all the major political figures in France were in favour of the proposed marriage, albeit for markedly different reasons. It was hardly surprising, therefore, that negotiations went ahead fairly smoothly and that by the opening of 1614 everything seemed to be concluded, save the formalities of a treaty.

At this critical moment, however, the princes of the blood took matters into their own hands by withdrawing from Court, and in 1615 they moved into open rebellion, in association with the Huguenots. James sent frequent couriers to France to find out what was happening. He also received envoys from the Huguenots and the princes, urging him to intervene on their behalf. In fact, for the greater part of 1615, James held the fate of France in his hands. Had he put himself at the head of the dissident movement in that country he could more or less have dictated his own terms for a settlement – one that would have excluded the Spanish marriages, to which he remained implacably opposed. But such a commitment ran counter to James's ingrained instincts. He regarded the princes as unreliable, which indeed they were, and his sympathy with the Huguenots on religious grounds was countered by his distaste for them as rebels against duly constituted authority. He therefore informed the dissidents that "as God had created him a monarch and absolute prince, the disobedience of subjects cannot please him". Nothing, he assured them, was dearer to him than the protestant religion, "and whenever that is concerned he will always be ready to stake his kingdoms and his life". In secular matters, however, the duty of subjects was to obey. He therefore exhorted the princes and the Huguenots to have recourse in the first instance to remonstrances and petitions. Only if these proved ineffective would he intervene "to defend the right cause".[2]

James's belief in the divinely ordained nature of secular authority was a major impediment to the working out of an effective foreign policy. Had he been more Machiavellian, he would have used it simply as part of his diplomatic armoury, to be employed or discarded as convenient. But James was not a cynic, and moral considerations played a significant part in his approach to international relations. He weighed up one possible course of action against another and saw the inherent weaknesses in all of them. Not surprisingly, he found it difficult, if not impossible, to commit himself, and inaction and irresoluteness became the hallmarks of his foreign policy. In 1615 he was working towards the creation of a league of states to contain Habsburg power and facilitate the peaceful resolution of all conflicts. He was lavish in his promises of assistance, but he lacked the means to carry them out, particularly after the failure of the Addled Parliament, and he put far too much trust in verbal or written assurances.

A case in point was the Treaty of Xanten, negotiated through Anglo-French mediation, which had put an end, for the time being at least, to the Cleves-Julich crisis. Unfortunately, neither the Emperor nor the Spanish governor of the Netherlands had been signatories to this agreement, despite the fact that they were key figures in the dispute, and they refused to hand back the strongholds in their possession. James sent for their representatives in London and asked if they would accept a formula that he would devise. After receiving a favourable response, he spent months trying to draw up a form of words which would be agreeable to all parties. The Habsburgs were quite content with this delay, since it gave them time to consolidate their position in the duchies, but the German protestant princes and the Dutch were appalled at James's apparent willingness to accept assurances of goodwill that were in stark contradiction to the behaviour of the parties concerned. The Elector of Brandenburg sent an envoy to London to press James for effective action, but in June 1615 the ambassador asked for permission to return home, "saying that he had wasted many months here, that His Majesty had several times promised to compel the Spaniards to restore the places, and had fixed a date, but many weeks had passed and no results appeared".[3]

After the death of Henri IV his allies were left to fend for themselves. The Duke of Savoy, whose state was of great strategic significance, acting as a buffer between France and Spanish-dominated Milan, was one of these, and he called on James to protect him. James responded by instructing his ambassador in Venice, Dudley Carleton, to arrange a truce between Savoy and Milan, whose governor was threatening to invade the duchy. Thanks in large part to Carleton's mediation, agreement was reached at Asti, on the basis that both sides should disarm. Carleton insisted that disarmament should take place simultaneously in the two states, but James, in his eagerness to secure a peaceful settlement, accepted the Spanish suggestion that the Duke should disarm first, on the understanding that Milan would then do likewise. When an envoy from Savoy arrived in London in September 1614, James assured him that the Duke's cause was his own, "that Spain is great enough and he cannot and will not permit her to become greater; that the annihilation of Savoy would be of too great prejudice not only to the princes of Italy but to those far off as well".[4]

As the months passed and it became clear that the Spaniards in Milan had no intention of disarming, James was called on to fulfil his promises. However, he proved reluctant to do so, telling the Savoyard ambassador that "he did not know what help he could give, because he had no money". The ambassador observed that James should have taken this into account when the treaty of Asti was being drawn up, especially since, on a number of occasions, "he had said that the Duke should hold fast by that treaty and he would help him. The King replied that it was true, but he had acted in the hope of peace and that there would not be fresh ruptures." James insisted that the primary responsibility for helping the Duke lay with Venice, but the ambassador pointed out that Venice was already doing more than enough, "and besides, His Majesty ought not to neglect his obligations because others are fulfilling theirs . . . The King replied that some princes are rich in money, like the King of Spain, some in jewels, some in ships and men. He had no money and could not possibly do what Venice is doing. The ambassador replied: 'Your Majesty is a powerful monarch in every respect, and recognised as such, and this would raise you higher.' But the King interrupted, remarking: 'Do not say so, for with all my forces and my three kingdoms together I could not do what the Republic is doing; but I will give the Duke what help I can.' "[5]

If James's protestations are taken at face value, they imply that he had an informed understanding of the *de facto* limits on his power, and therefore confined his role in international affairs to that of adviser, mediator and facilitator. Yet at other times, and in other contexts, he gave a different impression. In January 1621, for example, as the Bohemian crisis became ever more acute, he is said to have told his Council "that as the monarch of three large kingdoms he could very easily send one large army to Bohemia, one to Germany and one to Flanders, and do even more".[6] It has to be remembered that James had no personal knowledge of the Continent. Admittedly in 1589–90 he had dashed across the seas to Norway and Denmark to bring back his young bride, but that was the only occasion on which he ventured outside the bounds of Scotland and England. Unlike modern rulers he had none of the detailed statistical information which would have enabled him, had he so wished, to compare his resources with those of, for instance, France and Spain. His ambassadors in the various European capitals, whether they were resident or extraordinary, sent back detailed reports, but it is doubtful whether James did more than glance at them. When, in 1616, the Savoyard ambassador drew up a document for the King, setting out the needs of his ducal master, Secretary Winwood advised him not to present it, "because, being the length of a sheet, His Majesty would never read it".[7]

James seems to have assumed that all he needed to do in order to make his weight felt in European affairs was explain his position. In other words, exposition was not a prelude to action but an alternative, and the pen would have to do what the sword could never accomplish. This exalted view of the efficacy of the written word was appropriate for a scholar and philosopher, and it left James happy with the illusion of power without the costs and inherent risks of military involvement. His master plan to maintain peace in Europe by linking himself through marriage with the principal protestant and catholic states was part of this unconscious self-deception. Given that the maximum speed of communication was that of a galloping horse, diplomacy was of limited effectiveness. It could tidy up after events had been decided on the battlefield, but only rarely and in exceptional circumstances could it defuse a potentially dangerous situation. James's vision of himself as the peacekeeper of Europe was a noble one, but it took virtually no account of the realities of power. His occasional outbursts of temper and threats to intervene had some impact when they were first made, but as it became clear that they were no more than threats they were increasingly discounted.

This did not, perhaps, matter a great deal in the first fifteen years of James's reign as King of Great Britain, because the potential areas of conflict were far off and involved no direct British interests. But the situation changed dramatically with the outbreak of the Thirty Years War in 1618, for James's own daughter and son-in-law were in the eye of the storm. The sequence of events which led to war began in 1618 when the Bohemians, who had conformed to custom by electing as their king the Habsburg Archduke Ferdinand, heir-apparent to the Holy Roman Emperor, now renounced their allegiance and declared him deposed. They did so because Bohemia was religiously pluralistic, with a strong protestant element, whereas Ferdinand was a true child of the Counter-Reformation, committed to restore catholicism and extirpate all other forms of religion. The Bohemians knew that in rejecting Ferdinand they were taking a great risk. They hoped to minimise this by offering the vacant throne to someone who was not simply protestant himself but would rally behind him all the principal protestant states. The Habsburgs would have few reservations about suppressing an isolated revolt in Bohemia, but they would think twice – or so the Bohemians reckoned – before taking on the combined strength of protestant Europe. The obvious choice, from the Bohemians' point of view, was Frederick V, Elector Palatine, a nodal figure in the web of protestant connections, and in August 1619 they offered him the throne. Two days later the deposed Ferdinand was elected Holy Roman Emperor.

Frederick sent an envoy to James to ask for his advice on whether or not he should accept the Bohemians' offer. James took his time about replying. He abhorred rebellion, and rejected any suggestion that because Frederick was acting on behalf of the protestants his action was automatically justified. "What hath religion to do to decrown a king?" demanded James. "Leave that opinion to the Devil and to the Jesuits, authors of it and brands of sedition. For may subjects rebel against their prince in quarrel of religion? Christ came into the world to teach subjects obedience to the king, and not rebellion!"[8] James was not simply unclear in his own mind whether the rebels had any legal right to dispose of the Bohemian throne; he was also aware that by acting too hastily his son-in-law might set alight the whole of Europe. He therefore counselled caution, but his advice arrived too late. As James later summed it up, "he wrote to me, to know my mind if he should take that crown; but within three days after, and before I could return answer, he put it on".[9]

Frederick and Elizabeth arrived in Prague in the last days of October 1619, but they spent only one winter there before being driven out by imperial and Bavarian forces. They could not even take refuge in Frederick's hereditary territories, because in the summer of 1620 Spanish troops moved into the Rhine Palatinate and occupied about half of it. This put James in a difficult position, because in 1618 he had accepted a Spanish suggestion that he should act as mediator in the Bohemian conflict. He was also hoping to marry his son, Prince Charles, to a Spanish Infanta. The Spaniards had revived the idea of a marriage alliance in 1613, mainly in order to frustrate the proposed match with France, which at that time looked close to completion. Negotiations were set going by the newly arrived Spanish ambassador, Don Diego Sarmiento de Acuña, better known by his subsequent title of Count of Gondomar. He quickly established a close relationship with James – so close, it seemed, that many of James's subjects came to believe that their King was clay in the wily ambassador's hands. This was not, in fact, the case. Each man used the other for his own purposes, and mutual distrust was as much an element as mutual regard. What bound them together was the pursuit of common objectives – namely, the Spanish match and the maintenance of peace between the two states. When James's subjects attributed his hispanophile leanings to Gondomar's malign influence

they did so because they were unwilling to face up to the unpalatable fact that the King's approach to international affairs
was profoundly different from their own. He would have pursued his objectives whether or not Gondomar had been there
to encourage him.

Public opinion in England was strongly in favour of Frederick
and Elizabeth and profoundly anti-Spanish. James could not
remain impervious to this. He allowed volunteers to be raised
for service in the Palatinate, and some four thousand men
were sent there. He also appointed a Council of War to draw
up plans for intervention. This produced its report in February
1621 and gave its estimate that £200,000 would be required to
raise an army of 30,000 men and close on one million pounds
a year to keep it in the field. If anything, this was a conservative estimate, but the sheer size of the sums involved was calculated to make James draw back. However, he had already
summoned Parliament, and at the end of the first session, in
June 1621, the Commons passed by acclamation a resolution
that if the King's efforts at mediation "shall not take that good
effect which is desired . . . they shall be ready to the utmost of
their powers, both with their lives and fortunes, to assist him,
so as by the divine help of Almighty God . . . he may be able to
do that with his sword which by a peaceable course shall not be
effected".[10]

Nobody could doubt the Commons' commitment to the
protestant cause, but they, no less than James, used rhetoric
as a substitute for action. As proof of their goodwill they had
voted a mere two subsidies, which eventually brought in some
£160,000 – insufficient to raise an army, let alone maintain it.
If James had been less of an appeaser and less of a spendthrift
they might have voted more. If he had died much earlier and
been replaced by his eldest son, Prince Henry, the embodiment
of militant protestantism, they might have voted considerably
more. But they would never have provided sufficient funds for
Britain to play a major military role in Europe. They, and the
local communities they represented, simply could not conceive
of the levels of government financing that involvement in war
necessitated. James would have remained a pacifist no matter
how much he received, but even if he had been miraculously
transformed into a militant he would have found himself starved
of resources. In cash terms it made better sense to rely on
Spain than his own Parliament.

Envoys from friendly powers, even though they continually urged James to take action, realised that there was little chance he would do so. As early as January 1619 the Venetian ambassador had given his opinion that while James liked to pose as "the chief of a great union in Europe", in fact the English would "resolve upon nothing, and by offering a league as they have so often done, wish to bind others without binding themselves, or with little idea of carrying it into effect".[11] James showed increasing irritation as events spiralled out of control. When he was reminded that the Spanish general, Spinola, was poised to invade the Palatinate he burst out, "What do you know? You are ignorant. I know quite well what I am about. All these troubles will settle themselves, you will see that very soon. I know what I am talking about."[12] The Venetian ambassador warned James that the Spaniards seemed set to conquer the entire world, and that once they had done so they would show no mercy even to those who had previously fawned upon them, but the King insisted that the Spaniards already had more territories than they needed or desired. It was true they were using force to advance their aims, but that made it all the more necessary "to cut away their legs by accommodation and peace". When the ambassador pointed out that there was little chance of obtaining an acceptable settlement "unless we cut off the aforesaid legs with the sword, or at least accompanied our negotiation by vigorous action" the King made no comment other than a gesture "which seemed to me to speak very clearly to the effect that everything might be settled without recourse to arms".[13]

After the abrupt and embittered conclusion to the 1621 Parliament, James placed his entire hopes of securing a peaceful resolution of the problems of central Europe upon Spain. In order to bring the maximum pressure to bear upon the new King of Spain, Philip IV, he took the risky step – because of its inevitably unfavourable impact upon public opinion at home – of writing to Pope Gregory XV and urging him to advance the cause of peace and reconciliation. "It is truly to be wished, and by all means to be endeavoured", said James, "that this mis chief creep on no farther, but that these storms at the last ceasing, and the rancour being removed by which they were at the first raised, the hearts of those princes whom it any way concerns may be reunited in a firm and unchangeable friendship . . . This we have always had in our desires, and, to bring it to pass, have not hitherto spared any labour or pains." James expressed confidence in the Pope's willingness "to put your hand to so pious a work, and so worthy of a christian prince", and assured him that "if it shall take the desired effect in your days and by your assistance, Your Holiness shall worthily reap the glory and the reward".[14] James was transparently sincere in his desire for peace, and his willingness to cut across religious barriers is far more appealing today than the bigotry and intolerance of the vast majority of his subjects. But rulers cannot afford to become too detached from the opinions of those over whom they rule, and James was weakening the foundation of monarchy in a nation which defined itself in specifically protestant and passionately anti-catholic terms.

A Spanish marriage for Prince Charles was now, in James's eyes, a matter of urgent necessity, yet it was unclear, as always, whether the Spaniards were negotiating in good faith or merely going through the motions to keep James from intervening on the Continent while they consolidated their position by force of arms. John Digby, Earl of Bristol, James's special envoy to Spain, assured Prince Charles that "there is here either a sincere intention of giving His Majesty and Your Highness full satisfaction, both in the business of the match and of the Palatinate; or they are the falsest people upon the earth".[15] Digby obviously assumed that the Spaniards were basically trustworthy, but among his compatriots in England there were many who believed quite the contrary. It was almost certainly the Prince himself who decided to put the Spaniards to the test by arriving in Madrid without warning and demanding the hand of the Infanta. The dangers involved in allowing the heir to the throne to travel through France and Spain without an escort, and then offer himself as a virtual captive to his Spanish hosts, were so obvious that James would normally have dismissed the suggestion out of hand. But under enormous pressure from his son and his favourite, the Marquis of Buckingham, James succumbed, and in February 1623 the two men set off together on their extraordinary journey.

For the next eight months, James was dependent upon letters for news of what was happening, and there was a constant flow of messengers between Madrid and London – "they go up and down like a well with two buckets", commented Chamberlain.[16] Initial optimism that the marriage would be swiftly concluded gave way to gloom when it became apparent that there were still many difficulties in the way of a final agreement and that the Prince and Buckingham would have to stay on in Spain. This news, James told his two 'boys', "hath strukken me dead. I fear it shall very much shorten my days."[17] When Charles asked James to confirm that he would ratify any conditions to which the Prince assented in Madrid, James immediately agreed. These conditions included a promise to relax the penal laws against the catholics and never reimpose them, as a prelude to their abolition by Parliament. James, as he might have foreseen, had no choice but to accept. He did so in as secret a manner as possible, but the news soon became widely known. Public reaction was given voice in a letter said to be from Archbishop Abbot – though he strenuously denied authorship – imploring James to "take into your consideration what your act is, what the consequence may be. By your act you labour to set up the most damnable and heretical doctrine of the Church of Rome, the Whore of Babylon. How hateful it will be to God, and grievous to your good subjects, the professors of the gospel, that Your Majesty, who hath often disputed and learnedly written against those heresies, should now show yourself a patron of those wicked doctrines which your pen hath told the world (and your conscience tells yourself) are superstitious, idolatrous and detestable."[18] There could be no clearer indication that the credit balance that James had built up by his anti-catholic polemics over the course of his reign was now exhausted. Where religion was concerned, he was living on an overdraft.

The very fact that Charles and Buckingham were given a heroes' welcome when they returned from Spain without the Infanta shows what problems would have been created for James had the Spanish marriage ever been accomplished. But the King's delight at having his son and his favourite back home again was soon tarnished by the realisation that they were no longer content to leave the conduct of foreign policy in his hands. Their long sojourn in Madrid had convinced them that the Spaniards were not to be trusted and that the best policy for Britain was one of active involvement in an anti-Habsburg league. James was appalled at this transformation, and blamed it upon Buckingham, now a duke. When Charles had set out for Madrid, James told the Spanish agent, "he was as well affected to that nation as heart could desire, and as well disposed as any son in Europe. But now he was strangely carried away with rash and youthful counsels, and followed the humour of Buckingham, who had he knew not how many devils within him since that

151

journey."[19] Charles displayed his new-found confidence by pressing James to change course and take a stand against Spain – whereupon, according to one account, James burst into tears and asked, "Do you want to commit me to war in my old age and make me break with Spain?"[20]

This was exactly what Charles and Buckingham wanted, but they knew that James would not give in easily. Their initial efforts were focussed on persuading him to summon Parliament, in the hope that this body, once in session, would call for an end to negotiations and open the way to an alternative strategy by voting subsidies for war. They were successful, and the last Parliament of the reign assembled in February 1624. The King gave the customary opening address, but he broke with precedent by formally inviting the members to give him their advice "whether he should proceed any further in his treaties with Spain about the match of the Prince or concerning the restitution of the Palatinate".[21] In the debates that followed it quickly became clear that members wanted the negotiations broken off, but they were reluctant to vote supply until this was done, for fear that James might accept the subsidies but continue the negotiations. James, for his part, would not sever contacts with Spain until he was assured of subsidies, and it looked as though the old cycle of distrust would lead to deadlock in this Parliament as it had done so often in previous ones. Buckingham, however, persuaded James to make further concessions. Not only were any monies voted to be under the control of a committee of the Commons' own choosing; James also promised them, "on the word of a King, that although war and peace be the peculiar prerogatives of kings, yet as I have advised with you in the treaties on which war may ensue, so I will not treat nor accept of a peace without first acquainting you with it and hearing your advice, and therein go the proper way of Parliament in conferring and consulting with you".[22]

James was determined that if he did have to go to war he must be adequately funded. He proposed an initial grant of six subsidies and twelve Fifteenths, worth some £780,000, but the Commons could not comprehend such a sum, and even the Chancellor of the Exchequer, himself a member of the Lower House, admitted that the demand was "very fearful". However, he suggested that they should show goodwill by voting "so much as the present necessity requires".[23] This turned out to be three subsidies and three Fifteenths – i.e. £300,000 – to be used, among other specified objectives, for defence of the "true religion". James objected to this phrase, on the grounds that an anti-Habsburg league would have to include catholic as well as protestant states. He still hoped that war could be avoided, but if it did come about he wanted to confine British involvement to military operations in Germany designed to recover the Palatinate for his son-in-law and daughter. This could well be done without provoking an open breach with Spain, thereby leaving the way open for a negotiated settlement.

While members of the Commons professed their desire to see the Palatinate returned to its rightful ruler, they thought the best way to secure this was by a 'war of diversion' against Spain, and rather than ruling out religion as a motive they wanted to put it at the heart of their campaign. Although they reluctantly bowed to James's insistence that all mention of religion should be removed from the subsidy grant, they subsequently drew up a petition against recusants and made acceptance of this an implied precondition of the offer of subsidies. James had already drawn up instructions to his ambassador in Madrid to break off negotiations, but the moment he heard of the Commons' manoeuvre he halted its despatch. As he told his Secretary, "if I may be sure that they mean to keep their promises to me, let the packet go on; otherwise it were no reason I should be bound and they leap free and leave me naked and without help".[24] The problem was resolved and James accepted the offer of subsidies, but this did not mean that he had abandoned control over strategy: "I desire you to understand I must have a faithful and secret council of war that must not be ordered by a multitude, for so my designs might be discovered beforehand. A penny of this money shall not be bestowed but in the sight of your own committees. But whether I shall send twenty thousand or ten thousand, whether by sea or by land, east or west, by diversion or otherwise, by invasion upon the Bavarian or the Emperor – you must leave that to the King."[25]

Even before Buckingham left Spain he had made informal contact with France to discuss the possibility of a French marriage for Prince Charles. James had not altogether given up hope of the Spanish match, but the combined pressure of his son and favourite persuaded him to pursue the French option. At first the negotiations went smoothly, but a sudden change of ministers in France brought Cardinal Richelieu to power, and he insisted on a formal commitment on James's part to relax the penal laws against the catholics. James was most unwilling to give this, particularly since Charles had publicly promised in the House of Lords that no such provision would be contained in the marriage treaty. The problem was solved, in form at any rate, by the device of an *Ecrit Particulier*, in which James bound himself to free English catholics from persecution. It did not constitute part of the marriage treaty as such, but it met the minimum conditions that the French had laid down. If the French match and the accompanying military alliance were to be achieved, James had little alternative, but rumours of what he had done did little to still suspicions in Parliament and in the nation at large. As James's close friend, the Earl of Kellie, reported to another old friend of the King, the Earl of Mar, in September 1624, "the business does not now relish so well with the Parliament as it did before, since they begin to hear that matters for the catholics here must be in the same course that was concluded with Spain".[26]

In his letter, Kellie also referred to the arrival in London of the mercenary commander, Count Mansfeld. He was to lead an expedition for the recovery of the Palatinate consisting of twelve thousand English infantry. But after the successful conclusion of the marriage negotiations it was agreed that the French would meet half the costs of the expedition and also provide three thousand cavalry. James had initially insisted that Louis XIII should make a written commitment to support Mansfeld's expedition, for he had a deep distrust of French intentions, fearing that they wanted to involve him in operations which might lead to war with Spain while themselves remaining nominally uncommitted. In the end, James had to be content with Louis' verbal assurances, but in order to limit the risks of confrontation with Spain he instructed Mansfeld not to pass through any Spanish territories *en route* to the Palatinate. This alarmed the French, for the shortest way to the Palatinate was through the Spanish Netherlands, and if Mansfeld was forbidden to take this route he would either have to make a long detour through France or remain camped near Calais while an alternative strategy was worked out. The idea of having twelve thousand undisciplined English soldiers, conscripted from the dregs of the population, rampaging on French soil, was not one that appealed to Louis and his ministers. Their distrust of James was equal to, if not greater than, James's distrust of them, and they interpreted his latest intervention as a device to entrap them while he reopened negotiations with Spain. This was not an unfounded suspicion, because James was in fact awaiting the return to London of Gondomar, who had been despatched in great haste by Philip IV to detach the King from the warmongers surrounding him and guide him back into the paths of peace. Consciously or not, then, James had subverted Mansfeld's expedition, for the French withdrew permission for him to land in France, and at the last moment, and in the depths of winter, his force had to be diverted to Holland. Half the men found unsatisfactory accommodation ashore. The rest had to stay on shipboard, where infection set in and they dropped dead like flies.

It was fortunate for James that he died in March 1625, for he was temperamentally unsuited to lead Britain into war. He never stopped believing in the possibility of a negotiated settlement, and he was willing to go a long way down the road of appeasement in order to achieve this. Girolando Lando, who, as Venetian ambassador, had observed James at close quarters, gave a perceptive analysis of his attitude when he reported to the Doge and Senate in September 1622. The King, he explained, though "very acute and subtle in negotiation" was "slow in execution, being inclined to ambiguity and delay. This does not arise from his natural disposition, as he is hot, choleric and very fiery, but because he wants to persuade himself that he will get what he wants from spinning out time, or will at least postpone trouble."[27] There was a big contrast between James's position at home and the perception of him abroad. At home he commanded respect and obedience simply because he was King. He had no army and no police on which to rely, but long centuries of monarchical rule had given the sovereign a moral authority which, under normal circumstances, was as strong as anything that force alone could have provided. James's position as ruler over three kingdoms made him potentially a major player on the European scene, but his effectiveness abroad depended not on unquestioning acceptance but on how many ships, how many men, and how much money he could command. It also depended upon his willingness to deploy such resources in furtherance of his aims.

It quickly became apparent to the rulers of the European states that there was a wide and growing gap between appearances and reality where James was concerned. His threats turned out to be mere bluster, and instead of despatching fleets or armies he sent ambassadors. One reason for this, apart from

James's own temperament, was that the ships and men were not available. In the post-Armada years and the opening decade of James's reign the navy had been allowed to decline, and although Buckingham, as Lord Admiral, put an end to this, the perennial problem of underfunding remained. As for military forces, these had to be raised on an *ad hoc* basis and they were no match for the professional armies of Spain, France, or the United Provinces. If money had been plentiful it would have enabled the building of ships and the hiring of mercenaries, but James was crippled by debt and his appeals for aid to Parliament met, at best, a half-hearted response.

There were occasions on which James seemed to be aware of the constraints, both self-imposed and inherent in his position, that limited his capacity for effective action. One of these was recorded by the Venetian ambassador, who, in August 1620, ran James to ground at Salisbury, where the King was hunting, and informed him that the Spaniards had taken possession of the Valtelline. This was the Alpine pass which linked Italy with southern Germany, and by occupying it the Spaniards had secured the land route from Spain, via Milan, along which they could despatch their armies into central Europe and the Rhineland. The ambassador urged the King to take action to reverse this potentially dangerous development, but James confessed that "he did not know what he could do". According to the ambassador, James "seemed utterly weary of the affairs that are taking place all over the world at this time, and he hates being obliged every day to spend time over unpleasant matters and listen to nothing but requests and incitements to move in every direction and to meddle with everything. He remarked: 'I am not God Almighty'."[28] Little wonder, then, that at such times James preferred to escape from the harsh realities of the European situation into the delights of rural life. Lando believed there was "probably no Prince who excels him in aptitude for affairs if he will only give his mind to them", but added that "nothing is easier than to divert him from doing anything and prevent him from resolving upon any point . . . than to propose hunting during the fine weather, flying falcons, and such things".[29]

Given his love of peace and his deep reluctance to commit himself to any positive course of action that might subsequently entrap him, James's foreign policy made sense. While he spoke and thought of himself as an absolute King at home, he behaved abroad as the very model of Bagehot's constitutional monarch.

He reserved the right to be consulted, to encourage, and to warn, but he held aloof from direct intervention. In this role, he was, as Bagehot observed of constitutional monarchs in general, a man "who is most tempted to pleasure, and the least forced to business".[30] James was essentially a peacemaker and peacelover. He may genuinely have believed that his active intervention in European affairs, if and when it came about, would be decisive, but he preferred not to take the risk. Whether or not he realised that his resources could never sustain a forward policy, his caution reflected the true state of his affairs. James's subjects blamed him for his timidity, his lack of vision, and his failure to embrace the protestant cause, and the wider the gap between them, the more isolated James became. This undoubtedly weakened the monarchy, but a more adventurous policy might well have done even greater damage, as was demonstrated in the years following James's death. Charles I's active involvement in war led to humiliating defeats for which the King had to bear the blame. There is no reason to think that things would have been different under James. The truth is that the early Stuart state was not designed for war, and members of Parliament, even though they wanted their country to assume the leadership of the protestant world, believed – quite erroneously – that this could be done on the cheap, with loyal addresses substituting for hard cash. It was to take the transformation of the economy in the late seventeenth century, and the involvement of Parliament as an equal partner in government, to unlock Britain's latent resources and convert them into fleets and armies. James had little more than words to play with, and the great powers of Europe realised this and reacted accordingly. In April 1624 the Venetian ambassador reported that the Spanish envoys in England "display little or no apprehension about a rupture. They despise this kingdom as unwarlike, poor, disunited, under a timid King with an inexperienced Prince, and I know that they have called this movement [for war against Spain] the revolt of the mice against the cats."[31]

. . .

REFERENCES

1. *King James VI and I: Political Writings* ed. Johann P. Somerville (Cambridge University Press, 1994), pp. 133–4.

2. *Calendar of State Papers and Manuscripts relating to English Affairs existing in the Archives and Collections of Venice* ed. Allen B. Hinds, Vol. XIII *1613–1615* (1907), p. 542 [hereafter *CSPV*].

3. *CSPV*, Vol. XIII, p. 479.

4. *CSPV*, Vol. XIII, p. 185.

5. *CSPV*, Vol. XIV *1615–1617* (1908), p. 401.

6. *CSPV*, Vol. XVI *1619–1621* (1910), p. 516.

7. *CSPV*, Vol. XIV, p. 314.

8. *Commons Debates 1621* ed. Wallace Notestein, Frances Helen Relf and Hartley Simpson (Yale University Press, 1935), Vol. VI, p. 370 [hereafter *1621 Debates*].

9. *1621 Debates*, Vol. VI, p. 370.

10. John Rushworth, *Historical Collections* (1682), Vol. I, p. 36 [hereafter Rushworth].

11. *CSPV*, Vol. XV *1617–1619* (1909), p. 444.

12. *CSPV*, Vol. XVI, p. 376.

13. *CSPV*, Vol. XVI, p. 558.

14. *Cabala sive Scrinia Sacra* (1691), pp. 376–7 [hereafter *Cabala*].

15. Public Record Office *SP94* 25, 261.

16. *The Letters of John Chamberlain* ed. Norman Egbert McClure (American Philosophical Society, Philadelphia, 1939), Vol. II, p. 495.

17. British Library *Harleian MSS* 6987, 100.

18. Rushworth, p. 85.

19. *Cabala*, p. 276.

20. *Mémoires et Négociations Secrètes de M. de Rusdorf* (Leipzig, 1789) p. 146.

21. *Journals of the House of Commons 1547–1714*, Vol. I (1742), p. 670 [hereafter *CJ*].

22. Quoted in Robert E. Ruigh, *The Parliament of 1624* (Harvard University Press, 1971), p. 200 [hereafter Ruigh].

23. *CJ*, p. 741.

24. Public Record Office *SP14* 163, 30.

25. Ruigh, p. 231.

26. Historical Manuscripts Commission, *Supplementary Report on the Manuscripts of the Earl of Mar & Kellie* (1930), pp. 209–10.

27. *CSPV*, Vol. XVII *1621–1623* (1911), p. 441.

28. *CSPV*, Vol. XVI, p. 362.

29. *CSPV*, Vol. XVII, p. 441.

30. Walter Bagehot, *The English Constitution*, World's Classics (Oxford University Press, 1949), p. 75.

31. *CSPV*, Vol. XVIII *1623–1625* (1912), p. 265.

Chapter 8

KING AND GOVERNOR

. . .

ENGLAND

In early Stuart England the King ruled as well as reigned. James was an 'absolute' ruler in the sense that he exercised to the full all those powers which belonged to the sovereign. These included the appointment of the principal officers in the Church, state and judiciary. A change of monarch entailed a change of government, and as Elizabeth's reign drew towards its close there was increasing speculation about who would gain and who would lose from James's accession. The death of Lord Burghley in August 1598 opened the way to a struggle for power between his younger son and political heir, Robert Cecil, and the Queen's favourite, Robert Devereux, Earl of Essex. As far as the future was concerned, Essex seemed to hold the trump card, for he had already established contact with James and was pressing for the King of Scotland to be formally recognised as Elizabeth's successor – something which, so far, the Queen had resolutely opposed. If Essex had been content to let time do its work he would have gained, under James, the high office which he longed for. But he was too impatient to wait upon events, and his impulsiveness, as well as his quest for military glory, led him to disaster. He accepted command of the Queen's forces in Ireland, only to realise, too late, that by absenting himself from Court he had left the way open for the Cecilians to cement their hold on power. He therefore ignored the Queen's express commands and returned to England, to halt the further erosion of his position. Among the allies to whom he appealed for help was the King of Scots.

James was not sure whether Essex's discontent with the Queen's government was widely shared. There was no question, of course, of putting Elizabeth's life in danger, but if Essex succeeded in forcing her to change course and appoint him as her chief minister, James would stand to gain. He therefore decided to send his close friend, the Earl of Mar, to London to represent his interests, instructing him to follow the advice of Essex and his associates and, "if that actually they perform their promises on their part ... to give them full assurance of my assisting them accordingly".[1] However, while Mar was preparing to leave Edinburgh, news arrived that Essex had been arrested after leading an armed uprising against Elizabeth's government. James thereupon modified his instructions, leaving it to Mar to weigh up the evidence after his arrival in London and act accordingly. Should Mar come to the conclusion that the opponents of Robert Cecil still had a good chance of success and were only lacking in someone to lead them, then he was to assure them "I shall be as willing and ready to supply that place as they can be to desire me." If, on the contrary, Mar found that the revolt against the Cecilians had totally collapsed, he was to use "all the means ye can to get me a party there and assure them that I can neither with honour nor surety disguise myself any longer".[2]

James was understandably afraid that his association with the disgraced Essex might prejudice his chances of succeeding Elizabeth, but he remained uncertain about the best strategy to pursue. In April 1601 he instructed Mar to become "well and surely informed of the people's present disposition and inclination and to conform your behaviour accordingly". If popular discontent was directed "only against the present rulers in the Court", Mar was to concentrate on maintaining good relations with the Queen. If, on the other hand, "the discontentment be grown to that height that they are not able any longer to comport either with prince or state", then Mar must be very careful neither to act too precipitately nor to hold back too long, for fear that "by suffering them to be overthrown for not declaring myself in time, they were forced to sue to other saints". But the most important task which James imposed upon Mar was to clear him of all complicity with Essex's rebellion and to persuade the Queen not to do anything that might prejudice James's right of succession.[3]

James was not prepared to sit back and be a passive observer of events. He told Mar "to obtain all the certainty ye can of the

town of London, that in the due time they will favour the right;
next, to renew and confirm your acquaintance with the Lieutenant of the Tower; thirdly, to obtain as great a certainty as ye can
for the fleet . . . and of some seaports; fourthly, to secure the
hearts of as many noblemen and knights as ye can get dealing
with and to be resolved what every one of their parts shall be at
that great day; fifthly, to foresee anent [i.e. about] armour for
every shire, that against that day my enemies have not the whole
commandment of the armour and my friends only be unarmed;
sixthly, that . . . ye may distribute good seminaries [i.e. seedbeds]
through every shire, that may never leave working in the harvest
till the day of reaping come; and generally to leave all things
in such certainty and order as the enemies be not able in the
meantime to lay such bars in my way as shall make things
remediless when the time shall come".[4]

This letter demonstrates that James could act both decisively
and ruthlessly when his interests were at stake. In effect he was
instructing Mar to prepare the ground for rebellion in England in James's favour should the King's enemies attempt to
bar his succession. The greatest enemy of all was the Queen's
Secretary of State, Robert Cecil, Essex's opponent and destroyer,
but Mar was to "plainly declare to Master Secretary and his
followers" that if they acted in an unfriendly manner towards
James, they should do so in the knowledge that "when the
chance shall turn I shall cast a deaf ear to their requests; and
whereas now I would have been content to have given them, by
your means, a full assurance of my favour if at this time they
had pressed to deserve the same, so now, they condemning it,
may be assured never hereafter to be heard".[5]

Whether James's threats had the required effect, or whether
Cecil, surveying all the possibilities, concluded that his best
interests lay in securing James's peaceful accession, a remarkable transformation of the political scene now took place.
Cecil made known to Mar that he was ready to do all he could
to promote James's cause and offered to open a secret correspondence with the King. James was delighted, for this meant
that the major roadblock on his way to the English throne had
been removed and that the great prize was now firmly within
his grasp. He wrote to Cecil to assure him of his "thankful
acceptance of his plain and honourable dealing" and to promise
"his constant love to him in all times hereafter". As soon as it
pleased God that James should "succeed to his right, he shall

no surelier succeed to the place than he shall succeed in bestowing as great and greater favour upon [Cecil] as his predecessor doth bestow upon him".[6] Following Cecil's advice, James now gave up any thought of building up his own party in England. Elizabeth was approaching seventy, and in the course of nature would soon be removed from the scene. It made sense for James to wait on events, and he assured another of his English correspondents that "it never was, is, nor shall be my intention to enter that kingdom in any other sort but as the son and righteous heir of England, with all peace and calmness, and without any kind of alteration in state or government as far as possible I can".[7]

When James at last ascended the English throne in 1603, he created Cecil a baron. He demonstrated his continuing favour by making him a viscount in 1604 and Earl of Salisbury in 1605. James also confirmed Cecil in office as Secretary of State and Master of the Wards, and in 1608, following the death of the Earl of Dorset, he appointed him Lord Treasurer. Not since the days of Wolsey had so much power been concentrated in the hands of one man. Cecil was now indisputably the King's chief minister, but James could also turn for advice to the Privy Council, of which Cecil was the principal member. The Privy Council was the early Stuart equivalent of a modern Cabinet, consisting as it did of the principal office holders, but it also included the Archbishop of Canterbury, the Lord Chief Justice, the Master of the Horse and household officials who would not now be regarded as political figures. Elizabeth had preferred to keep her Council small, and at her death it contained no more than thirteen members. James immediately doubled its size, to make it more representative and to repay some of the political debts he had incurred as the price of his peaceful accession.

One of the problems confronting James was whether and how to incorporate his principal Scottish advisers into the new regime. Many Scots, of all degrees and conditions, had followed James south, hoping for rich pickings from the change in their master's fortunes, but although, as already mentioned (see above, p. 82), the Scots did well in purely financial terms, they were treated far less generously where the grant of offices was concerned. A total of 158 Scots eventually gained positions in James's government and household, but many of these were minor posts. While James, on the last lap of his journey to London, was resting at Theobalds, Robert Cecil's palatial house north of the capital, he appointed six of his closest Scottish advisers to the English Privy Council, but only two of these played any significant role. Edward Bruce, Lord Kinloss, who had accompanied the Earl of Mar on his visit to London shortly before James's accession, became Master of the Rolls, while George Home, later Earl of Dunbar, briefly held the office of Chancellor of the Exchequer. On the other hand, Scots were highly prominent in the royal household, where they held the offices of Lord Steward, Keeper of the Wardrobe, Keeper of the Privy Purse, Groom of the Stool, and Captain of the King's Guard.

The Privy Council might be called upon to consider major political issues – though James would often decide such matters by himself or in consultation with Cecil – but most of the time it dealt with routine administrative business, much of it of little significance. James was only too happy with this state of affairs, since it freed him from tedious chores and enabled him to escape from London. In January 1605 James informed the Council that he had resolved "to remove sometimes to places distant from this city and our houses nearest to it, with some small company to attend us in our sports and private journeys, only used for preservation of our health". He commanded the members, in his absence, to meet once every week, as well as on Sundays after the sermon was over, wherever Queen Anne was in residence, so that his subjects could be assured of "some certain place where they shall receive despatch in all those things which do depend upon our own directions to you or upon the provisional power which we have given you".[8]

In his letter, James reminded the Councillors that if, in their judgment, his presence was needed in town, he would immediately return. However, he kept such visits as brief as possible, describing one of them as "like a flash of lightning, both in going, stay there, and returning".[9] In 1604, when he was on his summer progress and obviously in high good humour, he painted a picture of Cecil and his fellow Councillors guiding the state again under Queen Anne as they had formerly done under Queen Elizabeth. "Ye sit at your ease and directs all. The news from all the parts of the world comes to you in your chamber. The King's own resolutions depends upon your posting despatches. And when ye list ye can (sitting on your bedsides) with one call or whistling in your fist make him to post night and day till he come to your presence."[10] One of the occasions which entailed James's return to town was the arrival of the

Constable of Castile in August 1604, to sign the Treaty of London. Prior to this, however, the King was determined to fit in as much as possible of his progress, which would take him to the country seats of his greater subjects and allow him to indulge to the full in the pleasures of the chase. "I lose all this year's progress if I begin not to hunt there upon Monday come eight days," he told Cecil, "for the season of the year will no more stay upon a king than a poor man, and I doubt if the Constable of Castile hath any power in his commission to stay the course of the sun."[11]

When James talked of hunting "there" he was referring to Theobalds, the enormous mansion which Lord Burghley had built just north of London, in the middle of excellent hunting country, and which had passed by descent to Robert Cecil. James called on Cecil "to provide for no other entertainment for me there than as many stags as I shall kill with my own hunting . . . And since ye have been so much used these three months past to hunt cold scents through the dry beaten ways of London, ye need not doubt but it will be easy for you to harbour a great stag amongst the sweet groves about your house."[12] James found Theobalds much to his liking and was overjoyed when Cecil presented it to him in 1607. Theobalds now became a royal palace, and to show his gratitude James gave Cecil the royal manor of Hatfield, where Salisbury constructed the great house in which his descendants still live.

James's favourite residences, apart from Theobalds, were Royston and Newmarket – both of them within relatively easy reach of London, though not in the depths of winter, when the country roads would often become impassable. The King's House at Royston, which James created out of two inns, with later additions, is described by Howard Colvin as 'rather more than a lodge', but 'in no sense a palace. It was a royal seat for the sole purpose of hunting.'[13] The King's residence at Newmarket also included an earlier inn, but the whole building subsided in 1613, when James was showing the area to his son-in-law, the Elector Palatine, and an entire new block was constructed, costing not far short of £5,000. The accommodation at Newmarket, as at Royston, was subsequently expanded, most notably in 1620 when the Prince's Lodgings were erected to a design by Inigo Jones. When James went hunting he would always have a secretary with him, and sometimes a Privy Councillor, but government business took second place to sport and had to be crammed in either before James set out for the chase or after he returned from it. James despatched such business swiftly, but the hard labour of translating his wishes into action fell upon the ministers or courtiers who were in attendance. The Earl of Worcester, on one occasion, complained that since his departure from London "I have not had two hours [out] of twenty-four of rest but Sundays, for in the morning we are on horseback by eight and so continue in full career from the death of one hare to another until four at night; then for the most part we are five miles from home; by that time I find at my lodging sometimes one, most commonly two packets of letters, all which must be answered before I sleep."[14]

The greatest strain was upon Cecil, who had not only to conduct government business in London but also to make regular reports to his absent master. James was grateful for having such a devoted and efficient servant, and showed this by referring to him as "my little beagle" – nicknames drawn from the hunting field were always a sign of James's approbation. "Although I be now in the midst of my paradise of pleasure", he told Cecil in the spring of 1604, "yet will I not be forgetful of you and your fellows that are frying in the pains of purgatory for my service."[15] Eighteen months later James excused himself for not writing on the grounds of "lack of matter, for I daily hear of so great diligence and carefulness in all the Council, and of your so continual consultations upon all my affairs, as I protest I was never so void of care for all my great turns".[16] There were a number of occasions when the relationship between the King and his principal minister seemed to cool, but after one of these, in 1607, James assured Cecil that "I think as well of you and trust as much in you as of any servant that ever did, does, or shall serve me, *in saecula saeculorum* [i.e. world without end], amen".[17]

The King was never merely a puppet in the hands of his Councillors, nor was he solely dependent upon them for advice. The Gentlemen of the Bedchamber were a rival source of influence, for by virtue of their constant attendance upon the King they were well placed to make their views known and advance the interests of their clients. Until the emergence of George Villiers as favourite (see below, p. 171) the Gentlemen were invariably Scottish, and they became an object of suspicion and even hatred for those Englishmen who felt that their abilities had remained unknown, and their chances of promotion blocked, because of this alien presence at Court. Their resentment was given voice by Sir John Holles, who had formerly been a Gentleman of the Privy Chamber and was frustrated in his desire for high office. "The Scottish monopolize his [James's] princely person," he complained, "standing like mountains betwixt the beams of his grace and us", and he pleaded with James to ensure that "his Bedchamber may be shared as well to those of our nation as to them".[18] There was, of course, some truth in Holles's complaint, but it is hardly surprising that James should have chosen his fellow-countrymen as his body servants. Moreover, the Bedchamber provided him with information and advice which prevented him from becoming a puppet in the hands of his Councillors.

James was aware of this pitfall, and therefore insisted on being informed about what the Council was proposing to do, and in matters that were of particular interest to him, such as the Hampton Court Conference, he took the initiative himself. Generally speaking, however, he was content to leave business in Cecil's hands. This included the managing of Parliament, but here James fell into a trap of his own making, for by elevating Cecil to the peerage he removed him from the House of Commons, which was a much larger body than the Lords and far more difficult to control. Cecil's father, Lord Burghley, had conducted affairs from the Upper House, but this was not so easy after Elizabeth gave way to James, particularly since the major business of the first Parliament was the Anglo-Scots union – an objective close to James's heart but abhorrent to many of the English political nation. Moreover, Cecil had learned from the struggle with Essex that power could never be taken for granted and that rivals must be discouraged or eliminated. This was probably one reason why the crown was so poorly represented in the Lower House. In 1604, when James's first Parliament opened, there were only two Councillors in the Commons, both of them mediocre. By 1606 the number had fallen to one, and although Sir John Herbert was a Secretary of State, the fact that he was commonly referred to as 'Mr Secondary Herbert' suggests that he was not regarded as belonging in the first rank. In these circumstances it is hardly surprising that Sir Edward Hoby, who had been a member of Parliament under Elizabeth as well as under James, was of the opinion that "the state scorneth to have any Privy Councillors of any understanding in that House".[19]

Robert Cecil could hardly be blamed for Parliament's refusal to approve the union, but he was directly responsible for the proposed Great Contract of 1610 (see above, p. 86), which was designed to solve James's financial problems by persuading the Commons to vote the crown a permanent land tax. Cecil obviously overrated his influence, for the Commons proved recalcitrant and drove a much harder bargain than he had anticipated. Moreover, in the course of debates in the Lower House there was a degree of public discussion of the crown's affairs, and of implied criticism of the King, which James found deeply distasteful: "our fame and actions have been daily tossed like tennis balls amongst them, and all that spite and malice durst do to disgrace and infame [i.e. slander] us hath been used. To be short, this Lower House by their behaviour have perilled and annoyed our health, wounded our reputation, emboldened all ill-natured people, encroached upon many of our privileges, and plagued our purse with their delays."[20]

Although James assured Cecil that the failure of the Contract had not diminished his favour towards him, the old, easy relationship – on the King's side at any rate, for Cecil always remained scrupulously deferential – had gone for good. James blamed Cecil for trusting too much in Parliament, "this rotten reed of Egypt", and told him, "your greatest error hath been that ye ever expected to draw honey out of gall, being a little blinded with the self-love of your own counsel in holding together of this Parliament, whereof all men were despaired (as I have oft told you) but yourself alone".[21] Sir Francis Bacon, who was no friend to Cecil, told the King after his death that Cecil had been fertile in ideas but weak in carrying them through, "and though he had fine passages of action, yet the real conclusions came slowly on".[22] James apparently shared this view, or became converted to it, for some years later, when he appointed a new Lord Treasurer, he complained that Cecil, instead of attending to the needs of the royal revenue, "was wont to entertain him with epigrams, fine discourses, and learned epistles, and other such tricks and devices, which yet he saw would pay no debts".[23]

Cecil's virtual monopoly of power died with him, for James seems to have concluded that great ministers eclipsed the glory of great kings. He therefore left the Treasury in commission, appointed a nonentity as Master of the Wards, and made it known that he would not choose a new Secretary for some time, "since he is prettily skilled in the craft himself, and till he be thoroughly weary will execute it in person".[24] Power and influence were now more widely distributed, though the Howard family did particularly well. Henry Howard, Earl of Northampton and Lord Privy Seal, was James's principal adviser until his death in 1614; Charles Howard, Earl of Nottingham, was Lord Admiral; Thomas Howard, Earl of Suffolk, was Lord Chamberlain of the Household until 1614, when James appointed him Lord Treasurer. The Howards were not a homogeneous group, but in general they had catholic sympathies and favoured an alliance with Spain as an alternative to reliance upon Parliament. This put them at odds with another group, even more loose-knit, which was committed to the advancement of the protestant cause in association with Parliament. Its principal members were George Abbot, Archbishop of Canterbury, and William Herbert, Earl of Pembroke.

Both the catholic and the protestant lords had to take into account a third major contestant for power and patronage in the immediate post-Cecil years. This was the royal favourite, Robert Carr, one of the many Scots who followed James to England. Knighted in 1607, he became Viscount Rochester in 1611 and Earl of Somerset two years later. Ever since his encounter, at the age of thirteen, with Esmé Stuart, whom he created Duke of Lennox, James had rarely between without one or more male favourites, but although Lennox, with the King's encouragement, played a major political role in Scottish affairs, this was not the case with his successors. Carr's significance sprang from the fact that he had ambitions which extended beyond the hunting field or the royal bedchamber, and he was the first of James's favourites to be appointed a Privy Councillor. He also carried out the functions of Secretary after Salisbury's death, thereby easing the burden on the King, and held this office until the appointment of Sir Ralph Winwood in 1614. Carr lacked the ability to become a political figure in his own right, but he chose as his confidant and adviser Sir Thomas Overbury, a far more effective operator. Overbury hoped to advance his own and his patron's interests by tacking between the other two groups without becoming committed to either of them. However, this high-risk strategy lost its *raison d'être* when Carr fell in love with Suffolk's daughter, Frances Howard, Countess of Essex.

Northampton and Suffolk saw their chance to attach the favourite to their interests by promoting a marriage between

Carr and Frances, but this was out of the question so long as Frances remained the wife of the Earl of Essex. With their backing, therefore, she began proceedings to have her marriage annulled on the grounds that witchcraft had rendered her husband incapable of sexual relations with her. In May 1613 James appointed a mixed commission of bishops and lawyers to examine and judge the case, and put pressure upon its members to give a verdict favourable to Frances. Archbishop Abbot, who chaired the commission, was upset by the way in which the proceedings were being organised. "What a strange and fearful thing it was", he complained, "that His Majesty should be so far engaged in that business; that he should profess that himself had set the matter in that course of judgment; that the judges should be dealt withal beforehand, and, in a sort, directed what they should determine . . . and as a dutiful servant to my most gracious master I wished in my heart that His Majesty's hand might be taken off the business." But James would not brook criticism of his attitude. He told Abbot he should have "a kind of faith implicit in my judgment, as well in respect of some skill I have in divinity, as also that I hope no honest man doubts of the uprightness of my conscience; and the best thankfulness that you that are so far my creature can use towards me is to reverence and follow my judgment and not to contradict it, except where you may demonstrate unto me that I am mistaken or wrong informed".[25]

Abbot continued to oppose the annulment of the marriage, but James added two more bishops to the commission to ensure that the verdict went the way he wanted. The public washing of a great deal of dirty linen did little for James's reputation. Chamberlain told Dudley Carleton that although he might seem to be speaking too plainly, "if you knew what indecent words and deeds have passed in the course of this suit, you would excuse it, and think me modest, for what would you say if you should hear a churchman in open audience demand of him [i.e. Essex] and desire to be resolved: whether he had affection, erection, application, penetration, ejaculation, with a great deal of amplification upon every one of these points?"[26] Not for the first time, James had allowed his emotions to override his reason, for where his favourites were concerned he would stop at nothing to ensure that their desires were satisfied.

The triumph of Carr, who was now firmly allied to the Howards and the 'Spanish faction', was anathema to the protestant lords, who therefore adopted the high-risk policy of promoting an alternative favourite – this time, an English one. They chose George Villiers, who made his appearance at Court in 1614 and immediately attracted James's attention. Carr sensed the danger but reacted badly by upbraiding the King and browbeating him. In an astonishingly frank letter, written in early 1615, James complained to Carr that he had "in many of your mad fits, done what you can to persuade me that you mean not so much to hold me by love as by awe, and that you have me so far in your reverence as that I dare not offend you, or resist your appetites. I leave out of this reckoning your long creeping back and withdrawing yourself from lying in my chamber, notwithstanding my many hundred times earnestly soliciting you to the contrary." If Carr reverted to his old kind behaviour he could be sure of retaining his hold on the King's affections. But James reminded him "that I am a freeman, if I were not a King. Remember that all your being, except your breathing and soul, is from me. I told you twice or thrice you might lead me by the heart and not by the nose. I cannot deal honestly if I deal not plainly with you. If ever I find that you think to retain me by one sparkle of fear, all the violence of my love will in that instant be changed into as violent a hatred. God is my judge, my love hath been infinite towards you; and the only strength of my affection towards you hath made me bear with these things in you and bridle my passions to the uttermost of my ability. Let me be met, then, with your entire heart, but softened by humility. Let me never apprehend that you disdain my person and undervalue my qualities; and let it not appear that any part of your former affection is cold towards me."[27]

Even if Carr had played his cards better he would not have been able to prevent Villiers's rise to favour, because the King was captivated by the twenty-three-year-old son of a Leicestershire knight, described by Bishop Goodman as "the handsomest-bodied man of England; his limbs so well compacted and his conversation so pleasing and of so sweet a disposition".[28] However, although Carr no longer had a monopoly of the King's favour he might have remained a figure of some standing at Court had it not been for the Overbury scandal. James had long been jealous of Overbury's influence on Carr and in 1613, in order to detach him from the favourite, he offered him a diplomatic appointment abroad. When Overbury high-handedly refused this offer, the offended King sent him to the Tower.

No doubt James assumed that a spell of imprisonment would change Overbury's attitude, but at this point Frances Howard intervened. She was not yet married to Carr and she believed, correctly, that Overbury was opposed to the marriage and would do all he could to frustrate it. She therefore arranged to have him poisoned, and in September 1613 Overbury died.

Foul play was not suspected at first, but two years later the rumours became so insistent that they reached James's ear and he appointed commissioners to investigate the matter. He also "made in the Council a great protestation before God of his desire to see justice done, and that neither his favourite . . . nor anything else in the world should hinder him". He intended to "use all lawful courses that the foulness of this fault be sounded to the depth, that for the discharge of our duty both to God and man, the innocent may be cleared and the nocent [i.e. guilty] may severely be punished".[29] Carr and his wife were sent for trial in May 1616. Frances pleaded guilty, her husband insisted upon his innocence, but both were condemned to death. James, despite his protestation, drew back from the shedding of noble blood. The Countess was pardoned but held prisoner in the Tower, along with her husband, until early 1622, when they were both released. Shortly before his death in 1625, James at last pardoned Carr. The whole episode had brought the Court, and by extension the King, into further discredit, but James had at least allowed justice to take its course. If he had not done so he might, as he told Carr, "have been thought to be the author of that murder, and so be made odious to all posterity".[30]

George Villiers's meteoric rise to favour was marked by the honours James showered upon him. Knighted in 1615, he was created Baron Whaddon and Viscount Villiers in 1616, and then became successively Earl (1617), Marquis (1618) and finally Duke (1623) of Buckingham. Honours were accompanied by offices, initially in the royal household, as Cupbearer (1614), Gentleman of the Bedchamber (1615), and Master of the Horse (1616). All these entailed close attendance on the King, and opened the way to influence over royal decisions, especially in patronage matters. Buckingham's appointment to the Bedchamber was particularly significant, since it marked the first breach in the Scottish monopoly of that institution. Villiers went some way towards meeting Sir John Holles's demand by securing the appointment of more English Gentlemen, but he had always to take account of James's preferences, for the King liked familiar faces and was averse to change. Outside the household, Buckingham was appointed to both the English and Scottish Privy Councils in 1617, but his most important office was that of Lord Admiral, conferred on him in January 1619.

Buckingham owed everything to the King, and there was no exaggeration in his letter of thanks for his dukedom in which he expressed his gratitude to James, who had "filled a consuming purse, given me fair houses, more land than I am worthy of to maintain both me and them, [and] filled my coffers so full with patents of honour that my shoulder cannot bear more".[31] He used his influence with James to promote the interests of his friends and kindred, and swiftly built up a patronage empire which had no rival. Yet he never attained a monopoly of patronage in James's reign. There were other figures at Court – such as James's Lord Chamberlain, William Herbert, Earl of Pembroke – who were major patrons and defended their interests in a most determined manner. There was also, of course, the King, whose views on certain major appointments did not necessarily coincide with the favourite's. When, in early 1619, James was considering the choice of a new Secretary of State, Buckingham put his weight behind two of his clients, neither of whom, however, was selected. It was the King who decided upon Sir George Calvert, and all Buckingham could do was to go along with this. Similarly, in 1621, Buckingham's candidates for the major office of Lord Keeper were rejected by the King, who was determined to appoint a churchman, and chose John Williams, at that time Dean of Westminster. James's preferences, then, were always a deciding factor, but he was not interested in the multitude of lesser offices which needed filling, and was quite content that Buckingham should have the disposal of them, often in return for payment.

Buckingham also acted as James's agent in the selling of titles of honour, a practice which had begun before his rise to favour but which he systematised and vastly increased. Government and administration in early modern states were based on patron–client relationships, in which the lubricant was usually money. Corruption was therefore endemic, not least because it was so hard to define. Many practices which would today be regarded as immoral, if not illegal, were then accepted without comment. There *was* a line, however indeterminate, which divided the acceptable from the non-acceptable, but during

James's reign it may have become hazier. Buckingham had been given a royal licence to make money both for himself and the crown, but his activities added to the aura of sleaze which hung around James's Court. Whether in fact there was more corruption under James than under Elizabeth is well nigh impossible to decide, but James's own lax attitude towards money and his lack of understanding of financial affairs left the field open to unscrupulous operators.

Following the death, in October 1617, of Sir Ralph Winwood, who had been Secretary of State for three years, James used Buckingham as his unofficial secretary, much as he had earlier employed Carr. As Gondomar reported in 1620, the King "shows him everything and gives him account of everything, desiring to keep him informed and make him capable of handling negotiations".[32] In effect, Buckingham was James's apprentice, learning the mysteries of statecraft and diplomacy of which the King had a lifetime's experience. In his early years at any rate, Buckingham had no cause to question James's judgment, nor was he well placed to do so since his entire position depended upon retaining the King's goodwill. But there are indications that from about 1620, as the crisis over the Palatinate and Bohemia deepened, Buckingham began to chafe at the bit and favour a more committedly anti-Habsburg approach. However, he remained a servant, not a master, and although there were some people who professed to believe that he twisted James round his finger, the truth is that James, as always, took his own decisions and made his own policy. This, after all, was his God-given duty.

Buckingham acted as the King's messenger, and thereby served as his scapegoat. In late 1620, for example, there was an outpouring of anti-Spanish sentiment in England when the Spanish general, Spinola, took his army into the Palatinate and began occupying it. Gondomar was accused of deliberately deceiving James about Spinola's intentions, but strenuously denied this. In response to his insistence, James instructed Buckingham to write to the ambassador, confirming that he had never given misleading information about Spinola's objectives. Gondomar published the letter, in the hope of diverting blame from himself, but the only effect was to transfer it to Buckingham, who was assumed to be behind James's initiative. By using his favourite in this way, whether or not he did it consciously, James was divesting himself of the responsibility for unpopular actions and shielding himself from public anger. Only after Buckingham's return from Spain in late 1623 did the favourite move into open confrontation with the King on fundamental policy issues, and even then he and Prince Charles had to proceed with great care. During the last eighteen months of his life James fought a very effective rearguard action to preserve his control of foreign policy. His freedom of action was circumscribed not merely by the pressures of public opinion and from within his own family, but also by the unfolding of events on the Continent, yet he never became a cipher.

In those spheres for which he was directly responsible, Buckingham proved himself a highly effective administrator. His predecessor as Lord Admiral, Charles Howard, Earl of Nottingham, had won fame and glory as commander of the English fleet against the Armada in 1588, but he was now over eighty and had allowed the navy to run down. As early as 1608 a commission had been appointed to enquire into the state of the navy and see what needed to be done to improve things, but its recommendations were largely ignored. Ten years later another commission was at work, headed by Lionel Cranfield, the London merchant and financier. Buckingham, as Lord Admiral, took Cranfield under his wing and assured him of his support. As James later informed Parliament, "Buckingham laid the ground and bare the envy. [Cranfield] took the laborious and ministerial part upon him . . . and he himself many a time protested unto me that he had not been able to do me any service in the ministerial part if Buckingham had not backed him in it."[33] The commissioners came to the conclusion that if an effective attack was made on waste and corruption it would be possible to halve costs and yet build two new ships every year as well as repair two old ones. Buckingham responded by persuading the King to make the commission permanent and give it control over naval administration. He also appointed as his principal adviser in naval matters Sir John Coke, a member of the Navy Board under Elizabeth and a man of exceptional capacity and probity. There was no sudden or miraculous transformation of the navy under Buckingham, for shortage of money remained endemic and corruption could never be totally eliminated. But a steady programme of repair and new construction was put into effect, and the navy was in far better shape at James's death than it had been when he came to the throne.

Buckingham had been so impressed by Cranfield that he continued to act as his patron and brought him into the Villiers circle by providing one of his relatives as Cranfield's second wife. Cranfield's talents as a financier, combined with Buckingham's support, gave him credit with the King, who in 1621 appointed him Lord Treasurer and a year later created him Earl of Middlesex. Another of Buckingham's clients was Sir Francis Bacon, who had long been held back from high office – or so he believed – by the jealousy of Robert Cecil, and now pinned his hopes on the favourite, to whom he professed his devotion. Bacon's strategy paid off, for in 1617 James appointed him Lord Keeper. A year later he gave Bacon the superior title of Lord Chancellor and raised him to the peerage. Here again the favourite's patronage had eased the way into royal service of a most talented individual, but it could not save Bacon when the Commons, in their investigation into the abuse of monopolies in 1621, came across evidence that he had taken bribes. A number of Buckingham's relatives were monopoly profiteers, and rather than expose them and himself to further scandal the favourite was willing to sacrifice Bacon – thereby showing the downside of patronage from the point of view of the client who had become a liability. James, who was also in danger of being tarred with the monopoly brush, adopted a similar pose of high-minded disinterestedness. "So precious unto me is the public good", he informed the House of Lords, "that no private person whatsoever, were he never so dear unto me, shall be so respected by me . . . as the public good."[34]

Not all of Buckingham's clients were as worthy of office as Cranfield and Bacon, nor did he act entirely out of altruism. He expected loyalty and, where appropriate, thankofferings, from those he promoted, but the mixture of public considerations and private interests was characteristic of political systems throughout Europe, and kindred and patronage ties operated in much the same way as party allegiances do today. This did not alter the fact, however, that by the end of James's reign Buckingham had become, in the eyes of the public, the symbol, if not the cause, of everything that had gone wrong during the course of it. No sooner was James dead than the attack on him began. Sir John Eliot, speaking in the Parliament of 1626, complained that the King's "treasures are exhausted, his revenues are consumed, as well as the treasures and abilities of the subject. And though many hands are exercised and divers have their gleanings, the harvest and great gathering comes to one. For he it is that must protect the rest. His countenance draws all others to him as his tributaries, and by that they are enforced not only to pillage for themselves but for him, and to the full proportion of his avarice and ambition . . . This cannot but dishearten, this cannot but discourage, all men well affected, all men well disposed to the advancement and happiness of the King."[35] Eliot, of course, had his own agenda and was far from dispassionate in his criticism. In many respects Buckingham had vindicated the trust James placed in him and, in return for the enormous benefits he had received, had served the King to the best of his abilities. James, like Charles after him, would no doubt have rejected Eliot's criticism as totally unjustified and prompted by frustrated ambition, but the very existence of a favourite, particularly one as dominant as Buckingham, served to foment discontent among those members of the political nation who blamed him – and, by implication, the King – for their exclusion from office and influence.

The emergence of a powerful favourite left the Privy Council with a diminished role, since although Buckingham was a member of this body he never had the close relationship with it that Robert Cecil, Earl of Salisbury, had preserved. Yet even under Salisbury the Council had never played any significant part in the formulation, as distinct from the execution, of policy. Once or twice a year the King would take part in its deliberations – he was present, for instance, in 1618, when the decision to transfer control of the navy to the commissioners was ratified – but generally speaking he left the Council alone to deal with routine administration. Major policy decisions he kept to himself, and this meant there was less scope for conflicting opinions to make themselves known, and perhaps too clear a line drawn between those who were and those who were not in the King's confidence.

James managed to hold the various factions in balance for the first fifteen years of his reign in England, but the deteriorating situation in Europe after 1618 hardened attitudes all round. Even if the Privy Council had had a more constructive role this would not have made any significant difference, for it could not create harmony where none existed. Change came about in 1624 only because the Court itself was split, with the favourite and the heir to the throne espousing a policy of intervention against the wishes of the reigning monarch. Failing to win support from the Council, they took the struggle into the broader forum of Parliament, where they secured sufficient backing to drive James gradually back from his entrenched positions. By so doing they demonstrated the limited political effectiveness of the major institutions of English government. Neither the Privy Council nor Parliament could assert an independent role against the King; the only way in which to change policy was to change the King's mind. Had James been cast in the same mould as his contemporaries, Louis XIII of France and Philip IV of Spain, he would have been content to reign while his current favourite or favoured minister ruled. But James was not prepared to take a back seat, and although he came under increasing pressure in the last year or two of his life he remained the key figure in British politics. It was upon his choice and his decision that everything else, in the last resort, depended.

.   .   .

SCOTLAND

After 1603 James, as he frequently reminded himself and others, was ruler of three kingdoms, and although he made his home in England he kept a close watch on Scotland and Ireland and never relinquished control of policy to his delegates there. As far as Scotland was concerned he took pride in the fact that "here I sit and govern it with my pen. I write, and it is done, and by a clerk of the Council I govern Scotland now, which others could not do by the sword."[36] This was, in fact, a remarkable achievement and the effective rule of an absentee king demonstrates the extent to which James had tamed the Scottish nobility and broken the hold of the militants on the Kirk. Responsibility for maintaining order in Scotland now rested with the Scottish Privy Council, in which a core of office-holders played a key role. James did not exclude members of the old nobility as long as they were prepared to serve him faithfully, but he made greater use of men from a lairds or gentry background, frequently lawyers, whom he raised to the peerage. The Council was kept on a short leash, however, for one of James's first actions upon arrival in England was to improve the postal service between his two kingdoms, and some sixty royal missives were despatched every year from London to Edinburgh. The Council usually implemented James's orders without question, but his main interest was in religious matters and he left the regulation of the economy increasingly to the Council. As the years passed, the Council also became adept at blunting measures of which it disapproved: as the Earl of Mar told James's successor in 1626, "a hundred times your worthy father has sent down directions unto us which we have stayed, and he has given us thanks for it when we have informed him of the truth".[37]

The principal task of the Scottish Privy Council was the maintenance of order. There were two regions which were particularly lawless. The first of these were the former borderlands between England and Scotland, and in 1605 a joint body of English and Scots commissioners was appointed to restore the rule of law, with a small police force at their disposal. This proved to be highly effective, and in 1609 the Lord Chancellor of Scotland declared that "all these ways and passages betwixt . . . Scotland and England" had been rendered "free and peaceable", and that the whole area was now "as lawful, as peaceable and as quiet as any part of any civil kingdom of Christianity".[38] There was an element of wishful thinking in this claim, for the borderlands were still prone to violence. The police force remained in existence until 1621, when James ordered it to be dissolved as part of an economy drive, but its absence soon came to be regretted.

At the other end of Scotland, the highlands and islands were regions where the authority of the crown was subordinate to that of clan chieftains. James regarded the highlanders, much as he did the Irish, as little better than savages, and favoured a policy of severe repression, confiscation of property and resettlement by lowlanders. However, James did not have either the soldiers or the money with which to carry out his policy, and in any case Ireland, after 1603, offered better prospects to any Scots willing to become colonists. Repressive measures were enforced, not least against the unruly MacGregors, who were faced with the threat of virtual extermination if they did not bow to the royal will. Elsewhere, however, James allowed his Council in Scotland to employ gentler measures. In so doing it made use of the bishops whose dioceses covered the areas in question. This policy was apparently justified when Andrew Knox, Bishop of the Isles, summoned a meeting at Iona in 1609 at which the highland chiefs accepted the Statutes of Icolmkill, whereby they agreed to maintain order in the King's name and to embrace the reformed faith, with all its built-in disciplinary mechanisms. In Orkney, on the other hand, peaceful means were of no avail, for the Earl of Orkney ruled the territory as a quasi-independent prince and ignored the efforts of James Law, Bishop of Orkney, to integrate him into the Icolmkill system. The Council therefore summoned the earl to Edinburgh, and promptly imprisoned him. When, in 1615, his son raised a rebellion in protest, Orkney was executed. By this mixture of force and persuasion, royal authority and the rule of law were imposed upon the highlands and islands.

In Scotland generally the main threat to order came from what an act of Parliament of 1609 called "the ungodly and barbarous and brutal custom of deadly feuds".[39] An earlier act of 1604 had prescribed severe penalties for lairds found guilty of feuding, and the royal government had been very successful in reducing its incidence. Indeed, one observer, in 1605, went so far as to declare that "there are very few in Scotland who have any grievances at all, compared to the number in former times. For the King's wise authority has so ordered it that, God be thanked, never was there less disturbance in this country than at the present time."[40] But James was aware that feuding could quickly break out again if steps were not taken to eradicate it completely, and he decided to follow the English example of appointing local gentlemen as Justices of the Peace with responsibility for maintaining order in their shires. The 1609 act explicitly authorised him to nominate "some godly, wise and virtuous gentlemen of good quality . . . to be commissioners for keeping His Majesty's peace . . . [with] power and commission to oversee, try, and prevent all such occasions as may breed trouble and violence among His Majesty's subjects or forcible contempt of His Majesty's authority and breach of his peace".[41] Commissioners were duly appointed, but although they acted as a counterweight to the hereditary sheriffs, they never acquired the major role in local government that their English equivalents took for granted. Kirk sessions proved a more effective mechanism for maintaining order, and the elected elders, whether or not they were appointed commissioners, exercised an authority that no merely secular official could match.

Because James intended to rule Scotland directly, after 1603 as before, he never appointed a viceroy or Lord Deputy, as in Ireland. His principal minister there was Alexander Seton, a distinguished lawyer and judge whom James created Earl of Dunfermline. He had been named as one of the 'Octavians', the eight auditors of the Exchequer appointed by James in 1596 to restore his finances, and masterminded their reform programme. He also won the King's approval for the skilful way in which he defended Scottish interests in the negotiations for a statutory union of the two kingdoms which he conducted with Robert Cecil, Earl of Salisbury. Dunfermline retained power because he retained James's confidence, but he lost this in 1606 over the question of how to deal with the hard-line presbyterians. James made little effort to conceal his intense dislike of what he regarded as an unruly faction within the Kirk. As a young man he was reported as saying that "he had been brought up among a company of mutinous knave ministers, whose doctrine he had never approved",[42] and some twenty years later he informed the bishops assembled for the Hampton Court Conference that although he had "lived among puritans and was kept for the most part as a ward under them, yet since he was . . . ten years old he ever disliked their opinions."[43] Nevertheless, while he was only King of Scotland James did not dare risk an open break with the presbyterians. For one thing they commanded a wide measure of public support, and, for another, he needed them as allies against a turbulent nobility. This explains why, in 1589, he took umbrage at Richard Bancroft's notorious Paul's Cross sermon, in which the bishop claimed that episcopacy was of divine origin and made unflattering references to Scottish presbyterianism. By way of riposte, James assured the general assembly of the Scottish Church that he thanked God for having been born into the Kirk, and compared the anglican service to "an evil said Mass in English".[44]

Relations between James and the presbyterians reached their high point in 1592, when the 'Golden Act' gave presbyteries a formal role in the appointment of ministers. It was now only a matter of time – or so it seemed to the triumphant presbyterians – before the Kirk was entirely remodelled along lines of which they approved, but James had retained a number of trump cards in his hand. Although the Kirk had secured the nominal right to annual assemblies, it was left to the King to decide where and when they should assemble. Moreover, the office of bishop had not been abolished, and James continued to fill vacancies in the episcopate; by 1605 only three of the thirteen Scottish sees were without a bishop. However, although James's appointees held the name of 'bishop' they were little more in practice than ordinary ministers temporarily graced with this title. What James needed was time for the idea of episcopacy to become accepted and for the bishops themselves to assert their authority. This would not be easy so long as they were liable to be called to account by a general assembly of the Kirk, but after his accession to the English throne James felt strong enough to take a much firmer line against the presbyterians, particularly now that the Scottish nobles had been reduced to order. A general assembly of the Kirk had been summoned to meet at Aberdeen in July 1604, but James put this off until the following year. Then, in June 1605, he postponed it yet again, without fixing an alternative date. This was too much for the Melvillians – the hard-line presbyterians – and just under thirty ministers defied James's explicit orders by gathering at Aberdeen and constituting themselves an assembly.

It was this act of defiance which led to Dunfermline's fall from grace, for he was apprehensive about driving the presbyterians into open opposition and urged the King to show leniency towards the defiant ministers. James, however, had no intention of condoning overt disobedience, and he therefore turned to his old acquaintance, Sir George Home, Earl of Dunbar and Lord Treasurer of Scotland. Dunbar did as he was ordered by orchestrating the trial of the ministers and securing the conviction of the most prominent. James was delighted, and thereafter Dunbar became his principal agent for the governance of his northern kingdom, commuting at least once a year between London and Edinburgh.

There seems little doubt that James was highly impressed by the ceremonious gravity of anglican services when he experienced them at first hand, and had all his predilections in favour of episcopacy confirmed. Hoping that a similar experience might win over even the most recalcitrant presbyterians, he invited Andrew Melville and a number of other militants to London in August 1606. The experiment was not a success. Melville used the occasion to preach in favour of the ministers imprisoned for taking part in the Aberdeen meeting and to demand that general assemblies of the Kirk should be free to determine their own times and places of assembly. He also sneered at the 'Romish rags' worn by Bancroft, now Archbishop of Canterbury, and criticised the ornate furnishings of the royal chapel. James responded by sending Melville to the Tower, where he remained until 1611, when he was allowed to go into permanent exile. The same fate was decreed for the imprisoned ministers. James had effectively decapitated the presbyterian leadership in Scotland, and he followed up this *coup* by summoning a convention of ministers to Linlithgow, where they were bribed and bullied into agreeing that in future every presbytery should be presided over by a bishop, acting as its chairman or 'moderator'. James later insisted that the convention had also accepted the right of bishops to act as moderators of synods, which were made up of representatives from a number of presbyteries.

One reason for the ineffectiveness of the episcopate in Scotland was its poverty. The Reformation had laid open the Church to unmerciful plunder, and much of its wealth had passed into lay hands. This transference of property had been sanctioned by the Act of Annexation of 1587, but James was determined that what one Parliament had done, another should now undo. In July 1606, therefore, Dunbar went north to preside over a meeting of Parliament which, under heavy pressure from him and other of the King's agents, passed an act "anent [i.e. concerning] the restitution of the estate of bishops" which revoked the Act of Annexation so far as it concerned episcopal lands. The laity were the apparent losers from this measure, but in fact they held on to a great deal of what they already owned. Moreover, the King used the abbey lands in his possession to endow new peerages, which he conferred on his principal followers. In this way he created an aristocracy of service which acted as a counterweight to the old nobility and was fully supportive of the crown's interests. The erection of temporal lordships out of former ecclesiastical property was in effect a huge bribe given to the laity at the expense of the Church, but what remained was used to endow the bishops. Further improvement in their status came in 1608, when Dunbar took with him to Scotland his chaplain, George Abbot, future Archbishop of Canterbury, who was remarkably successful in persuading many Scots that there were only minimal differences between the English and Scottish churches, and that such things as ceremonies and forms of government were 'matters indifferent' which the crown had the right to regulate. A year later the Scottish Parliament passed an act restoring the bishops "to their former authority, dignity, prerogative, privileges and jurisdiction" and confirming their right to administer justice "in all spiritual and ecclesiastical causes".[45]

Dunbar's greatest triumph came in 1610, a year before his death, when James decided to convene a general assembly of the Kirk at Glasgow. There was a danger, as always, that it would be hijacked by the radical minority of Melvillian ministers, but Dunbar was now a past master in the art of rigging such meetings, and he used all the means at his disposal to ensure that the moderates would be in control. Well-affected ministers who lived far from Glasgow had their expenses paid by the crown, and presbyteries were 'persuaded' to choose as their representatives men who would be in sympathy with the King's policies. When the assembly elected John Spottiswoode, Archbishop of Glasgow, as its moderator, the adoption of the government's programme was assured. Members duly voted to restore diocesan bishops to their traditional functions, giving them a role similar to that of their counterparts in England. James had already ordered the setting up of Courts of High Commission in the two Scottish archiepiscopates of Glasgow and St Andrews, which strengthened the authority of the bishops over the clergy in their dioceses. All they now lacked was formal consecration, which could not be carried out in Scotland since the virtual suspension of episcopacy for such a long period meant that there were no consecrated bishops still alive. Spottiswoode and two fellow bishops were therefore sent to England to be formally consecrated, and on their return north they performed the same function for the remainder of the Scottish episcopate.

The restoration of episcopacy in his native land was a personal triumph for James. As he rightly said, it had been "our own proper motion, not suggested or procured by importunity or suiting of others".[46] It provoked surprisingly little opposition, not least because there was no attempt to dismantle the presbyterian system where it had taken root. James presumably hoped and assumed that as the Scots became used to episcopacy they would voluntarily embrace it, so that presbyterianism would wither on the vine. This might conceivably have happened if James had been content to leave time to do its work, but he was by now so persuaded of the superiority of the anglican form of worship that he wished to introduce it to his native land. When he left Scotland it had been with the promise that he would return every three years, but shortage of money, as well as his immersion in English affairs, had kept him in London. In 1617, however, he made the great journey north and took up residence at the Palace of Holyrood House, where an organ was installed in the royal chapel and English carpenters were preparing to set up carved wooden statues of the apostles.

This led to complaints of idolatry, and such was the outcry that even Archbishop Spottiswoode urged restraint. James reluctantly agreed to postpone the work, but only on grounds of lack of time. He told the bishops not to deceive themselves "with a vain imagination of anything done therein for ease of your hearts, or ratifying your error in your judgment of that graven work, which is not of an idolatrous kind, like to images and painted pictures adored and worshipped by papists, but merely intended for ornament and decoration of the place where we should sit".[47] Services in the royal chapel were conducted with all the ceremony of which the English church was master, 'with singing of choristers, surplices, and playing on organs'.[48] James intended this as a means of instruction, for he hoped that the presbyterians who came to watch would go away converted. Many of them, however, had quite the opposite reaction, being convinced that popery had entered among them.

Much greater alarm was caused when it became known that James was proposing to move the Kirk closer to anglican forms by getting it to accept what became known as the Five Articles. These were, that communicants should kneel when they received the sacraments; that communion should be administered in private houses if sickness or other considerations made this appropriate; that private baptism should be likewise permitted; that feast days such as Christmas and Easter should be duly celebrated; and that children should be brought before bishops to undergo the rite of confirmation. James also called on the Scottish Parliament to acknowledge that "whatever His Majesty should determine in the external government of the Church, with the advice of the archbishops, bishops, and a competent number of the ministry, should have the force of law".[49] This aroused fears that James intended to impose the Five Articles upon the Scottish Church, and a number of clergy, led by David Calderwood, its future historian, made a formal protest.

The King summoned the protesters before him and defended his position with his customary vigour. In response to Calderwood's statement that he had been a minister for twelve years, James commented, "Indeed, when I went out of Scotland ye were not a minister. I heard no din of you till now. But hear me, Mr Calderwood. I have been an older keeper of the general assembly than ye. A general assembly serves to preserve doctrine in purity from error and heresy, the Kirk from schism, to make confessions of faith, to put up petitions to the King and Parliament.

But as for matters of order, rites and things indifferent in Kirk policy, they may be concluded by the King, with advice of the bishops and a choice number of ministers."[50] Calderwood was not persuaded by James's argument, and said he could give only passive obedience to the King's command. This was not enough for James, who refused to accept that obedience could be qualified. "I will tell thee, man, what is obedience. The centurion, when he said to . . . this man 'Go!', and he goeth; to that man, 'Come!', and he cometh. That is obedience!"[51]

James had no intention of abandoning the Five Articles. On the contrary, he ordered a general assembly of the Kirk to meet at St Andrews, after his departure from Scotland, to make formal acceptance of them. However, even the bishops had doubts about the wisdom of trying to enforce practices upon the Scots which were likely to provoke opposition. Hostility focussed upon kneeling at communion, for this was alien to the Scottish reformed tradition and smacked of popery. So did the celebration of feast days, which was another bone of contention. In the end, the assembly took no action on the Articles, which amounted to a rejection of them. James, whose patience was always limited, warned the members of the consequences. "Since your Scottish Church hath so far contemned my clemency," he told them, "they shall now find what it is to draw the anger of a King upon them."[52] In January 1618 the Scottish Privy Council, in response to James's instructions, ordered that henceforth Good Friday, Easter Day, Ascension Day, Whitsunday and Christmas should be observed as both holy days and holidays. Later that year a general assembly met at Perth, by the King's command. Its purpose, as James informed the bishops, was to undo "the disgrace offered unto us in that late meeting at St Andrews". James accepted the desirability of obtaining the general consent of the ministers to the proposed changes, but reminded the bishops that he had an "innate power . . . by our calling from God . . . to dispose of things external in the Church, as we shall think them to be convenient and profitable for advancing true religion amongst our subjects".[53] Archbishop Spottiswoode, using methods he had no doubt learned from Dunbar, had secured a majority of moderates in the assembly, and the Five Articles were given the formal acceptance that James had demanded.

This did not mean, of course, that the Articles were immediately and willingly adopted by the ministers of the Kirk. Many refused to put them in execution, and James, according to the Earl of Kellie, was "wonderfully offended at the matter, and I think is resolved to come himself in person if they be not settled to his contentment otherways".[54] James did not, in fact, go north again, but he ordered the High Commission to take action against refractory ministers. In 1621 he further strengthened his position by persuading the Scottish Parliament to ratify the Articles, but it did so only after he had promised to make no more innovations. By this date, however, the gathering crisis in Europe had shifted James's attention elsewhere, and he could no longer direct a sustained campaign of enforcement of the Articles in Scotland. In this respect James left an unfortunate legacy to his son, and one that proved to be Charles's undoing.

Given the fact that the Five Articles were bound to arouse opposition in Scotland, the question arises why James pushed ahead with them. It may be that his long absence from his native land had left him increasingly out of touch with Scottish sentiment and practice in matters religious, but his return visit in 1617 gave him the opportunity to experience public reactions at first hand. An alternative explanation is that the flattery and assurances of devotion heaped upon James in England, particularly by the bishops, went to his head and led him to assume that he had only to make his will known for it to be immediately accepted. In his campaign to secure the adoption of the Five Articles, James won only a partial victory, but he was used to setbacks and skilled in the art of making tactical retreats in order to prepare a position from which he could subsequently advance. If James had lived longer he might well have succeeded in his long-term aim of bringing the Scottish Church ever closer to the pattern of its English counterpart. In James's eyes, it made no sense to have united kingdoms without a united Church. Since religion and politics, the clerical and the secular, were so closely interwoven, the Church and state needed to be closely aligned, and since God had appointed the King to rule over both, it was the King's duty as well as his right to reduce areas of contention and iron out differences. James had a successful record in this respect. He had defeated the militant presbyterians in Scotland and isolated the hardline puritans in England. In both cases he had taken his stand on the centre ground and secured the obedience, if not always the full-hearted support, of the moderate majority. His achievement was threatened by the outbreak of religious war in Europe, which raised religious passions to such a temperature that compromises and imposed solutions were no longer acceptable. Yet James's aim of uniting the churches of England and Scotland was by no means dishonourable, nor was it doomed to failure. A single British Church in a united British state would have had much to be said for it, and James had shown a pertinacity in pursuing his objective and a mastery of both strategy and tactics that might well have brought it about.

. . .

IRELAND

James did not have personal knowledge of his third kingdom, Ireland, but he was aware of the close links between it and his native land. Scots had been migrating to Ireland since the thirteenth century, but the pace increased in the second half of the sixteenth century, when a steady trickle of islanders moved into Ulster, though they gained a livelihood as mercenaries rather than settlers. They were looked on with mixed feelings by the English rulers of Ireland, who regarded them as an impediment to the imposition of effective English rule. The English presence in Ireland was largely confined to the Pale, a strip of land which spread north along the coast from Dublin for fifty miles or so and extended some twenty miles inland. Beyond the Pale stretched the Irishry, occupied by Gaelic-speaking clans headed by chieftains. The most powerful families were those of the 'Old English', descended from the Anglo-Norman adventurers who had invaded Ireland in the twelfth century. There was considerable rivalry between the principal Old English dynasties, of which the most important were the Butlers, under the Earl of Ormond, and the FitzGeralds, under the Earl of Kildare. However, the dominance of the Old English had been threatened in Henry VIII's reign by his strategy of anglicising and ennobling the principal Irish chieftains; the head of the O'Neill clan, for instance, was created Earl of Tyrone.

The Old English had long regarded themselves as the natural allies and agents of the London government, and during the first fifty years of Tudor rule the Earls of Kildare had a virtual monopoly of the office of Lord Deputy. But the Reformation transformed the situation, since the crown became committed to protestant men and policies, while the Old English, like the

Gaelic Irish, remained firm in their catholic faith. Under Elizabeth the government abandoned the policy of 'civilising' the Irish chieftains, and decided to impose the English language, English law and English administration upon the whole of Ireland. This threat to their traditions deeply angered the native Irish, and the 1590s saw the outbreak of major rebellions against English rule. The most dangerous of these was the Ulster rising, led by the Earl of Tyrone. Elizabeth had to despatch a large army to the province, under the command of her favourite, the Earl of Essex, but instead of fighting Tyrone he negotiated a truce with him and promptly returned to England. It was left to his replacement, Charles Blount, Lord Mountjoy, to bring the revolt to an end, shortly before Elizabeth's death. James continued Mountjoy in office as Lord Deputy until June 1604, when he recalled him to England, created him Earl of Devonshire, and made him his principal adviser on Irish affairs. The new Lord Deputy was Sir Arthur Chichester, formerly governor of Carrickfergus.

The catholic population of Ireland had high hopes of James, who was the son of a catholic martyr. An Irish Jesuit reported that when the news of Elizabeth's death reached Waterford, Cork and Clonmel, the principal towns of the kingdom, "the [protestant] ministers' books were burned and the ministers themselves hunted away, and . . . thereupon masses and processions were celebrated as frequently and upon as grand a scale as in Rome itself".[55] This picture was confirmed by an English observer a year or two later. The entire country, he declared, was swarming with "priests, Jesuits, seminaries, friars and Romish bishops" and he gave his opinion that "if there be not speedy means to free this kingdom of this wicked rabble, much mischief will burst forth in a very short time".[56] The upsurge of catholic activity in Ireland had been prompted by the belief that James would grant freedom of worship, but in June 1605 he issued a proclamation making plain that he would never do anything to "confirm the hopes of any creatures that they should ever have from him any toleration to exercise any other religion than that which is agreeable to God's word and is established by the laws of the realm".[57] This announcement was not simply a reaction to events in Ireland. James was known to be opposed to compulsion in matters of belief, and English as well as Irish catholics had been hoping for a measure of toleration. But the King had to take into account majority opinion among his protestant subjects, who already feared he was too soft on 'popery'. He therefore ordered all catholic priests to leave his kingdoms.

In Ireland such an order was unenforceable, for the priests had widespread popular support and "every town, hamlet and house was to them a sanctuary".[58] Elements in the Dublin government were in favour of repressive measures, but they could only be carried out piecemeal against selected individuals. More often than not these were Old English, deeply loyal to the crown while remaining catholic, and they protested to James and the Privy Council in London. James could hardly condemn his administrators in Ireland for trying to carry out his commands and enforce the law, yet he recognised the futility of compulsion in the Irish context, especially as it ran counter to his deepest instincts. "He would much rejoice", he said, "if the Irish catholics would conform themselves to his religion, yet he would not force them to forsake their own."[59] James would have preferred a campaign of protestant evangelisation to win over the catholics, but an investigation into the state of the anglican Church in Ireland showed it was incapable of such a crusade. Protestant clergy were thin on the ground, and often the churches to which they were attached were no more than roofless shells. They rarely spoke the Irish language and were therefore unable to communicate with their parishioners, who ignored them in favour of the catholic priests. Too many protestant clergy were mere time-servers, with no sense of mission, and defined their spiritual duties in terms only of the English community.

Chichester was determined to extend English influence into Ulster, but this brought him up against Tyrone, who had been treated generously after the defeat of his rebellion and allowed to retain his estates. Another of the chieftains who also saw his power base threatened by Chichester's ambitions was Rory O'Donnell, created Earl of Tyrconnell in September 1603. What both men resented most of all was the fact that they were no longer virtual sovereigns in their own domains. Whether or not they were in touch with Spanish agents and plotting rebellion, as their enemies alleged, makes little difference. They were survivors from an older Gaelic Ireland that was fast disappearing, and all that the future promised was continuing diminution of their influence and authority. Rather than face this prospect they decided to seek their fortunes abroad, and in September 1607 they left Ireland for ever.

The 'Flight of the Earls' deprived Ulster of its natural leaders and opened up a whole range of possibilities. Chichester wanted to take advantage of the situation by extending the English military presence through the establishment of garrisons. But James had more grandiose ideas. He had already tried out the policy of settlement, or 'plantation', in the Scottish islands as a means of imposing order on what he regarded as the savage natives, and he could see the advantage of employing the same strategy in Ireland. By seizing the Earls' lands and offering them to English and Scottish settlers, he could speed up the 'civilising' process in Ireland and gradually reduce the size of the expensive army which he had to maintain there. Secular considerations were reinforced by religious ones, for, as James told Chichester, "the settling of religion [and] the introducing [of] civility, order, and government amongst a barbarous and unsubdued people" would be accounted "acts of piety and glory, and worthy always of a Christian prince to endeavour".[60]

The policy of plantation which was now firmly adopted led to an inflow of settlers. They are usually referred to as the 'New English', but were really 'New British', since they came from Scotland as well as England. Unlike the Old English, they were aggressively protestant. They were also different in that they despised the native population and its traditions, and regarded the law merely as a convenient way of confirming their property rights and subjugating their tenants. James had assumed that the English and Scottish 'undertakers' would bring tenants with them from the mainland, to replace the native Irish, who would be concentrated in areas where they would be more easily 'civilised'. In practice, however, the undertakers found it cheaper and more efficient to employ native labour, so many Irish stayed put, even though they were ruthlessly exploited by their new masters. James was angry at the way in which his plans for the plantation were being frustrated. In a letter to Chichester written in March 1615 he complained that the majority of the undertakers had done "nothing at all, or . . . to so little purpose that the work seems rather to us to be forgotten by them and to perish under their hand than any whit to be advanced by them: some having begun to build and not planted, others begun to plant and not build, and all of them in general retaining the Irish still upon their lands, the avoiding [i.e. expelling] of which was with us the fundamental reason of that plantation". James ordered Chichester to confiscate all those lands whose owners had failed to fulfil the terms of the settlement "and to bestow them upon other men, more active and worthy of them than themselves". In a postscript in his own hand, James reminded Chichester that he expected "that zeal and uprightness from you that ye will spare no flesh, English nor Scottish, for no private man's worth is able to counterbalance the perpetual safety of a kingdom which this plantation being well accomplished will procure".[61] Unfortunately for James, threats of confiscation were counter-productive, for the settlers would be unwilling to commit themselves fully to their undertaking if they were likely to have the fruit of their labours taken away from them. The King, unlike his officials in Dublin, underestimated the difficulties confronting the undertakers in settling vast tracts of land in which the native Irish were still a presence and English and Scottish settlers were in short supply. In practice, there was little he could do to change the pattern of settlement in Ulster. The men who 'adventured' their lives and fortunes in the plantation were driven by self-interest rather than considerations of state, and it was they, and not the distant crown, who determined the nature of what was in fact if not in name the colony of Ireland.

One of the consequences of the Ulster plantation was the prospect of a protestant majority in the Irish Parliament, when that body should next be summoned. Hitherto the catholics had been predominant, but the creation of new parliamentary boroughs in Ulster threatened to undermine their influence and open the way to repressive anti-catholic legislation. The Old English lords appealed to James against the way in which "beggarly cottages" were being given the franchise so that "by the votes of a few elected for that purpose, under the name of burgesses, extreme penal laws should be imposed upon your subjects".[62] When the Parliament nevertheless went ahead, in 1613, the Old English members of the Lower House, who were now in a minority, challenged the validity of the returns from the new boroughs and refused to take any further part in proceedings until the King had delivered judgment on the issue. In April 1614 the representatives of the Old English were in London, where James gave them audience. His initial response was distinctly unfavourable – "my sentence is that you have carried yourselves tumultuously, and that your proceedings have been rude, disorderly, and worthy of severe punishment"[63] – but, as was frequently the case, he moderated his opinion after due reflection. When he made his final decision some months later, he disallowed a number of returns and reduced the protestant majority in the Irish Lower House to a mere six. The Old English felt they had gained a victory – as, in a sense, they had – but in fact James had conceded nothing of importance, apart from the withdrawal of the proposed anti-catholic legislation. The Irish Parliament had been turned into a protestant body, and was to remain so.

Although James was far less paranoid in his attitude towards catholics than the vast mass of his English and Scottish subjects, he nevertheless shared their assumption that acceptance of papal headship of the Church was incompatible with loyalty to the crown. The Old English seemed to be proof of the contrary, but James was unable to reconcile their expressions of devotion with their continued support for the Pope. "Surely I have good reason for saying that you are only half-subjects of mine?" he asked them. "For you give your soul to the Pope, and to me only the body; and even it, your bodily strength, you divide between me and the King of Spain . . . Strive henceforth to become good subjects, that you may have *cor unum et viam unam* [i.e. one heart and one way], and then I shall respect you all alike."[64] When they returned to Ireland, the Old English took part once again in debates and demonstrated their loyalty by voting for the subsidy bill, but James never summoned another Parliament in Ireland. He did not relish the prospect of future encounters with opposition delegations, and in any case the powers of the prerogative in Ireland were sufficiently extensive to make parliaments unnecessary.

The plantation of Ulster, despite the fact that it had not been carried out in the way the King intended, had demonstrated the effectiveness of colonisation in taming the native Irish and strengthening the protestant interest. James was more than ever convinced that the extension of plantations would be the best solution for the whole of Ireland. What he had in mind was not an Ulster-style subjugation of the existing Irish population but a regrouping of it in defined areas where agriculture could be practised instead of herding, and a more ordered way of life established. English and Scottish immigrants would be encouraged to settle in the areas vacated by the Irish, so that they could demonstrate to their neighbours the advantages of their superior techniques both of cultivation and of civilisation. The native Irish would thereby be brought up to the higher standards prevailing in England and Scotland. But as always in Ireland, there was a yawning gap between aims and achievements. A leading Irish historian refers to a survey of 1622 'which found that the plantations amounted to little more than the superimposition of a substantial number of absentee landlords upon the "inferior Irish" of Wexford and the midlands'. This, he concludes, was 'an inexorable consequence of the way in which the scheme had been administered. Under local control, James's policy of interspersed planting was converted into a new, predatory form of surrender and regrant directed towards the enrichment of the New English.'[65]

Following the recall of Sir Arthur Chichester in 1615, after he had served as Lord Deputy for more than eleven years, James appointed Oliver St John as his viceroy. St John, who was himself an 'undertaker' in Ulster, with land grants amounting to thousands of acres, had been Chichester's close friend and adviser and was in many ways well suited to his new office, but he owed his appointment to the patronage of Buckingham, the unpopular royal favourite, and this tarnished his reputation. St John, whom Sir Francis Bacon described as "a man ordained of God to do great good to that kingdom",[66] rigorously enforced the laws against catholic priests and recusants at the same time as he pushed ahead with the plantation policy. He thereby made enemies among the Old English, who could exert considerable political influence in Whitehall and Westminster, and although his hard-line policies appealed to English protestants they distrusted his dependence upon the favourite. Increasing criticism of St John persuaded James to recall him in April 1622, but he retained the King's favour and was elevated to the peerage. The new Lord Deputy was Henry Cary, Viscount Falkland, who, as it happened, was also one of Buckingham's clients. Falkland attempted to follow the same course as his predecessor, and in early 1623 he issued a proclamation ordering all catholic priests to leave the kingdom. But he was unfortunate in his timing, because negotiations for a marriage between Prince Charles and a Spanish Infanta were now moving into the critical phase, and toleration for catholics was part of the price that James had to pay. When the Prince returned from Spain without his bride, a more hard-line approach was once again permissible, but expulsion of catholic priests, however desirable in theory, was never a practical possibility, given the degree of support for them among the Irish population.

As always, the only really effective means of reducing that level of support was an evangelising campaign by the protestant Church. James was in favour of this, but it would have needed money on a scale far beyond royal resources. Ireland cost the crown much more than it received, and attempts to plug the gap of some £20,000 a year were either ineffective or counter-productive. In 1622 James authorised the setting up of a Court of Wards in Ireland, designed to enforce the crown's feudal rights over landowners and to ensure that the income they generated was duly credited to the Exchequer. This had the effect of marginally improving the crown's finances, but only at the cost of alienating the principal Old English landowners, whose heirs were barred from possession as long as they remained catholic. An attempt to increase the yield from Customs was more promising, and in 1613 they were farmed out to an English syndicate for an annual rent of £6,000. Five years later the Irish Customs farm was granted to Buckingham, on condition that he shared the profits with the crown. This, once again, produced an increase in the royal revenue, but the link with an unpopular royal favourite, who had his own clients to satisfy and was not too scrupulous about the way in which they enriched themselves, brought the whole system into disrepute. In the closing years of James's reign Buckingham was becoming more and more involved in Irish affairs, and his influence, on the whole, was malign. His personal ambitions, which included the building up of a large landed estate, often ran counter to the requirements of efficient administration, and both St John and Falkland had to modify their policies in order to satisfy his need for money and the demands of his patronage system.

The only attempt during James's reign to conduct a thorough examination of Irish finances and administration came with the appointment of Lionel Cranfield as Lord Treasurer of England in 1621. He promoted the setting up of a commission of English and Irish officials charged with investigating Irish affairs and making recommendations for their improvement. The commissioners were at work in Ireland during the interregnum between St John's departure and the arrival of Falkland, and they swiftly produced a report revealing widespread incompetence and corruption. Cranfield reacted with his customary vigour and proposed a range of reforms which, if they had been carried out, would have eliminated many of the worst abuses. But Cranfield was not given the time he needed to put his programme into

effect. As Lord Treasurer he was opposed to English intervention in the Thirty Years War and therefore welcomed the prospect of a Spanish marriage for Prince Charles as the best way
of preserving peace between the two powers. Reports from Spain
that Buckingham was becoming increasingly sceptical about the
chances of such a match, and moving towards a more bellicose
stance, led Cranfield to take the dangerous course of not
simply opposing the favourite's policy but putting forward one
of his young relatives to replace him in the King's affections.
Unfortunately for Cranfield he badly miscalculated, and when
Buckingham returned to England he organised the parliamentary impeachment that led to the Lord Treasurer's downfall. With
Cranfield went the best hope of reforming Irish government in
James's reign.

It is tempting to write off James's rule in Ireland as a failure,
but any verdict must depend upon the standards which are
applied. James hoped to anglicise the Irish and turn them into
civilised protestants, but he did not have sufficient resources
to do this himself. He therefore encouraged plantation, in the
hope that private individuals would perform this task at minimum cost to the crown. What he envisaged was transforming
the Irish from itinerant herdsmen and bandits into a stable
peasantry, secure in their property but living alongside English
and Scottish settlers who would set them an example and help
them cast off their primitive attitudes and improve their conditions. There was nothing wrong with this ideal, but it was virtually impossible to achieve. Settlement in Ireland involved big
risks for those willing to undertake it, and it is hardly surprising
that their main objective was personal enrichment. Far from
elevating the natives, they depressed them into quasi-serfdom.
If James was, in this sense, betrayed by the settlers, the same is
also true of the established Church, which in general preferred
to take the easy course of attending to the spiritual needs of
the colonists rather than winning over the native Irish.

It never occurred to James, any more than it had to his Tudor
predecessors, that liberty of worship might be the best way to
make the Irish into loyal subjects. The English state, as it had
emerged in the sixteenth century, was so imbued with protestantism that the two could not be separated, and anglicisa-
tion was accompanied by virulent anti-catholicism. Looking back
from the twentieth century it is clear that the whole premise of
colonisation was misjudged, and that plantation solved nothing;

on the contrary it created more, and more intractable, problems for future British governments. Yet by the standards of his own day James had achieved a limited degree of success. The New English were not the ideal settlers from his point of view, but they were at least English and protestant, and these, by definition, were virtues. He could look forward to the day when the whole of Ireland would be transformed by plantation, which, as the word implies, promised growth and development. If the mere presence of English settlers was an essential first step on the way to producing an anglicised and protestant Ireland, then James had gone some way towards this goal.

. . .

REFERENCES

1. *Letters of King James VI & I* ed. G.P.V. Akrigg (University of California Press, 1984), pp. 169–70 [hereafter *Letters*].
2. *Letters*, p. 170.
3. *Letters*, pp. 173–4.
4. *Letters*, pp. 175–6.
5. *Letters*, p. 176.
6. *Letters*, p. 179–80.
7. *Letters*, pp. 206–7.
8. *Letters*, p. 247.
9. *Letters*, p. 242.
10. *Letters*, p. 234.
11. *Letters*, p. 233.
12. *Letters*, pp. 232–3.
13. *The History of the King's Works* ed. H.M. Colvin, Vol. IV: *1485–1660 (Part II)* (1982), p. 237.
14. Quoted in David Harris Willson, *King James VI and I* (Jonathan Cape, 1956), pp. 185–6 [hereafter Willson].
15. *Letters*, p. 227.
16. *Letters*, p. 269.
17. *Letters*, p. 289.
18. Historical Manuscripts Commission, *Report on the Manuscripts of the Duke of Portland*, Vol. IX (1923), p. 113. See also Neil Cuddy, 'The Revival of the Entourage: The Bedchamber of James I, 1603–1625' in David Starkey (ed.), *The English Court: From the Wars of the Roses to the Civil War* (Longman, 1987).
19. *The Court and Times of James the First* [ed. Thomas Birch] (1848), Vol. I, p. 60 [hereafter Birch].
20. *Letters*, p. 319.

21. *Letters*, p. 317.
22. *The Works of Francis Bacon* ed. James Spedding (1874), Vol. XI, pp. 279–80.
23. Birch, Vol. I, pp. 335–6.
24. *The Letters of John Chamberlain* ed. Norman Egbert McClure (American Philosophical Society, Philadelphia, 1939), Vol. I, p. 355 [hereafter Chamberlain].
25. *Cobbett's Complete Collection of State Trials*, Vol. II (1809), pp. 815 and 862.
26. Chamberlain, p. 475.
27. J.O. Halliwell, *Letters of the Kings of England*, Vol. II (1846), pp. 129–31.
28. Godfrey Goodman, *The Court of King James the First* (1839), Vol. I, pp. 225–6.
29. Quoted in Willson, p. 353.
30. Quoted in Willson, p. 353.
31. British Library *Harleian MSS* 6987, 153.
32. *Documentos Ineditos para la Historia de España* (Madrid, 1936–45), Vol. II, p. 274.
33. *Journals of the House of Lords 1578–1714* (1767), Vol. III, p. 344 [hereafter *LJ*].
34. *LJ*, p. 69.
35. Quoted in Samuel R. Gardiner, *History of England from the Accession of James I to the Outbreak of the Civil War 1603–1642* (1883), Vol. VI, p. 80 [hereafter Gardiner].
36. Quoted in Willson, p. 313.
37. Quoted in Maurice Lee, *Government by Pen: Scotland under James VI & I* (University of Illinois Press, 1980), p. 115.
38. Quoted in Gordon Donaldson, *Scotland: James V to James VII* (Oliver & Boyd, 1965), pp. 227–8 [hereafter Donaldson].
39. *The Acts of the Parliaments of Scotland* (1814), Vol. IV, p. 434 [hereafter *APS*].
40. Quoted in M. Perceval-Maxwell, *The Scottish Migration to Ulster in the Reign of James I* (Routledge & Kegan Paul, 1973), p. 21 [hereafter Perceval-Maxwell].
41. *APS*, p. 434.
42. Quoted in David George Mullan, *Episcopacy in Scotland: The History of an Idea, 1560–1638* (John Donald, Edinburgh, 1986), p. 88 [hereafter Mullan].
43. J.R. Tanner (ed.), *Constitutional Documents of the Reign of James I* (Cambridge University Press, 1930), pp. 61–2.
44. Quoted in Willson, p. 108.
45. *APS*, p. 430.
46. Quoted in Mullan, p. 122.
47. Quoted in Gardiner, Vol. III, p. 224.

48. David Calderwood, *The True History of the Church of Scotland from the Beginning of the Reformation unto the End of the Reign of King James VI*, Wodrow Society, Edinburgh (1842–49), Vol. VII, pp. 246–7 [hereafter Calderwood].

49. Quoted in Gardiner, Vol. III, p. 226.

50. Calderwood, p. 262.

51. Calderwood, p. 263.

52. Quoted in Donaldson, p. 209.

53. Calderwood, pp. 308–9.

54. Historical Manuscripts Commission, *Supplementary Report on the Manuscripts of the Earl of Mar & Kellie* (1930), p. 93.

55. Quoted in Richard Bagwell, *Ireland under the Stuarts*, Vol. I: *1603–1642* (1909), p. 7 [hereafter Bagwell].

56. Quoted in Bagwell, p. 18.

57. Quoted in Bagwell, p. 19.

58. Quoted in T.W. Moody, F.X. Martin, F.J. Byrne (eds), *A New History of Ireland*, Vol. III: *Early Modern Ireland 1534–1691*, p. 191 [hereafter *New History*].

59. Quoted in *New History*, p. 190.

60. Quoted in Perceval-Maxwell, p. 75.

61. *Letters*, pp. 332–5.

62. Quoted in *New History*, p. 213.

63. Quoted in *New History*, p. 215.

64. Quoted in *New History*, p. 217.

65. Aidan Clark in *New History*, pp. 221–2.

66. *Dictionary of National Biography sub* ST JOHN, Oliver.

Chapter 9

THE WISEST FOOL IN
CHRISTENDOM?

Henri IV's pithy dismissal of James as a ruler has echoed down the centuries and made a substantial contribution to the generally unfavourable verdict on the first King of Great Britain. Henri, who was no intellectual himself, in fact described James as the 'most learned' fool, thereby displaying a contempt for abstract theorising not uncommon in men of action. Of James's learning there can be no doubt, and when this was allied to his natural intelligence it gave him good grounds for trusting his own judgment. Observers had noted James's skill in argument while he was still a child. Fontenay reported that he "grasps and understands quickly; he judges carefully and with reasonable discourses; he restrains himself well and for long. In his demands he is quick and piercing, and determined in his replies. Of whatever thing they dispute, whether it be religion or anything else, he believes and maintains always what seems to him most true and just."[1]

Yet Fontenay's pen picture of the young King also highlighted elements in James's character and behaviour which made him seem undignified if not downright foolish. Because he had never been taught how to behave properly he was "very rude and uncivil in speaking, eating, manners, games, and entertainment in the company of women". Moreover, he had a peculiar manner of walking: "his gait is bad, composed of erratic steps, and he tramps about even in his room".[2] Weldon confirms this observation. James, he said, walked in a circular fashion, and all the while his fingers were "fiddling about his cod-piece". Weldon also claims that James's tongue was "too large for his mouth, which ever made him speak full in the mouth, and made him drink very uncomely".[3] Weldon was, of course, a hostile witness, but the case notes of the King's distinguished physician, Theodore de Mayerne, confirm that James had problems in walking and was a clumsy rider. Some recent writers have deduced from this that the King was a victim of porphyria, the 'royal disease' which was later to affect George III; but an alternative, and perhaps more convincing, explanation is that he suffered from 'mild cerebral palsy with athetoid features (the irregular writhing movements) somewhat prominent in addition to spasticity'.[4]

James was probably the best-educated ruler ever to sit on an English or Scottish throne, and the only one with any claim to be a political philosopher. He constructed a formidable theoretical justification of monarchy as the most valid form of government, but was he, as Henri implied, a failure when it came to the practical business of ruling? Did he behave in such a ludicrous way that he invited the contempt not only of his fellow monarchs but of his subjects as well?

This charge has some force behind it when James is seen from an overseas perspective. Fontenay had remarked on "his ignorance and lack of knowledge of his . . . little strength, promising too much of himself and despising other princes",[5] and this remained characteristic of James even as a mature ruler. He never seems to have perceived how wide a gap there was between his own estimate of his influence and his actual weight in the European power balance. His pursuit of peace and his desire to put an end to the rifts within christendom were admirable objectives, but even with three kingdoms at his command James had insufficient strength to exert any significant pressure on major figures like the Kings of France and Spain. It was not only his relative poverty which made him a factor of diminishing importance in European great-power politics. So also did his temperament, because he resorted naturally to verbal arguments rather than force of arms and was content with reassuring statements even when they bore little relation to events on the ground.

As for James's subjects, they had – or so it would appear – almost as much reason to belittle him as his fellow monarchs, for at home as abroad there was a perceptible gap between James's theory of kingship and his actual practice. Far from attending to the duties of state he spent days and weeks in the country, abandoning himself to the delights of the chase. He continued, as Fontenay had noted, to love "indiscreetly and inadvisedly",[6] promoting favourites who were widely regarded as worthless and allowing them to enrich themselves in ways that antagonised his subjects and tarnished his reputation. Moreover, in spite of his insistence upon the Godlike nature of his position he failed to impose discipline upon his followers. No sooner did Prince Charles ascend the throne than he announced his intention to reform the Court. He did so because, during the reign of his "most dear and royal father", he had become aware of "much disorder in and about his household, by reason of the many idle persons and other unnecessary attendants following the same", which had occasioned "much dishonour to our house".[7] Charles also put an end to another of his father's practices, namely the sale of titles, for this lowered the prestige of the nobility upon whom the King relied for assistance in governing, and brought the sleazy practices of the market place into what should have been a dignified and honourable transaction.

If aspects of James's rule were condemned even by his dutiful son, it might seem impossible, indeed a waste of time, to propound a defence of them. Yet here again it is revealing to look at James from a European perspective, and this time the comparison is much to his advantage. James's passion for hunting was characteristic of early modern monarchs, who spent hours in the saddle in pursuit of stags and other prey.[8] Not only did hunting provide healthy recreation for the ruler. It also developed his courage, endurance and cunning, and brought him into contact with the country dwellers who made up the majority of the population. Admittedly, when James was out with the hounds he was not easy to track down, and the frequent complaints in the Venetian ambassadors' letters that hunting took precedence over business echo Fontenay's observation that the young James was "too lazy and too thoughtless over his affairs, too . . . devoted to his pleasure, especially hunting". But James did not accept this criticism. On the contrary, he told Fontenay that "although he spent much of his time hunting he could do as much business in one hour as others would in a day".[9] This could be regarded as mere boasting on the part of a precocious boy, but in fact many of the problems which confronted James as a mature ruler were not susceptible to either a swift or an easy solution, and there was a great deal to be said for postponing decisions upon them. Moreover, in London even more than in Edinburgh James was subject to constant pressure from place-seekers and advice-offerers. It is hardly surprising, therefore, that he was impatient to escape from town and "enjoy the solitude and liberty of some of his distant places".[10]

James's passion for hunting extended to country life in general, which he believed had positive virtues, transcending the brittle values of metropolitan society. London, for which he had little love, was already becoming the great wen, and he issued a number of proclamations designed to limit its growth. Other proclamations ordered the gentry and nobility to leave the city, where they wasted their time and money in pursuit of the latest fashions, and return to their country seats. There they should keep up hospitality, as their forefathers had done, and maintain the established order in Church and state. In 1622 James used the device of a Horatian elegy to drive home his message, as well as hone his poetic skills:

"The country is your orb and proper sphere.
There your revenues rise; bestow them there."[11]

James was no less assiduous than Elizabeth in progressing around the southern part of England every year, honouring selected subjects with his presence and displaying himself to his people.[12] The first progress began in August 1603, when James and Anne went westwards as far as Winchester and Southampton before turning north towards Oxford. In subsequent years the King – sometimes accompanied by the Queen – went on a western progress, a northern progress or a midlands progress. The royal couple stayed in palaces or hunting lodges belonging to the crown, and also in private houses, as long as these were big enough. Hinchingbrooke, just outside Huntingdon, was a particular favourite, for James much enjoyed the company of its owner, Sir Oliver Cromwell, as well as the good hunting in the vicinity. Wherever the King went, he visited the principal towns in the locality. In 1614, for example, he was given a formal reception at Nottingham and Leicester, and in the following year he went twice to Cambridge. The journey to Scotland and back in 1617 was really an extended progress. *En route*, James made a formal entry into Lincoln, where he passed his hand over a hundred sufferers from the 'King's Evil' – a form of scrofula that was supposed to be curable by the royal touch. In York, James 'touched' another seventy persons in the minster, and after attending a dinner and banquet, dubbed eight knights.

More knighthoods were bestowed after his official reception at Durham. Progresses, large or small, were a means of putting the King on display and enabling him to distribute honours, healing, and whatever else was appropriate. James may not have relished public appearances in the way that Elizabeth did, but he appreciated the value of moving around his kingdom and making personal contact with his subjects.

On his return from Scotland James passed through Lancashire, where the magistrates had just attempted, on religious grounds, to suppress conventional Sunday amusements. James resented this, partly because Lancashire still had a high proportion of catholics who would now be able to tar the Church of England with the puritan, killjoy brush, but even more because of his instinctive feeling for traditional values. Lancashire was not unique in its official attitude towards sabbath games, and in 1618, therefore, after returning to London and consulting with his bishops, James issued the Declaration of Sports, in which he expressed his indignation at the fact that "his subjects were debarred from lawful recreations upon Sundays after evening prayers". He feared that "if these times were taken from them, the meaner sort who labour hard all the week should have no recreations at all to refresh their spirits". To counter this restrictive impulse, James now gave specific sanction to such pastimes as "dancing, either men or women; archery for men; leaping, vaulting or any other such harmless recreation" and also to "May games, Whitsun ales and Morris dances and the setting-up of maypoles".[13]

James has been blamed for indiscriminately expanding both the knightage and peerage, thereby cheapening titles of honour. It is indeed the case that he was lavish in his grants of knighthood. In 1603 alone he created well over nine hundred knights, which was more than Elizabeth had done during the entire course of her reign. As for the English peerage, it numbered fifty-five at the death of Elizabeth, but by 1625 James had added sixty-five new titles, as well as expanding the Irish peerage. No doubt James was over-generous, and the transition from famine to abundance too abrupt, but titles of honour should reflect the structure of society and the distribution of wealth, both of which had changed dramatically during the Tudor period. Elizabeth had been too conservative, too mean perhaps, in giving formal recognition to these changes. When, at James's arrival in London, Richard Martin – a noted lawyer and member of

Parliament – addressed him on behalf of the sheriffs, he made a pointed reference to "the neglected and almost worn-out nobility" and expressed the hope that with the accession of a new sovereign they would once again be "as bright diamonds and burning carbuncles . . . [in the] . . . kingly diadem".[14]

A more serious charge against James is that of selling titles, and here again the facts are not in dispute. A new title, that of baronet – in effect a hereditary knighthood – was created in 1611 and offered to anyone prepared to pay the required price. Peerages went on sale four years later, and the market expanded considerably after Buckingham became favourite and systematised the process, to the enrichment of himself as well as his royal master. Yet here again James was acting in a way that was typical of early modern monarchies. In France it was public appointments, or 'offices', that were sold, but the big attraction of them from the point of view of the purchaser was that they either conferred nobility automatically or opened the way to it. The French crown deliberately created offices simply in order to sell them, even though their proliferation silted up the channels of administration. The device seems crude by present-day standards, as well as self-defeating, but the governments of early modern states were faced with increasing expenditure and a circumscribed range of fiscal possibilities. There was inbuilt resistance to taxation, particularly among the richer elements of the population, and rulers had to choose methods of raising money that would create the minimum amount of disaffection. Only for brief periods of time, as during the English Republic and in France under Louis XIV, were governments sufficiently powerful to override opposition and levy taxes more or less at will.

The sale of titles under James was not merely a result of extravagance. Baronetcies, for instance, were created for the specific purpose of maintaining an army in Ireland, to preserve British rule there. The profits from the sale of peerages, on the other hand, merely served to increase the amount of ready money at the King's disposal. Not all the money paid for honours reached the King; Buckingham and other intermediaries took a substantial commission. But even this apparently dubious practice represented a saving to the King, for monarchs were expected to be 'bountiful', and when a ruler licensed a favoured subject to enrich himself at the public's expense he thereby avoided the need to part with his own resources. Here again, the assumptions behind the functioning of *ancien-régime* states were very different from those of our own day.

The same is true of patronage. Buckingham, who became the greatest of the patrons apart from the King himself, was justly accused of giving plum positions to members of his family and close circle. But such practices were standard in contemporary Europe. Richelieu, to make the most obvious comparison, was notorious for the way in which he inserted his 'creatures' – i.e. clients who were utterly devoted to his service – into key posts in the administration. This was a period when bureaucracies were small and the idea of 'public service' in its infancy. Men served the state in the expectation of making money out of it, and there was no clear line between the private and the public domain. Even quite humble officials were expected to use their own resources in carrying out government business, and it made sense for them to recoup their outlay as and when they could, for while governments might acknowledge debts they were all too frequently unable or unwilling to repay them. This applied to all levels of the administration, including the highest. Buckingham, for example, made a fortune as the King's favourite but he also spent huge sums in the service of the state. Following his assassination it took many years to disentangle the public and private elements in his finances, and even then a great deal of uncertainty remained.

Clientage systems were not necessarily harmful. Without them the inherently inefficient administrative machinery of the Renaissance monarchies would probably not have been able to function. Nor were favourites necessarily the villains of historical legend. Monarchy became an increasingly complex business as the range of the state expanded, and kings varied in their capacity to manage it. Where the sovereign was either incapable or temperamentally unsuited to his role, the favourite became a substitute ruler, less than a king but more than a prime minister.[15] Lerma and Olivares in Spain, and Richelieu and Mazarin in France are the prime examples of 'favouritism' as a political institution, but James was never prepared to let go the reins of government in the way that Philip IV and Louis XIII did. Generally speaking, his favourites had little or no political significance. The exception is Buckingham, though even he never had a completely free hand while James was alive. Buckingham was exceptional simply because he had the will and capacity to become a political figure in his own right. James may have chosen him because he had well-shaped legs and shining white teeth, but he developed in a way that bore a closer resemblance to Olivares or Richelieu than to his predecessor in the King's favour, Robert Carr, Earl of Somerset. It was for this reason that he was so widely distrusted and feared. It is often assumed that the hatred which Buckingham inspired was something personal and peculiarly English, but in fact the reaction to him was typical of that to all early modern favourites. They were hated because they were so powerful, because they used the royal authority to cut through red tape and get things done instead of preserving the *status quo*. They represented, in short, that aspect of absolute monarchy which was potentially an agent for change, for innovation. When the Commons impeached Buckingham in 1626 they were making a profoundly conservative gesture. They did the same, but more effectively, in 1641 when they destroyed the Earl of Strafford who had succeeded Buckingham as the embodiment of 'thorough' government.

The very existence of royal favourites under James has been taken as evidence that standards of behaviour in public life were declining and that corruption was becoming ever more insidious. This may indeed have been the case, but there is no way of proving it. Elizabeth I and her chief minister, Lord Burghley, believed that public morality was already in decline during the closing years of the Queen's reign, and fears about the corrupting influence of royal favourites were inspired by Leicester and Robert Cecil long before Somerset and Buckingham appeared on the scene. Ben Jonson's *Sejanus his Fall*, which deals with the relationship between the Emperor Tiberius and his evil favourite, might well be taken as delivering a coded message about James and his minions, but it was conceived, and partly written, while Elizabeth was still on the throne. We are so accustomed to think of Elizabeth as Gloriana, the semi-divine ruler worshipped and adored by her people, that we forget how unpopular she had become by the end of her reign, and how tarnished her reputation. Once again, Richard Martin offers a corrective. It was his duty, he told James, to "make known to an uncorrupted king the hopes and desires of his best subjects . . . The people shall every one sit under his own olive tree and anoint himself with the fat thereof, his face not grinded with extorted suits nor his marrow sucked with most odious and unjust monopolies. Unconscionable lawyers and greedy officers shall no longer spin out the poor man's cause in length, to his undoing and the delay of justice. No more shall bribes blind the eyes of the wise, nor gold be reputed the common measure of men's worthiness . . . No more shall Church livings be pared to the quick, forcing ambitious churchmen (partakers of this sacrilege) to enter in at the window by simony and corruption, which they must afterwards repair with usury and make up with pluralities."[16]

James did not meet all the high hopes which were pinned on him. If anything, his reign saw the lawyers becoming even more unconscionable and the royal officers ever more greedy. Yet he put an end to the plunder of the Church and did as much as was in his power to ensure that simony and pluralism no longer disfigured it. He also took action against monopolists in response to parliamentary pressure in 1621, and three years later accepted a statute which restricted his right to make the grants from which they profited.

It is often said that James, by contrast with Elizabeth, lacked the common touch and failed to cultivate public opinion. This is certainly not the case where the political nation – the upper section of British society – was concerned. James's writings and speeches, which were widely circulated, were calculated attempts to win support for his views among the people who mattered. This applied even to his pamphlet war against catholic controversialists, especially Cardinal Bellarmine, for by upholding the 'true faith' in so open a manner he established his protestant credentials even more firmly. James had always been adept at defending specific aspects of his policies. In 1582 he published a "Declaration of the King's Majesty's will anent [i.e. concerning] Religion" and three years later followed this up with a "Declaration of the King's Majesty's intention and meaning towards the late Acts of Parliament", which justified the legislation passed in 1584 to restrain the presbyterians. After taking action against the Melvillians in 1606 he issued a "Declaration of the just causes of His Majesty's proceedings against those ministers who are now lying in prison", but, rather surprisingly, he did not appeal to the public at large after the collapse of the Great Contract in 1610 or the Addled Parliament in 1614. Only in 1621, as already mentioned (see above, pp. 69–70), did he issue both a proclamation and a declaration explaining why he had dissolved a Parliament on which such high hopes had been built.

It would be absurd to suggest that James was an ideal ruler, or that his long reign in Scotland and Britain was an unqualified success. He was the victim of his own defects of character as well as changing circumstances. Yet while in many respects James was a fairly typical early modern monarch, there were aspects of his rule and personality which singled him out. Probably the most striking of these was his lack of fanaticism in matters religious. James was, and remained until the end of his life, a convinced protestant, but he recognised the futility of trying to force his own beliefs upon other people. Elizabeth is credited with saying that she did not wish to make windows into men's souls, but the statement could just as well have been made by James. He denounced the papacy when it claimed the right to intervene in secular affairs, but he never regarded the Pope as being beyond the pale of civilised communication. In like manner he denounced the errors of the Roman Catholic Church, but was prepared to acknowledge its redeeming features and accept that it was a valid spiritual institution. James disliked extremists of all sorts, whether they were catholic or protestant, and he was more successful than Elizabeth in preventing the puritans from taking over the Church of England. Yet he managed to retain all but a minority of puritans within his Church, and despite uncompromising rhetorical assertions he was content with a minimum of conformity. In fact, James deliberately used rhetoric, not only in religious matters, as a smoke-screen behind which he could turn apparently sharp-edged policies into actions that were characterised by compromise and ambiguity. In this way he went as far as any ruler could – and a good deal further than most – towards establishing a *modus vivendi* which preserved outward harmony between groups whose opinions were diametrically opposed.

James was unashamedly absolutist by inclination, and a stout defender of the royal prerogative. There was nothing absurd about this. With the exception of Venice and the United Provinces, monarchy was the standard form of government throughout Europe, and there was no obvious alternative to it. Western societies were under enormous strain from population growth, religious tensions, inflation, and the spiralling costs of defence, and "the authority of a king", to use Wentworth's words, was "the keystone which closeth up the arch of order and government, which contains each part in due relation to the whole".[17] Take it away or enfeeble it and the whole construction, the work of many centuries, would come crashing to the ground. Students of Aristotle, who included James and most of the political nation, knew that monarchy was better than oligarchy and infinitely preferable to democracy. 'Rule by the people' was a contradiction in terms, since the people were patently incapable of ruling themselves. Even the property-owners, the people who mattered, were unsuited to government. Nobody could have suspected before the 1640s that Parliament, and in particular the five hundred or so wrangling members of the Lower House, could assume power and successfully direct policy – for a time, at least.

Government was a matter for kings, and James had no doubt of his capacity for it, but once again there was a blurred area between his rhetoric and his practice. As long as his subjects accepted the principle that his powers derived from God and could not be questioned, James was perfectly content to acknowledge and uphold their traditional rights. His aim was to maintain the balance between the authority of the crown and the liberties of the subject which was at the heart of government in both Scotland and England. While in theory he was – or might have become – an innovator, he was committed in practice to the preservation of the *status quo*. His repeated professions of his desire to uphold the law and to rule justly were not without their effect. In contrast to his Tudor predecessors and Stuart successors he was never confronted with a major revolt in any of his kingdoms after he ascended the English throne. He also achieved the not inconsiderable feat of dying in his bed, unlike his mother, Mary, Queen of Scots, and his son and successor, Charles I, who both met their end on the scaffold. There are no grounds for calling the first truly British sovereign 'James the Great', but he deserves to be remembered as 'James the Just' or 'James the Well-Intentioned'. Given the fact that the vast majority of rulers merit no such appellation, James's subjects were lucky to have him as their king.

. . .

REFERENCES

1. *Calendar of State Papers relating to Scotland and Mary, Queen of Scots 1547–1603* ed. William K. Boyd, Vol. VII: *1584–1585* (Edinburgh, 1913), p. 274 [hereafter *CSPS*].
2. *CSPS*, p. 274.
3. [Sir Walter Scott, ed.] *Secret History of the Court of James the First* (Edinburgh 1811), Vol. II, p. 2.

4. A.W. Beasley, 'The Disability of James VI & I', *The Seventeenth Century*, Vol. 10, No. 2, 1995.
5. *CSPS*, p. 274.
6. *CSPS*, p. 274.
7. James Larkin (ed.), *Stuart Royal Proclamations*, Vol. II: *Royal Proclamations of King Charles I 1625–1646* (Clarendon Press, 1983), p. 37.
8. See Philippe Salvadori, *La Chasse sous l'Ancien Régime* (Paris, 1997).
9. *CSPS*, pp. 274–5.
10. *Calendar of State Papers and Manuscripts relating to English Affairs existing in the Archives and Collections of Venice* ed. Allen B. Hinds, Vol. XVII: *1621–1623* (1911), p. 185.
11. Quoted in Leah S. Marcus, 'Politics and Pastoral: Writing the Court on the Countryside' in Kevin Sharpe and Peter Lake (eds), *Culture and Politics in Early Stuart England*, Problems in Focus (Macmillan, 1994), p. 144.
12. See John Nichols, *The Progresses, Processions, and Magnificent Festivities of King James the First*, 4 vols (1828) [hereafter Nichols].
13. S.R. Gardiner (ed.), *The Constitutional Documents of the Puritan Revolution 1625–1660* (Clarendon Press, 1906), p. 101. See also Patrick Collinson, 'Elizabethan and Jacobean Puritanism as Forms of Popular Religious Culture' in Christopher Durston and Jacqueline Eales (eds), *The Culture of English Puritanism 1560–1700* (Macmillan, 1996).
14. Nichols, Vol. I, p. 131.
15. See Roger Lockyer, 'An English *Valido*? Buckingham and James I' in Richard Ollard and Pamela Tudor-Craig (eds), *For Veronica Wedgwood These: Studies in Seventeenth-Century History* (Collins, 1986). Also Francisco Tomas Valiente, *Los Validos en la monarquia española del siglo XVII* (Madrid, 1963).
16. Nichols, Vol. I, pp. 130–1.
17. J.P. Kenyon (ed.), *The Stuart Constitution 1603–1688*, 2nd edn (Cambridge University Press, 1986), p. 16.

BIBLIOGRAPHICAL ESSAY

1. *General*

The only full-length biography of James based upon a wide range of primary and secondary sources is D.H. Willson's *King James VI and I* (Jonathan Cape, 1956), but, as explained at the beginning of Chapter 1, it is now outdated and badly needs replacing. The best recent account is that by Maurice Lee, Jnr, *Great Britain's Solomon: James VI and I in his Three Kingdoms* (University of Illinois Press, 1990). The second edition of S.J. Houston's *James I* in the Seminar Studies in History series (Longman, 1995) provides an excellent summary of recent work on James and has an extensive bibliography. Jenny Wormald has written an important article on 'James VI & I: Two Kings or One?', *History*, Vol. 68, 1983. A generous selection of James's letters is now available in G.P.V. Akrigg (ed.), *Letters of King James VI & I* (University of California Press, 1984). The most recent article on James's health is A.W. Beasley's 'The Disability of James VI & I' which appeared in Vol. 10 of *The Seventeenth Century* (1995). James's wife is the subject of Ethel Carleton Williams's *Anne of Denmark* (Longman, 1970) and also of an article by Leeds Barroll, 'The Court of the First Stuart Queen' in Linda Levy Peck (ed.), *The Mental World of the Jacobean Court* (Cambridge University Press, 1991). The best study of her eldest son is by Roy Strong: *Henry Prince of Wales and England's Lost Renaissance* (Thames & Hudson, 1986).

2. *Political thought*

The political works of James I have recently been made available in an edition by Johann P. Somerville, *King James VI and I: Political Writings*, Cambridge Texts in the History of Political Thought (Cambridge University Press, 1994). Jenny Wormald considers two major works in 'James VI and I, *Basilikon Doron* and *The Trew Law of Free Monarchies*: The Scottish Context and the English Translation', printed in *The Mental World of the Jacobean Court* (see section 10). James Doelman

211

challenges some of her conclusions in ' "A King of Thine Own Heart": The English Reception of King James VI and I's *Basilikon Doron*' in Vol. 9 of *The Seventeenth Century*, 1994. Another relevant article is by Linda Levy Peck, 'Kingship, Counsel and Law in Early Stuart Britain', in J.G.A. Pocock (ed.), *The Varieties of British Political Thought, 1500–1800* (Cambridge University Press, 1993). Kevin Sharpe discusses 'Private Conscience and Public Duty in the Writing of James VI and I' in John Morrill, Paul Slack, and David Woolf (eds), *Public Duty and Private Conscience in Seventeenth-Century England* (Clarendon Press, 1993). He also considers the political significance of James's theological writings and poetry in 'The King's Writ: Royal Authors and Royal Authority in Early Modern England' in Kevin Sharpe and Peter Lake (eds) *Culture and Politics in Early Stuart England* (Macmillan, 1994).

3. Constitutional ideas and assumptions

There are a number of recent studies of political thought in the early Stuart period, which deal among other things with James's views on absolutism. Two are by Glen Burgess: *The Politics of the Ancient Constitution* (Macmillan, 1992) and *Absolute Monarchy and the Stuart Constitution* (Yale University Press, 1996). There is also an article by Burgess on 'The Divine Right of Kings Reconsidered', published in Vol. CCCCXXV of the *English Historical Review*, 1992. Burgess's arguments are criticised by J.P. Somerville in 'The Ancient Constitution Reassessed: The Common Law, the Court and the Languages of Politics in Early Modern England' in R. Malcolm Smuts (ed.), *The Stuart Court and Europe: Essays in Politics and Political Culture* (Cambridge University Press, 1996). Somerville's own views are to be found in his book on *Politics and Ideology in England 1603–1640* (Longman, 1986) and his essays on 'James I and the Divine Right of Kings: English Politics and Continental Theory' in *The Mental World of the Jacobean Court* (see section 10); 'Ideology, Property and the Constitution' in Richard Cust and Ann Hughes (eds) *Conflict in Early Stuart England: Studies in Religion and Politics 1603–1642* (Longman, 1989); and 'The Ancient Constitution Reassessed: The Common Law, the Court and the Languages of Politics in Early Modern England' in Malcolm Smuts's *The Stuart Court and Europe*, listed above. Conrad Russell's article on 'Divine Rights in the Early Seventeenth Century' which appears in *Public Duty and Private Conscience* (see section 2), is also relevant.

4. The union

The union of crowns and the attempted union of states are discussed in Bruce Galloway, *The Union of England and Scotland 1603–08* (John Donald, 1986); Brian P. Levack *The Formation of the British State: England, Scotland, and the Union 1603–1707* (Clarendon Press, 1987); and Conrad Russell 'The Anglo-Scottish Union 1603–1643: A Success?' in Anthony Fletcher and Peter Roberts (eds), *Religion, Culture and Society in Early Modern Britain* (Cambridge University Press, 1994). Jenny Wormald considers the question of what James actually meant by 'union' in her article 'James VI, James I and the Identity of Britain' in Brendan Bradshaw and John Morrill (eds), *The British Problem c.1534– 1707: State Formation in the Atlantic Archipelago*, Problems in Focus (Macmillan, 1996).

5. Parliament

The nature of James's relationship with his parliaments has come under close scrutiny in recent years. A new interpretation was adumbrated by Conrad Russell in 'Parliamentary History in Perspective 1604–29', *History*, Vol. 61, 1976, and fleshed out in *Parliaments and English Politics 1621–1629* (Clarendon Press, 1979). Russell discusses 'The Nature of a Parliament in Early Stuart England' in Howard Tomlinson (ed.), *Before the English Civil War: Essays on Early Stuart Politics and Government* (Macmillan, 1983). He turns his attention to the earlier years of James's reign in 'English Parliaments 1593–1606: One Epoch or Two?' in D.M. Dean and N.L. Jones (eds), *The Parliaments of Elizabethan England* (Basil Blackwell, 1990), and *The Addled Parliament of 1614: The Limits of Revision* (University of Reading, 1992). Russell's views are to some extent rebutted in Thomas Cogswell's *The Blessed Revolution. English Politics and the Coming of War, 1621–1624* (Cambridge University Press, 1989); 'A Low Road to Extinction? Supply and Redress of Grievances in the Parliaments of the 1620s', *Historical Journal*, Vol. 33, 1990; and 'Phaeton's Chariot: The Parliament-Men and the Continental Crisis in 1621' in J.F. Merritt (ed.), *The Political World of Thomas Wentworth, Earl of Strafford, 1621–1641* (Cambridge University Press, 1996). A sustained attacked upon 'revisionism' is made by the contributors to J.H. Hexter (ed.), *Parliament and Liberty: From the Reign of Elizabeth to the English Civil War* (Stanford University Press, 1992). Hexter also contributed a study of 'The Apology' of 1604 to the volume edited by Richard Ollard and Pamela Tudor-Craig, *For Veronica Wedgwood These: Studies in Seventeenth-Century History* (Collins, 1986). Further consideration of the Commons' view of their role is provided by Pauline Croft in 'Annual Parliaments and the Long Parliament', *Bulletin of the Institute of Historical Research*, Vol. 59, 1986.

6. Finance

There has been little recent work on the royal finances under James. The standard full-length study of this topic is still F.C. Dietz's *English Public Finance 1558–1641* (New York, 1932), but Menna Prestwich's *Cranfield: Politics and Profits under the Early Stuarts* (Clarendon Press, 1966) is a mine of information. Conrad Russell's 'Parliament and the King's Finances' in the collection of essays he edited under the title of *The Origins of the English Civil War* (Macmillan, 1973) is most illuminating. So also is the essay by G.L. Harriss on 'Medieval Doctrines in the Debates on Supply, 1610–1629' in Kevin Sharpe (ed.), *Faction and Parliament: Essays on Early Stuart History* (Clarendon Press, 1978). David Thomas's essay on 'Financial and Administrative Developments' in *Before the English Civil War* (see section 5) is useful, as is J.D. Alsop's 'The Privy Council Debate and Committees for Fiscal Reform, September 1615', *Historical Research*, Vol. 68, 1995. Pauline Croft considers various aspects of the crown's revenue in 'Wardship in the Parliament of 1604', *Parliamentary History*, Vol. 2, 1983; 'Parliament, Purveyance and the City of London, 1589–1608', *Parliamentary History*, Vol. 4, 1985; and 'Fresh Light on Bate's Case' [Impositions], *Historical Journal*, Vol. 30, 1987. Eric Lindquist covers part of the same ground in 'The Failure of the Great Contract', *Journal of Modern History*, Vol. 57, 1985, and 'The King, the People and the House of Commons: The Problem of Early Jacobean Purveyance', *Historical Journal*, Vol. 31, 1988. The declining value of the crown's landed revenue is brought into sharp relief in R.W. Hoyle (ed.), *The Estates of the English Crown, 1558–1640* (Cambridge University Press, 1992).

7. *Religion*

The best accounts of the Jacobean Church are to be found in Patrick Collinson's *The Religion of Protestants: The Church in English Society 1559–1625* (Clarendon Press, 1982); Kenneth Fincham, *Prelate as Pastor: The Episcopate of James I* (Clarendon Press, 1990); and Kenneth Fincham (ed.), *The Early Stuart Church, 1603–1642* (Macmillan, 1993). The physical setting for anglican worship is described in a most illuminating essay by George Yule, 'James VI and I: Furnishing the Churches in his Two Kingdoms' in Anthony Fletcher and Peter Roberts (eds), *Religion, Culture and Society in Early Modern Britain* (Cambridge University Press, 1994). The Hampton Court Conference has given rise to a number of articles, most recently Frederick Shriver, 'Hampton Court Revisited: James I and the Puritans', *Journal of Ecclesiastical History*, Vol. 33, 1982, and Patrick Collinson, 'The Jacobean Religious Settlement: The Hampton Court Conference' in *Before the English Civil War* (see section 5). James's initial attitude towards English puritanism is the subject of B.W. Quintrell's 'The Royal Hunt and the Puritans 1604–05', *Journal of Ecclesiastical History*, Vol. 31, 1980. The development of his attitude is analysed in Kenneth Fincham and Peter Lake, 'The Ecclesiastical Policy of King James I', *Journal of British Studies*, Vol. 24, 1985. James's view of the nature of episcopal authority is discussed by J.P. Somerville in 'The Royal Supremacy and Episcopacy "Jure Divino", 1603–40', *Journal of Ecclesiastical History*, Vol. 34, 1983. James's reaction to the emergence of Arminianism within the United Provinces is considered by Christopher Grayson, 'James I and the Religious Crisis in the United Provinces 1613–19', and John Platt, 'Eirenical Anglicans at the Synod of Dort', both in Derek Baker (ed.), *Reform and Reformation: England and the Continent c.1500–c.1750*, Ecclesiastical

History Society, Studies in Church History (Blackwell, 1979). There is no adequate account of James's attitude towards the Roman Catholics, but W.B. Patterson's essay on 'King James's Call for an Ecumenical Council' in C.J. Cuming and Derek Baker (eds) *Councils and Assemblies*, Ecclesiastical History Society, Studies in Church History (Cambridge University Press, 1971) illustrates his desire to reunite Christendom.

8. *Foreign policy*

There is no single book on James's foreign policy, but Thomas Cogswell's *The Blessed Revolution* (see section 5) has much to say about Anglo-Spanish relations, as does Roger Lockyer's *Buckingham: The Life and Political Career of George Villiers, First Duke of Buckingham 1592–1628* (Longman, 1981). Cogswell also has an essay on 'England and the Spanish Match' in *Conflict in Early Stuart England* (see section 3). The political ramifications of the Spanish Match are considered by Peter Lake in 'Constitutional Consensus and Puritan Opposition in the 1620s: Thomas Scott and the Spanish Match', *Historical Journal*, Vol. 25, 1982. Charles H. Carter's 'Gondomar: Ambassador to James I', *Historical Journal*, Vol. 7, 1964, is still relevant, and Simon Adams's essay 'Spain or the Netherlands? The Dilemmas of Early Stuart Foreign Policy' in *Before the Civil War* (see section 5), sets out the problems very clearly. Adams also deals with Anglo-French relations, in 'The Road to La Rochelle: English Foreign Policy and the Huguenots 1610–1629', *Proceedings of the Huguenot Society of London*, Vol. XXII, 1975. For the pre-1610 period there is Maurice Lee's *James I and Henri IV: An Essay in English Foreign Policy 1603–10* (University of Illinois, 1970). Parliamentary attitudes towards foreign policy are dealt with by Simon Adams, 'Foreign Policy and the Parliaments of 1621 and 1624' in *Faction and Parliament* (see section 6), and by Robert Ruigh, *The Parliament of 1624: Politics and Foreign Policy* (Harvard University Press, 1971).

9. *Ministers and favourites*

There is no recent work on the Privy Council in James's reign, nor has the structure and functioning of the Court been fully analysed. Neil Cuddy deals with one aspect of the Court in his essay on 'The Revival of the Entourage: The Bedchamber of James I, 1603–1625' in David Starkey (ed.), *The English Court: From the Wars of the Roses to the Civil War* (Longman, 1987). He also considers the impact of the Scots in 'Anglo-Scottish Union and the Court of James I, 1603–25', *Transactions of the Royal Historical Society*, 5th series, Vol. 39, 1989. Pauline Croft has an essay on 'Robert Cecil and the Early Jacobean Court' in *The Mental World of the Jacobean Court* (see section 10). She has also published an invaluable 'Collection of Several Speeches and Treatises of the Late Lord Treasurer Cecil' in the *Camden Miscellany*, Vol. XXIX, Camden 4th series, Vol. 34 (Royal Historical Society, 1987). Other articles by Croft on James's principal minister include 'The Religion of Robert Cecil', *Historical Journal*, Vol. 34, 1991; 'The Reputation of Robert Cecil: Libels, Political Opinion and Popular Awareness in the Early Seventeenth Century', *Transactions of the Royal Historical Society*, 6th series, Vol. 1, 1991; 'Serving the Archduke: Robert Cecil's Management of the Parliamentary Session of 1606', *Historical Research*, Vol. 64, 1991; and 'The Parliamentary Installation of Henry, Prince of Wales', *Historical Research*, Vol. 65, 1992. Another leading figure and courtier is the subject of Linda Levy Peck's *Northampton: Patronage and Policy at the Court of James I* (George Allen & Unwin, 1982). Peck is also the author of *Court Patronage and Corruption in Early Stuart England* (Unwin Hyman, 1990). There is no major work on Robert Carr, Earl of Somerset, but the less savoury aspects of his fall from grace are brought under the spotlight in David Lindley, *The Trials of Frances Howard: Fact and fiction at the Court of King James* (Routledge, 1993) and Anne Somerset, *Unnatural Murder: Poison at the Court of James I* (Weidenfeld & Nicolson, 1997). George Villiers, Duke of Buckingham, who succeeded Carr as favourite, is the subject of Roger Lockyer's biography (see section 8). Buckingham's principal agent in running the navy was Sir John Coke, whose career is dissected in Michael B. Young's *Servility and Service: The Life and Work of Sir John Coke*, Royal Historical Society Studies in History (Boydell Press, 1986). Another of Buckingham's *protégés* was Lionel Cranfield, Earl of Middlesex, of whom the classic account is that by Menna Prestwich (see section 6). Yet another was Francis Bacon, whose political life still remains to be written. His fall is considered in Damien X. Powell, 'Why Was Sir Francis Bacon Impeached? The Common Lawyers and the Chancery Revisited: 1621', *History*, Vol. 81, 1996. James's role as a patron of architecture is considered *en passant* in Howard Colvin's magnificent study of *The History of the King's Works*, Vol. III *1485–1660* (Part I) and Vol. IV *1485–1660* (Part II) (HMSO 1975 and 1982). J. Newman also discusses this topic in 'Inigo Jones and the Politics of Architecture' in *Culture and Politics* (see section 2).

10. *Scotland and Ireland*

A general background to James's rule in Scotland is provided by Jenny Wormald in *Court, Kirk, and Community: Scotland 1470–1625*, The New History of Scotland, Vol. 4 (Edward Arnold, 1981). Gordon Donaldson's *Scotland: James V to James VII* (Oliver & Boyd, 1965) is invaluable, as is Maurice Lee's *Government by Pen: Scotland under James VI & I* (University of Illinois Press, 1980). An important aspect of Scottish religious history is dealt with by David George Mullan in *Episcopacy in Scotland: The History of an Idea, 1560–1638* (John Donald, 1986). James's attitude towards the presbyterians in his native land is the subject of an article by Jenny Wormald, 'Ecclesiastical Vitriol: The Kirk, the Puritans and the future King of England' in John Guy (ed.), *The Reign of Elizabeth I: Court and Culture in the Last Decade* (Cambridge

University Press, 1995). Scottish attitudes to the union with England are discussed in Roger A. Mason (ed.), *Scots and Britons: Scottish Political Thought and the Union of 1603* (Cambridge University Press, 1994). James's attitude towards the Scottish Church and its relationship with its English counterpart is the subject of John Morrill's essay on 'A British Patriarchy? Ecclesiastical Imperialism under the Early Stuarts' in *Religion, Culture and Society* (see section 4). For Ireland, the key work is T.W. Moody, F.X. Martin and F.J. Byrne (eds), *A New History of Ireland*, Vol. III: *Early Modern Ireland 1534–1691* (Clarendon Press, 1991). For the connection between Scotland and Ireland there is M. Perceval-Maxwell's *The Scottish Migration to Ulster in the Reign of James I* (Routledge & Kegan Paul, 1973). Also useful is Alan Ford, *The Protestant Reformation in Ireland, 1590–1641* (Four Courts, Dublin, 1997).

CHRONOLOGY

1559   May. John Knox returns to Scotland from Geneva.

1560   July. Under terms of Treaty of Edinburgh, both England and France withdraw forces from Scotland.

Aug. Scottish Parliament accepts protestant Confession of Faith.

1561   Aug. Following death of her husband, Francis II, King of France, Mary Stuart returns to Scotland.

1565   July. Mary Stuart marries Henry, Lord Darnley.

1566   March. Murder of Rizzio.

June 19. Birth of James VI in Edinburgh.

1567   Feb. Murder of Darnley.

May. Mary marries Bothwell.

July 24. Abdication of Mary. James becomes King of Scotland.

July 29. James crowned at Stirling. Earl of Moray regent.

1568   May. Mary flees to England.

1570   Jan. Assassination of Moray.

Earl of Lennox, Darnley's father, becomes regent.

George Buchanan appointed James's tutor.

1571   Sept. Lennox killed in skirmish. Earl of Mar becomes regent.

1572   Oct. Death of Mar. Earl of Morton becomes regent.

Nov. Death of John Knox.

1574   Andrew Melville returns to Scotland from Geneva.

1578   March. End of regency. James assumes power.

2nd Book of Discipline establishes presbyterian system in Scotland.

1579   Sept. Arrival in Scotland of Esmé Stuart, Seigneur d'Aubigny, subsequently created Earl (1580) and Duke (1581) of Lennox.

1581   June. Execution of Morton.

1582   Aug. Ruthven Raid. Lennox returns to France and dies there in 1583.

Sept. Death of George Buchanan.

1583 June. James escapes from Ruthven raiders.
1584 Scottish Parliament passes 'Black Acts'.
1586 July. Treaty of friendship between England and Scotland signed at Berwick.
James given pension by Elizabeth.
1587 Feb. Execution of Mary, Queen of Scots.
Scottish Parliament passes Act of Annexation of episcopal property.
John Maitland of Thirlestaine appointed Chancellor.
1589 James sails to Norway and marries Anne of Denmark.
1590 James and Anne return to Scotland.
1592 Scottish Parliament passes 'Golden Act'.
1594 Feb. Birth of Prince Henry.
1596 Aug. Birth of Princess Elizabeth.
1598 Publication of *The True Law of Free Monarchies*.
1599 *Basilicon Doron* printed for private circulation.
1600 Aug. Gowrie conspiracy.
Nov. Birth of Prince Charles.
James secures election of three Scottish bishops.
1601 Jan. Rebellion of Earl of Essex in London.
Feb. Execution of Essex.
Sept. George Home (later Earl of Dunbar) appointed Lord Treasurer of Scotland.
1603 March 24. Death of Queen Elizabeth. James accedes to English throne.
April. Presentation of Millenary Petition.
May. James arrives in London.
1604 Jan. Hampton Court Conference.
March. Opening of James's first Parliament in England.
June. Commons draw up *Form of Apology and Satisfaction*.
Aug. Treaty of London puts end to war between England and Spain.
Sept. James issues ecclesiastical Canons.
Oct. James proclaims himself King of Great Britain. Sir Arthur Chichester appointed Lord Deputy of Ireland.
Dec. Following death of Whitgift in February, Richard Bancroft becomes Archbishop of Canterbury.
1605 Nov. Gunpowder Plot.
Illegal assembly of presbyterian leaders at Aberdeen.
1606 Jan. Parliament reassembles. Passes anti-catholic legislation.
March. Alexander Seton, Earl of Dunfermline, appointed Lord Chancellor of Scotland.
July. Scottish Parliament revokes Act of Annexation.
Nov. Bate's Case in Court of Exchequer.
1607 April. Alexander Melville imprisoned in Tower of London.

Sept. Earls of Tyrconnell and Tyrone flee Ireland. Plantation of Ulster begins.

1608   May. Earl of Salisbury appointed Lord Treasurer.

1609   April. Spain agrees twelve-year truce with United Provinces.

1610   Feb. Parliament reassembles.

May. Assassination of Henri IV of France.

June. Negotiations between James and Commons over terms of proposed Great Contract. General Assembly of Kirk at Glasgow votes for restoration of episcopacy.

1611   Jan. Death of Dunbar.

Feb. Dissolution of James's first Parliament.

March. Robert Carr created Viscount Rochester.

April. George Abbot becomes Archbishop of Canterbury, following death of Bancroft in November 1610. Andrew Melville goes into exile in France.

1612   May. Death of Robert Cecil, Earl of Salisbury.

Nov. Death of Henry, Prince of Wales.

1613   Feb. Princess Elizabeth marries Frederick V, Elector Palatine.

May. Opening of Irish Parliament.

Sept. Earl of Essex divorce proceedings. Poisoning of Sir Thomas Overbury.

Nov. Robert Carr, Viscount Rochester, created Earl of Somerset.

Dec. Marriage between Somerset and Frances Howard (formerly Countess of Essex).

1614   April–June. James's second or 'Addled' Parliament.

July. Thomas Howard, Earl of Suffolk, appointed Lord Treasurer.

1615   Aug. Dissolution of Irish Parliament.

Nov. Sir Arthur Chichester recalled from Ireland.

1616   Jan. George Villiers (knighted in April 1615) appointed Master of the Horse.

May. Somerset and his wife found guilty of Overbury's murder.

July. Oliver St John appointed Lord Deputy of Ireland.

Nov. Sir Edward Coke dismissed as Chief Justice. Replaced by Sir Henry Montagu.

1617   Jan. George Villiers created Earl of Buckingham.

March. Francis Bacon appointed Lord Keeper.

May–Aug. James revisits Scotland.

James issues *Declaration of Sports*.

1618   May. Defenestration of Prague. Outbreak of Thirty Years War.

July. Dismissal of Suffolk as Lord Treasurer.

Aug. General Assembly of Kirk at Perth accepts the Five Articles.

Nov. Opening of Synod of Dort.

1619   Jan. Buckingham appointed Lord Admiral.

Aug. Bohemians elect Frederick V, James's son-in-law, as king.

Election of Ferdinand II as Holy Roman Emperor.

Nov. Coronation of Frederick V in Prague.

1620   Aug. Spanish troops invade Palatinate.

Nov. Defeat of Frederick V at Battle of White Mountain.

1621   Jan–June. James's third Parliament in session. Attack on monopolies.

March. Death of Philip III of Spain. Accession of Philip IV.

May. Overthrow of Lord Chancellor Bacon.

July. Appointment of John Williams, Bishop of Lincoln, as Lord Keeper.

Aug. Resumption of war between Spain and United Provinces.

Sept. Lionel Cranfield appointed Lord Treasurer.

Nov. Parliament reassembles.

Dec. The 'Protestation' of the Commons.

1622   Feb. Dissolution of James's third Parliament.

April. Recall of Oliver St John from Ireland. Replaced as Lord Deputy by Viscount Falkland.

Sept. Lionel Cranfield created Earl of Middlesex.

1623   March–Sept. Prince Charles and Buckingham in Spain.

May. Buckingham created Duke.

1624   Feb–May. James's fourth (and last) Parliament.

March. James breaks off negotiations with Spain.

Dec. James ratifies treaty of marriage between Prince Charles and Henrietta Maria, sister of Louis XIII of France.

1625   Jan. Mansfeld's expedition sails from Dover.

March 27. Death of James I.

0 — 50 miles
0 — 80 km

N

Berwick

1

Newcastle
upon Tyne

2   5   Durham

Whitehaven

4

3

Ripon •   6

York

Hull

3   Leeds

Liverpool

Manchester   Sheffield

Chester   10   Lincoln

7   8   9
          Derby   Nottingham

12   King's Lynn
          Norwich
Shrewsbury

Leicester   14   15
11   18   13
          Coventry   20   21   Great
16   19   Yarmouth
Warwick   Bury St. Edmunds   Ipswich
Worcester   17   Northampton   Cambridge   22

23

25   Colchester
Gloucester   Oxford   26   27   28
24

31   LONDON
Bristol   Reading   32

Bath   30   33   Chatham
29   Salisbury   38   34   Canterbury
          39

Tiverton   37   Portsmouth
36   Exeter

ISLE OF
WIGHT

35   Plymouth

Counties of England

1	Northumberland	14	Rutland	27	Hertfordshire
2	Cumberland	15	Norfolk	28	Essex
3	Lancashire	16	Herefordshire	29	Somerset
4	Westmorland	17	Worcestershire	30	Wiltshire
5	Durham	18	Warwickshire	31	Berkshire
6	Yorkshire	19	Northamptonshire	32	Greater London
7	Cheshire	20	Huntingdonshire	33	Surrey
8	Derbyshire	21	Cambridgeshire	34	Kent
9	Nottinghamshire	22	Suffolk	35	Cornwall
10	Lincolnshire	23	Bedfordshire	36	Devon
11	Shropshire	24	Gloucestershire	37	Dorset
12	Staffordshire	25	Oxfordshire	38	Hampshire
13	Leicestershire	26	Buckinghamshire	39	Sussex

Map 1. England

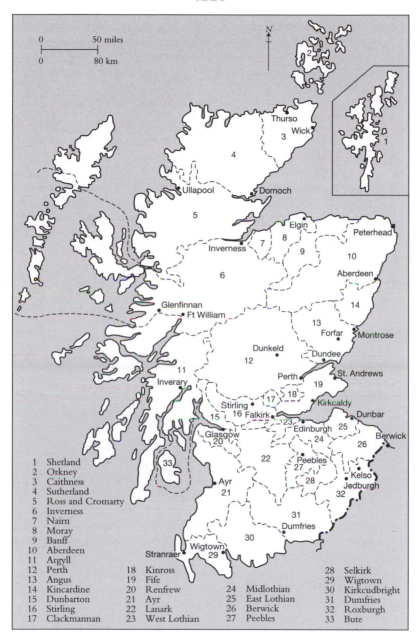

0   50 miles
0   80 km

Thurso
Wick
3
4
Ullapool
Dornoch
5
Elgin
7   8
Inverness   9
6   10
Aberdeen
14
Glenfinnan
Ft William   13
Forfar   Montrose
Dunkeld
12   Dundee
Perth   St. Andrews
11   19
Inverary   18
17
Stirling   Kirkcaldy
15   16 Falkirk   Dunbar
Glasgow   23
20   Edinburgh   25
24   Berwick
26
22   Peebles
33   27
28   Kelso
Ayr   Jedburgh
21   32
31
Dumfries
30
Stranraer   Wigtown
29

1   Shetland
2   Orkney
3   Caithness
4   Sutherland
5   Ross and Cromarty
6   Inverness
7   Nairn
8   Moray
9   Banff
10 Aberdeen
11 Argyll
12 Perth   18 Kinross   28 Selkirk
13 Angus   19 Fife   29 Wigtown
14 Kincardine   20 Renfrew   24 Midlothian   30 Kirkcudbright
15 Dunbarton   21 Ayr   25 East Lothian   31 Dumfries
16 Stirling   22 Lanark   26 Berwick   32 Roxburgh
17 Clackmannan   23 West Lothian 27 Peebles   33 Bute

Map 2. Scotland

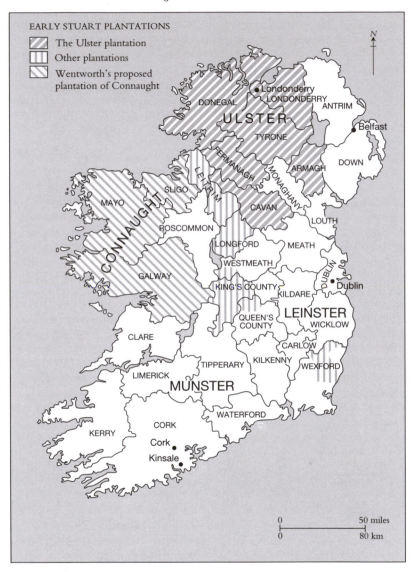

Map 3. Ireland

INDEX